SOCIAL CHANGE IN '

DEMOCRACY AND CORRUPTION IN EUROPE

The *Social Change in Western Europe* series developed from the need to provide a summary of current thinking from leading academic thinkers on major social and economic issues concerning the evolving policies of Western Europe in the post-Maastricht era. To create an effective European Union, governments and politicians throughout the region must work to provide satisfactory social, economic and political conditions for the populations of Europe, and each volume affords an opportunity to look at specific issues and their impact on individual countries.

The series is directed by an academic committee composed of Arnaldo Bagnasco (Turin University), Henri Mendras (CNRS, Paris) and Vincent Wright (Nuffield, Oxford), assisted by Patrick Le Galès (CNRS, Rennes), Anand Menon (University of Oxford) with the support of Michel Roger and Olivier Cazenave (Futuroscope in Poitiers). This group forms the *Observatoire du Changement en Europe Occidentale* which was launched in Poitiers (France) in 1990 with the generous funding of the Fondation de Poitiers headed by René Monory.

SOCIAL CHANGE IN WESTERN EUROPE
IN THE SAME SERIES

SOCIAL CHANGE IN WESTERN EUROPE

DEMOCRACY AND CORRUPTION IN EUROPE

edited by
DONATELLA DELLA PORTA
and
YVES MÉNY

PINTER
London and Washington

PINTER
A Cassell Imprint
Wellington House, 125 Strand, London WC2R 0BB
PO Box 65, Herndon VA 20172

First published in Great Britain in 1997

British Library Cataloguing in Publication Data
A catalogue record for this book is available from the British Library.

ISBN   1 85567 366 5 (hb)
      1 85567 367 3 (pb)

Library of Congress Cataloging in Publication Data
Démocratie et corruption en Europe.   English
   Democracy and corruption in Europe / edited by Donatella Della
Porta and Yves Mény.
      p   cm. — (Social change in Western Europe)
   Includes bibliographical references and index.
   ISBN 1-85567-366-5 (hardcover). — ISBN 1-85567-367-3 (pbk.)
    1. Europe—Politics and government—1989-   2. Europe—Politics and
government—1945-   3. Political corruption—Europe—History—20th
century.   I. Della Porta, Donatella, 1956-   II. Mény, Yves.
III. Title.   IV. Series.
D2009.D4613 1997
320.94—dc20
                                         96–18572
                                           CIP

Typeset by Falcon Oast Graphic Art
Printed and bound in Great Britain by
Creative Print and Design Wales, Ebbw Vale, Gwent.

CONTENTS

LIST OF CONTRIBUTORS

Andrew Adonis is on the staff of the *Observer* and Associate Professor at Nuffield College, Oxford. He has published *Making Aristocracy Work: The Peerage and the Political System in Britain, 1884–1914* (1993), Oxford University Press; *Parliament Today* (1993), Manchester University Press (2nd edn); *A Conservative Revolution in the 1980s* (1994), Manchester University Press.

Jean-Marie Bouissou holds a research appointment at CERI – Centre d'études et de recherches internationales (FNSP, Paris) in addition to teaching appointments in Paris (INALCO and Université Paris-VII) and Rennes (Centre franco-japonais de management). Previously he was head of the Franco-Japanese Institute of Kyushu in Fukukoa. He is the author of *Le Japon depuis 1945* (1992), Armand Colin, and has recently published in the *Revue française de Science Politique* (1994): 'Les élections législatives au Japon (1993) – la chute du parti libéral-démocrate et la réconstruction du système politique'.

Jean Cartier-Bresson is Senior Lecturer in Economics at the Université Paris-XIII and a member of GREITD-CEDI. He further works as professional adviser to the Service central de prévention de la corruption.

Donatella Della Porta is Professor of Local Government at the University of Florence. Previously she held teaching and research appointments at Cornell University, the Wissenschaftzentrum in Berlin and the European University Institute in Florence. She has published *Lo scambio occulto. Casi di corruzione politica in Italia* (1992), Il Mulino; *Corruzione politica l'amministrasione pubblica* (1994), Il Mulino; *Social Movements, Political Violence and the State* (1995), Cambridge University Press; and *Movimentí collettivi e sisteme politico in Italia* (1996), Latersa.

Paul Heywood is Professor of Politics at the University of Nottingham and has recently published *The Government and Politics of Spain* (1995), New York, Macmillan. His previous publications include *Marxism and the Failure of Organised Socialism in Spain* (1990), Cambridge University Press and *'Governing a new democracy: the power of the prime minister in Spain'* in *West European Prime Ministers*, ed. G. W. Jones (1991), London, Frank Cass.

Jean-François Médard is a specialist in African politics and teaches at the Institut d'études politiques in Bordeaux. His most recent published work as editor is *Etats d'Afrique: formations, mécanismes, crises* (1991), Paris, Karthala.

Marie Mendras is a CNRS researcher at CERI – Centre d'études et de recherches internationales and a lecturer at the Institute of Political Science in Paris. She has edited *Un Etat pour la Russie* (1992), Brussels, Complexe and *La Russie et ses provinces* (1996), Geneva, CRES, and has published extensively on elections and state-building in Russia.

Yves Mény is Professor of Political Science – and director of the Centre Robert Schuman – at the European University Institute in Florence. He has directed a number of research projects in comparative European politics. His publications include *La corruption de la République* (1992a), Paris, Fayard, *Politiques comparées – les démocraties: Etats-Unis, France, Grande-Bretagne, Italie, RFA* (1993), Paris, Montchrestien (1987 1st edn); and, with Vincent Wright, *The Politics of Steel: Western Europe and the Steel Industry in the Crisis Years 1974–1984* (1987), Berlin/New York, De Gruyter.

Wolfgang Seibel is Professor of Political Science and Administration at the University of Constance. He has coedited *The Third Sector. Comparative Studies of Non-Profit Organisations* (1990), Berlin/New York, De Gruyter and *Zwischen Kooperation und Korruption. 'Abweichendes Verhalten' in der Verwaltung* (1992), Baden-Baden, Nomos.

Alberto Vannucci teaches at the University of Pisa. He has published *'La rivoluzione marginalista nelle scienze sociale: alcuni osservazioni'* in *Quaderni di Storia dell'Economia Politica*, (1990); *'La realtà economica della corruzione politica'* in *Stato e Mercato*, (1992).

INTRODUCTION: DEMOCRACY AND CORRUPTION

DONATELLA DELLA PORTA and YVES MÉNY

The fall of the Berlin Wall and the collapse of socialism crowned a 20-year period characterized by the 'triumphal march' of democracy, the dominant form of government in the Western world. However, the merits of the democratic model have in no way precluded the more lucid analysts from pointing out its imperfections.

Economists, political analysts and philosophers such as Schumpeter, Dahl, Sartori and Popper have done their best to induce disenchantment and demystification. While they recognize the pre-eminence of democracy, they do so with the irony of Churchill when he defined it as 'the worst of political systems, except for all the others', a definition taken up by the philosopher Noberto Bobbio in making the unassuming claim for it as 'a better system than those that have so far preceded and succeeded it' (Bobbio, 1987).

This guarded attitude on the part of philosophers and political specialists is in marked contrast to the somewhat brash and imperious assumptions made by most Western politicians to the effect that democracy cannot but be Western and that its intrinsic superiority makes it a universal model. From the 1970s onwards international relations and the exchange of trade tended to become identified with this all-conquering concept that has sealed the collapse of authoritarian regimes in Eastern Europe and the Third World.

Paradoxically, just when the myth of democracy appeared to be sweeping aside all before it, Western political systems were assailed by a multitude of problems, with political parties facing crisis after crisis in voter turnout as in the economy, and a crisis of 'values' as represented by the Western pantheon. Seen in this light, the growth of corruption over the last ten years or so and, more importantly, increased awareness of it in public opinion is a crucial expression of this crisis.

Nevertheless, evidence of the perverse effect of corruption on the functioning of political systems in general, and of democratic ones in particular, is not given universal credence. The functionalist analysis in the 1960s and 1970s sought to overlook moral connotations and value judgments in regard to democracy by stressing the beneficial effect which corruption might have on bureaucratic stalemate. Just as the school of organizational sociology had shown that, in France, the 'stalemate society' functioned thanks to the generalized practice of accommodation on the part of its participants, so American function- alists laid stress on the advantages of a degree of corruption in social- ist or developing countries in providing the means of lubricating machinery that was jammed. *Mutatis mutandis*, the argument was applied to Mediterranean societies already characterized by traditions of paternalism, clientelism and nepotism. Hence the issue was no longer open to doubt: corruption either had a function or else was so ingrained that any attempt to eradicate it was futile; better to accept it and try to curb its most glaring imperfections. Elsewhere, a general presumption of the absence of corruption tended to mask the prob- lem by a refusal to countenance it, corruption being non-existent or marginal. For instance, in France before the sequence of scandals and in the UK to a degree today, the customary refrain was often that cases of corruption are the exception rather than the rule. Corruption is seen as the lot of southern or developing societies while democracies, with sturdy bureaucratic traditions, experience no more than the odd scandal to which no society can be altogether immune.

During the 1980s, this panorama changed totally. A new realiza- tion of the problems of corruption took place all over Europe, Asia, Africa and former socialist countries. In autocratic regimes the de- nunciation of authoritarian methods or methods resorted to by the police was accompanied by corruption being highlighted by the leadership. In democracies successive scandals cast doubt on the integrity of the administrative and, especially, the political elite. In France, Spain, Italy, Germany and Denmark, opinion polls reflect growing mistrust of parties and politicians while elections provide an opportunity to reject parties that make up governments. Everywhere parties of protest or of right-wing populism are being spawned. This awareness and aloofness with regard to politics are doubtless a response to the growing problem of corruption, yet, as the Italian example shows, this itself does not explain the shift in public opinion;

year in year out a section of the press as well as prominent individuals engage in moral debate without eliciting more than polite indifference. To try to understand the renewed interest of the public in the problem of corruption, several factors have to be considered:

- disturbances in social equilibria brought about by the recession and by policies of deregulation and structural change;
- appearance of a social category with wealth newly and rapidly acquired through speculation or playing by the new rules, frequently in collusion with politicians. Economic and political factors being here intertwined, achievement in one field produces a knock-on effect in the other;
- arrogance on the part of those whose power is newly acquired whether in politics or the economy, such arrogance being more pronounced where politicians have been long excluded from office (note the non-communist left in France, Italy, Greece and Spain);
- the complementary rise of social forces that were hitherto largely held in check or lacked the muscle to stand up against the arrogance and corruption of the elites, and at the forefront the press, resurgent in Spain and Greece or more determined in France and Italy and increasingly inclined to take on power politics with investigative journalism. Faced with the vicious circle of corruption, denunciation of political malpractice by journalists and legal proceedings duly reported in the press contributed by degrees to the constitution of a virtuous circle involving press, public opinion, magistracy and political class. Everywhere eminent politicians or high-ranking civil servants have been obliged to resign or face prosecution, and almost everywhere a tightening up of rules, procedures and controls has taken place by way of reaction to the laxities and excesses of the 1980s;
- an increase in the financial needs of political parties and electoral organizations. Significantly, the 1970s and 1980s witnessed a widespread rise in legislation in respect of party financing and electoral campaigning, either in response to cases of scandal such as Lockheed or Flick, or to provide for the growth of factional groups (in Germany and Italy), or alternatively offset the staggering increase in the cost of electoral propaganda (in Japan and the USA). But far from resolving the problem, an increase in public funding merely whetted the appetite of politicians only too ready to turn their power and influence to monetary advantage. With the exception of the UK and, marginally, the USA with regard to

the presidential election, there was no attempt to resist pressure
from the political apparatus. Indeed, political parties cheerfully
resorted to self-serving practices;

- the development of a more incisive, investigative-type journalism
  which threw light on the darker side of politics and mobilized
  public opinion;
- determined action by the magistracy, in Italy especially, where
  the *Mani pulite* operation dealt a fatal blow to corruption in the
  twilight of the First Republic, but in France and Spain also.

The wave of scandals and the mounting number of cases of dubious
behaviour during the 1980s and the start of the 1990s, questionable
as regards both the law and public morality, have changed the nature
of the problem. In a number of countries seen as democratic, corruption no longer appeared to be a marginal or exceptional problem but
was seen as an endemic problem, a kind of meta-system which is
equally effective in operation as the official state-apparatus to which
it is attached and which nourishes it. A development of this order
requires a closer, more precise and comparative definition of corruption. Why is it that what appears scandalous in one society meets
with indifference in another? Why in some systems is corruption
more 'bureaucratic', while in others it is seen to be more 'political'?
Is it linked to social forms of organization, to the structure of politics
or to the dominance of certain groups or parties?

We would like to make it clear at the outset that this book is concerned with corruption only insofar as it affects public actors – politicians or civil servants. It goes without saying that corruption is rife in
the private sphere, but this sphere is deliberately excluded here in
spite of its evident bearing on corruption in the public sphere.
Corruption affecting public administration is more likely to develop
if civil society is vulnerable and the market weak; and one needs to
bear in mind that wherever a public actor is implicated there will
always be a private partner.

So corruption can be initially defined as a clandestine exchange
between two 'markets', the 'political and/or administrative market'
and the economic and social market. The exchange is an occult one
since it violates public, legal and ethical norms and sacrifices the
common good to private – personal, corporatist, partisan, etc. – interests. And such a transaction enables private actors to have access to
public resources (contracts, financing, decision-making, etc.) by
giving them an unfair advantage, because there is neither transparency nor competition. This procures present or future material

benefits to corrupt public actors either for themselves or for the organization of which they are members.

Corruption is powerfully in evidence at the interface of the public and private spheres, especially in sectors where public decision-making is not subject to rules that are strict or binding. In countries where democratic rights are upheld corruption has few opportunities to develop inasmuch as civil servants or politicians can only make a positive response to citizens provided the required conditions are met. Thus the issue of passports and payment of welfare benefits are subject to strict rules which leave the public servant no room for discretion. However, corruption on a small or large scale can arise wherever there is such opportunity. Assessing physical disability for the award of a pension, selecting the 'best' contract, on deciding how an investment should be allocated are decisions which cannot be contained in quasi-automatic procedures and which leave public servants and politicians significant room for manoeuvre, especially if the rules of procedure which are supposed to guarantee the due process of law are abided by neither in letter nor in spirit.

This definition is both more flexible than those habitually used in law, which, for example, single out misappropriation of public funds or misapplication of administration for personal gain, and narrower than the original sense that defines corruption as any adulteration of an initial state considered as ideal or pure. Hence it has the advantage of covering a variety of assumptions about corruption without being restrictively conditioned by legal or cultural considerations which are necessarily subject to marked variation in time and place.

A common definition for the areas explored does not mean, however, that problems, situations or ways of thinking are identical. Between the UK, which has been largely successful in eradicating corruption (though a number of practices would pose ethical problems on the continent), and Japan, where political corruption appears to be a way of life, or between German bureaucratic culture and Italian *arrangiarsi*, the contrast is striking. But beyond such differences that are related to the process of constructing democracy, the development of bureaucracy and the differences in national culture, common indicators and enduring features are to be found: these include mechanisms of exchange, gifts made and received, residual forms of patrimonialism, or structures, archaic or modernized, of nepotism or clientelism. And beyond its impact on the functioning of mechanisms and institutions, corruption, by striking at the very roots of democracy, compromises the values of the system. Corruption substitutes private interests for the public interest, undermines the rule of law, and denies the principles of equality and transparency in that it favours certain actors with secret and privileged access to public resources. The contributions that make up this volume together serve as a presentation of the imperfections of democracy.

1

FRANCE: THE END OF THE REPUBLICAN ETHIC?

Yves Mény

Political corruption in France, when considered from an historical perspective, seems to be no more than a marginal phenomenon whose appearance is cyclical and coincides with the major economic, cultural or political fractures that mark the country's history. But, leaving aside such periods of turbulence, it needs to be pointed out that there is general agreement among French politicians and high-ranking civil servants that corruption is a marginal occurrence. Presumably, such misplaced conviction is explained partly by the difficulty of supplying – except in legal terms – a precise definition of corruption and of even approximately assessing its magnitude:

- Generally corruption constitutes a violation of ethical norms that are protected by law. Certainly there are countless variations from one political system to another or one era to another as to the constituents of the 'code' governing what is or is not proscribed. What would pass for corruption in the USA may in France be considered as an agreement made between good fellows. What in France would constitute corruption may be considered virtually a moral obligation in Africa (he who holds power owes favours to his family and protégés). Moreover, such a code, which is cultural before being legal, invariably poses problems in borderline areas. For example, in France it is accepted that agreeing to waive a fine does not in itself imply corruption. Similarly, over a long period, hidden sources of political party funding were accepted or tolerated by political, administrative and intellectual elites as a whole. But this tolerance is susceptible to change with changing attitudes in public opinion or if excesses reach intolerable proportions. An American political scientist, A. Heidenheimer (1989), has drawn attention to the problem of borderline areas in making a distinction between 'white' corruption and 'grey' or 'black' corruption. White corruption is accepted by everyone, elites as well as the public at large; black corruption, similarly universal, is seen as corruption; grey corruption, however, meets with a range of responses. This is exactly what happened in France with regard to the funding of political parties. Whereas the elites based their views on a position that was really untenable, employing the specious argument that legitimate ends (parties, being necessary to a democracy, need money) justified the means, even when they contravene morality and the law, public opinion was shocked at the brutal disclosure of mechanisms it had no knowledge of and fell back on reflexes that were so common under the Third Republic – politicians are by definition corrupt.

• Representing as it does a violation of accepted standards, corruption is presumed to be clandestine. The secrecy surrounding what is transacted is both necessary and a source of scandal when the corrupt dealing is revealed. Hence those who participate in corrupt practices endeavour and are tempted to make them appear anodine or give them legal respectability. For instance, a mayor may allocate a subsidy to an association he controls, then put the funds to his own use, whilst observing the proper forms. The problems arise with misappropriation of public money, as was shown in a somewhat grotesque way by the case of Jacques Médecin or in another quite different context by the *Carrefour du développement* affair. In France the impenetrableness of transactions is furthered by the concentration of power in the hands of relatively few powerful decision-makers, mayors in particular whose power is virtually undivided. For those who, in resorting to corruption, enjoy privileged access to these decision-makers, the pickings are rich.

To complete the picture one needs to differentiate between the individuals and sectors concerned since the opportunities for corruption are not the same for all and vary in appeal from one sector to another. When Yann Gaillard (*Pouvoirs*, no. 31, 1984) declared that in France it is possible to obtain a number of administrative benefits without needing to pay or resort to corruption, he was right. Most people can exercise their rights without any problem. Even so, there have to be reservations that allow a distinction to be made between four different instances which are not in themselves normal.

In the first case, an individual may insist on obtaining a right that is guaranteed by law and constitutes an obligation on the part of the administration; however, delays or incompetence may prevent his obtaining satisfaction. So he has recourse to a contact, a politician, for example, i.e. to a channel that is not normal for these purposes, to bring influence to bear on his behalf. In other words, being able to exercise a right is not so easy a matter as it might at first appear: whereas everything might seem to be clearly laid down, there are procedures that come into play involving a possible exchange, the outcome of which cannot be quantified or determined in advance. There is no corruption but, in some cases, the setting up of a sort of dependency or clientelism, can lead to a climate that 'corrupts' the relationship between administration and subject in that it substitutes negotiation for an obligatory act.

Another hypothetical case is one where an individual requests a decision which the administration is free to take or not to take (a grant, a tax exemption, etc.) or, in the case of a bid or contract, can determine the beneficiary. In this instance, influence or pressure is not merely not excluded but may in the course of recognized lobbying become tainted with corruption. To the extent that the involvement of a well-placed politician may get things moving without affecting the vouchsafing of a right that is in any case recognized, influence applied to obtain a benefit that is not strictly due may well tend to become corrupt if it is not exercised in the open.

A third case is one where a decision in the applicant's favour depends on there being a set of contacts available. The ability to activate networks or have privileged access to those who take political administrative decisions clearly makes things a lot easier and removes the need of resorting to leverage or corruption to achieve one's aims. The demands of an influential politician or a forceful industrialist cannot be easily refused; compromises have to be found.

A fourth and final hypothesis is that no attempt is made to disguise corruption; rules and procedures are flouted because they apparently stand in the way of the desired objective or cannot provide a guarantee of its coming about. The incitement then must be particularly strong for an individual to resort to corruption. The economic or personal advantage involved must be considerable – e.g. winning a bid, or obtaining a residence permit or perhaps naturalization – and the person on whom the decision hangs has to be in a monopoly or a quasi-monopoly position, thus promising major advantages to the beneficiary. There is a marked propensity to resort to corruption in that it 'reduces uncertainty', and to set about eliminating the risk element in obtaining what is sought.

These characteristics account for the fact that cases of corruption appear with greater frequency where an official possesses mainly discretionary powers (i.e. police or finance) and where the costs of a decision going against the individual concerned are high (i.e. deportation or tax reappraisal). Corruption here goes hand in hand with misuse of authority. The official in question threatens to use powers and/or the legitimate violence he wields in the name of the state for illegitimate, i.e. private, ends. The corrupter and the person corrupted profit from the transaction to the detriment of the state which is ideologically devalued (through the wrongful behaviour of its agent) and financially defrauded (when financial settlement is made at its expense). The other sectors where corruption flourishes are ones where the government and private firms have a commercial contractual relationship. Procurement contracts are the characteristic sphere, which rather invalidates the neoliberal thesis that since corruption is linked to regulation, by deregulating one removes its principal cause. Further, this accounts for the fact that local authorities are in the front line as regards cases of corruption, as for example, in France where three quarters of civil investment is carried out by local authorities in their capacity as contractors. They are thus as much victims as culprits in the systematic bleeding of public works contracts in the course of recent years.

Perpetrators and mechanisms of corruption

Press reporting on corruption has often been and still is focused on minor officials. In the nineteenth century it was the gamekeeper, the customs official or the gendarme who was caught out now and again for some minor offence, which, taken out of context, seems ridiculous. Even now, most officials who are caught are low-ranking – prison warders who take bribes to make it easier for inmates to have outside contacts, administrative officials, e.g. in the Paris town hall or the *préfecture de police* accused of trafficking in identity cards or residence permits, police superintendents charged with 'protecting' bars in return for kickbacks or with extracting money from a taxi-driver afraid to lose his licence, or tax inspectors jailed for 'negotiating' the reduction of a tax adjustment or of a penalty for an overdue VAT settlement. Nothing of consequence, and generally involving only trifling sums (at most a few thousand pounds in the pocket of a dishonest official). The entire scenario is redolent of a third-world stereotype: the absence of a professional code of practice because the notion of public service is wanting, the effect of patrimonialization meaning that any post, any position of authority provides a licence for personal gain, manipulation of public regulations as a form of black-mail to serve private interests. And all this to beef up a salary structure that is held to be inadequate.

Against this, it is far harder to pinpoint social exchange corruption where a direct monetary exchange does not necessarily occur. Today corruption, like money, has shed its materiality. The flow is invisible and beyond a bank's power to trace. How is one to differentiate between the necessary alterations made to a land-use plan and the sort of manipulating linked to dubious objectives? How is one to tell the difference between legitimate dispensations and those accorded by preferential treatment? How can one be sure whether the localization of a public amenity, which constitutes a source of profit, is deter-mined by objective considerations or by the will to please certain pro-prietors or speculators? In most cases, there is no clear answer since proof of 'abuse of power' is difficult to obtain and there is a strong likelihood of either having to admit failure or in the absence of facts having to build a case based on assumptions. A single partial solution to the dilemma lies in increasing administrative transparency during the debate that takes place before a decision is taken. But, in spite of some procedural improvements, there is as yet little sign of such a development in France.

In relations between private individuals or between public servants and individuals, it is by no means unusual that corruption takes on the appearance of a sort of metasystem that seems at first glance com-patible with regulations, procedures and institutions, but is in fact a parasite grafted onto the system on which it feeds. Corruption may not be new but in its systematic and virtually institutionalized form it is a new phenomenon in France, just as in Italy, Spain, Germany and so on. In spite of the structural and cultural differences specific to each Western political system, one can point to common features: the requirement of meeting the enormous financial needs of the catch-all parties and the increasing expenses of electioneering, the ever-increasing penetration of market values of political and adminis-trative systems developed to meet other requirements. And in France one can include more specific elements, such as the interpenetration of the governing elites or the control over multiple positions of power (whether elected or not) by actors who are free to exert their influence equally at several levels.

Political parties in France have always been weak and are now even more so, in spite of a general belief among the public that they are all-powerful, or too powerful. They are in fact numerous, divided and undisciplined (except for the PCF which deals with disagreement by exclusion), and have never managed, except by fits and starts, to turn themselves into potent political machines where activist ardour matches a strong territorial and functional presence with a hierarchical organization and a strong back-up in terms of mass support and financial resources. Unlike German, UK, Italian or Scandanavian political parties, and with the notable exception, until recently, of the PCF, French political parties still remain archaic organizations.

This innate weakness, which has never been tackled, accounted for – but did not justify – the 'improvisations' which have enabled the parties to survive: *de facto* incorporation into the political status yet without their having legal organization or constitutional status; few members, hence few subscriptions, but generous (though not disinterested) benefactors on the right, or obliging municipalities on the left; a political system geared to *notables* where the personal vote counted for more than allegiance to an organization; and hence electoral campaigns depending more on an exchange of services than adherence to a programme. This hand-to-mouth system worked more or less until the Fifth Republic: parties in government had secret funds, the *patronat* had its 'good works', the *notables* 'made do', the left 'taxed' its elected members and activists, the Soviet Union and the USA provided a contribution, if the need arose, to their respective causes. The system started to look vulnerable during the Fifth Republic in particular, given the politics of communication adopted by successive governments. The need to mobilize opinion via plebiscite-type referendums as well as resorting to propaganda to make up for the Gaullists being thinly represented had their share in this change. From 1965 onwards, presidental elections by universal franchise played their part, each new election outdoing the cost of the previous one. Winning power meant mobilizing larger sums of money. Winning did not necessarily mean disposing of large funds, as Jacques Chaban-Delmas discovered in 1974; but being without it could result in defeat, as Raymond Barre experienced in 1988.

François Mitterrand was equally aware of this in 1971 at the time of the Epinay Congress, having participated in one presidential campaign and having the ambition to build a large modern left-wing party. But having neither the facilities provided by big business nor adequate subscriptions from members nor a proper mechanism for mobilizing resources as the Communist Party had through firms and municipalities, he had to find financial mechanisms to meet the new situation. Thus Urba-Conseil was set up in 1972. The mechanisms imported were in no way original, having been resorted to on occasion by other political parties; but there was at least one original feature: the centralizing of Socialist Party financial operations through consultancies (*sociétés d'études*), which as political insiders knew perfectly well were 'moles' working for the PS. These organizations worked on the simple principle of providing an intermediary function between those holding the resources (firms) and the beneficiaries (Socialist Party), making the flow of funds virtually mandatory where a voluntary set-up could not have delivered. Whether one takes a realistic or a supremely Machiavellian view, the main providers to the PS (or PC) as a rule had little liking for those on the receiving end of their generosity but were obliged to bite the bullet so as to have access to procurement contracts. In this instance, corruption loses its deviant, marginal, individual side and becomes normal, systematic and generalized.

Traditionally corruption tends to establish a dual relationship between a corrupting party and a corrupted party, effecting a secret exchange, monetary or other, so as to obtain what the observance of normal procedures fails to guarantee them. In the case of systematic corruption practised for the benefit of political parties, the technique is more complex and involves constraints that are often absent from traditional modes of corruption. Three elements are needed in order to pull off systematic corruption: an ultimate beneficiary, the political party; an intermediary, the politician; and a body with money to spend which, in collusion with the political party and in return for payment, entrusts the intermediary with the task of 'selecting' the contracting party from which to buy products or services.

This triangular relationship is frequent, not to say systematic, as regards public or private investment. But corruption comes into play through manipulating or misappropriating the interlinking process whereby resources which are at the same time financial, legal and representative of the community as a whole are put to the service of private – i.e. party – interests. And precisely because recourse to an intermediary body has every appearance of rationality and legitimacy, such misuse of public money is in effect unavoidable. If it has been exposed, the implication is that it has attained excessive proportions either because necessary precautions were not taken or because written evidence of the real destination of the funds being made available was carelessly left about.

This pattern then is simple and effective as it is virtually undetectable. A public body wishing to place a contract calls on the appropriate firms providing goods and services in the required sector. But a competing firm will have a greater chance of success if it uses the services and good offices of a consultancy firm, which after taking a percentage of the total of the contract will transfer the resources thus obtained to the beneficiary. In other words, the political party, in connivance with the authorities it controls, overturns the procedures. In place of the terms of competition provided for, it substitutes a monopoly (or oligopoly) for the benefit of one or more firms; it provides an *a priori* preferential guarantee of the result of a decision-making process that is theoretically open and transparent; and it incorporates a levy in its favour unknown to the taxpayers by adding to the cost of the investment or service or by a reduction in its quality. Legal experts may well talk of unilateral action or contract. In effect, public decision-making is auctioned off.

The firm's attitude is ambivalent. Whilst deploring the system it practises, it may even promote it on the grounds that it asks the lowest fee in return for privileged or monopolistic access to public orders. In other cases, however, directors of firms may apply ethical standards or display a preference for a competitive market or may hold the conviction that their products are in any event the best and the most competitive, and hence deplore a system that for them is just an organized racket. So much was confirmed by the deputy director of the Société auxiliaire d'entreprise (SAE) in a statement in March 1989 to those investigating the Marseilles discovery of faked invoices: 'Our subsidiaries are prevailed upon to make use of consultancies close to political parties so as to increase their chances of obtaining contracts'.[1] From being exceptional, the practice of forging invoices has become routine, or, to quote Alain Madelin: 'in the political world the bogus invoice is as necessary as is fresh air to a normally constituted human being!'[2]

The system of faked invoices introduced by the more or less fictitious consultancies connected with political parties is not the only instrument for financing political and electoral activity. A further one which has been used systematically is the 1901 statute on associations, which is susceptible to a number of interpretations in law. The problems and excesses created by uncontrolled use of this instrument have been revealed in a number of cases, the most celebrated of which is the *Carrefour du développement* affair, by virtue of the funds at stake, the personalities involved and the irresponsible use of public money.

Yet associations are most numerous and most active at local level, because the mayor, who is truly a local 'monarch' in most *communes* where his council's approval, combined with the impotence of the minority opposition ensure his predominance, is in a position that is virtually risk-free to transfer vast subsidies to associations which in most cases he chairs. Some of them perform perfectly respectable functions, such as economic development or cultural activity. Others are no more than screens to promote the mayor or the party in power. Alternatively, they are adept at combining both public and private activities. Many such associations have been carpeted over in recent years. However, they represent only the tip of the iceberg.

The structure of corruption

While taking care to reject the easy, sweeping allegation adopted by the Front National that all political parties are 'rotten to the core', how is one to begin to analyse a phenomenon that has become endemic? In my book *La corruption de la République* (1992a), I put forward five factors for consideration which clearly vary in their make-up and relative significance from one case to another. One might say that they constitute the ingredients of corruption *à la française*, implying that corruption as a universal phenomenon takes on different manifestations which have to be diagnosed and identified. Otherwise, introducing reforms will remain anodyne – as the 1988 and 1990 statutes suggest – a question of treating the symptoms and not the cause..

These factors are the following:

- Concentration of power in the hands of the executive. Since the French Revolution, every authoritarian regime has tried to place power in the hands of a single individual: dictator, emperor, head of state in central government, prefect and mayor in local government. Conversely, democratic regimes have sought, at times intemperately, to fragment political power. Under the Third and Fourth Republics, for instance, government was weakened but prefects and mayors were powerful and influential. The administration which was relatively autonomous acted as a counter-weight. With the Fifth Republic the 'monarchic' model came into its own, at the top first, then at the bottom where the mayors of the larger cities appropriated power in real terms. The 1982 statutes relating to decentralization generalized the model by extending it to the departmental or regional executive. By now the French have become so accustomed to the model's efficacity

(plebifying it constantly by re-electing their local elites) that they
have lost sight of its original or specific character. Frequently, the
party structure is too weak or too poorly integrated to be a vehicle
for corruption and the *notables* necessarily perform this function,
either directly, as in the case of Médecin or Boucheron, to mention two names that have been much in the news, or indirectly
and more discreetly via the people around them.

- Powerful national or local leaders need faithful servants, recruited
on a contractual basis or seconded from administrative posts by
virtue of their sympathies or loyalty. The inner circle, the private
office, increasingly and at every level replaces the normal administrative authorities which it controls, commands and sometimes
short-circuits. A dedicated collaborator takes on a task that an independent civil servant would refuse. After all, his appointment
has made him the eyes, ears and right hand of the leader he serves
and stands in for. Dedication to the individual has replaced
respect for the institution. The system has the advantage of being
dynamic and efficient. But if there is a slip-up, the institutional
system can hardly contain the abuses of procedure caused by this
interpenetration in the decision-making process. In this respect
the *Carrefour du développement* affair stands as an example of the
loss of control brought about by complicity between a minister
and the head of his private office.

- A third factor provides a ground for corruption in France, without constituting an act of corruption in itself. This is the transformation of the decision-making process from a decision reached
unilaterally to a generalized negotiation. The negotiation or
'contractualization' procedure has a number of attractions in that,
once a consensus has been reached, it is hoped that decisions will
be carried out more effectively. However, to avoid clientelist
irregularities (very noticeable, for instance, in the types of pact
reached over recent years) or clandestine arrangements, negotiations must be open and transparent.

- Unless these conditions are met, there is a considerable risk of a
generalized, more or less secret bargaining occurring, which,
despite initially appearing to be effective, gradually deteriorates
into full-blown corruption. Such a pattern of events has been
noticeable in the town-planning sector. Private promoters have
been required, in the name of partnership, to make their contributions to public funds − in itself quite normal − and then on
occasion they may be called upon to provide benefits, again for
public schemes but other than those in hand. If the private

investor is asked to contribute to party or campaign funds, all that is then required is for the last constraints upon personal corruption to be lifted and the political or administrative decision-maker to draw direct or indirect personal benefit from his position of power.

- A further element which favours the development of corruption derives from the failings or inadequacy of control mechanisms. This remark may appear improbable given that French administration with its fundamental mistrust of officials and public alike is bound up with pettifoggery and restrictive procedures. But the instruments applied are often toothless, such controls in general being merely formal – i.e. affecting only procedures, belatedly in the wake of contentious judgments, and uncertain. Added to this, the actors – politicians or civil servants – have themselves devised a range of let-outs and subterfuges to evade these already inadequate controls. Ostensibly with an eye for efficiency, a whole culture of accommodation and rule-bending has come into being. It is an attitude that can often find ready justification: it enables administrative paralysis to be avoided. But it also enables the conviction to grow that the norm exists to be violated or circumvented whenever it is inconvenient; sometimes to further desirable ends, yet frequently for less worthy reasons. Nonetheless, the internal but above all external control mechanisms are the ultimate defences in a system characterized by concentration of power, a low degree of participation and shady transactions. One's pessimism persists when one sees how too many decision-makers conduct themselves. Not only do they decline any form of personal responsibility (as was proposed in the case of mayors by the Defferre Bill, for instance) but they even, and increasingly, refuse to implement legal decisions that go against their interests.

- Lastly, the development of corruption cannot be understood without a reference to changing social values. What justification can be offered for an individual refusing to be party to corruption when he could derive personal or professional advantage by so doing? Can such a refusal be interpreted simply as the result of rationally setting favours hoped for against possible costs, i.e. penalties (see, for instance, Nye, 1967)? To consider the question only from a repressive perspective fails to provide a full explanation. Occasions for indulging in straightforward, risk-free corruption are innumerable, yet the majority of public servants and politicians eschew them. Why? Pizzorno[3] answers the question in terms of its 'moral cost'. The higher the moral cost the less likely the incidence of corruption. But what in a politico-administrative system causes variations in the moral cost? Pizzorno proposes interpreting such variations in terms of the moral recognition an individual acquires when confronted by corruption. Where, for example, there is a marked *esprit de corps* characterized by the defence of values such as the 'general good' and 'public service' which have been profoundly interiorized by those concerned, the cost of corruption is going to be high. Both from his own perspective and from that of his peers, an individual stands to lose a lot by giving way to corruption. Likely material rewards will not compensate for the moral loss resulting from violation of the group norms. (The same analysis can apply to other fields, the use of torture, for instance, or the practice of informing.)

Corruption is thus more likely to spread in cases where the 'immune defence systems' of the group tend to weaken and the 'moral cost' drops; as will occur when public behaviour is less prized than private, when producing results comes to matter more than observing standards, monetary values more than ethical or symbolic values. Viewed thus, the 1980s in France represented a period of upheaval. The left, which had put forward a programme and made much of the need for values, beat a hasty retreat and blithely reneged on all that it had lauded to the skies. However much its earlier Utopianism needed scaling down, the shock was probably too swift and too brutal to avoid the resultant collapse in a value-system which had until then been taken for granted.

Conclusion

The corruption that has blighted politics and administration over the last ten years has had profound repercussions on public opinion, parties and political life in general. It has given rise to not inconsiderable reforms of the ways in which parties and electoral campaigns are financed as well as changes in administrative procedure. But it appears equally clear that the ethical or legal implications have been sidestepped with the tacit accord of a large section of the political community.

In the short term, the impact of the several 'affairs' was devastating. In the *Luchaire* affair, just as in those of *Carrefour du développement* or the forged Marseilles invoices, the socialists were obliged to adopt a retaliatory strategy, especially when between 1986 and 1988 they had lost control over vital government machinery regarding the police and the justice system and the 1988 presidential battle was getting under way. The strategy was adroit and cynical, with François Mitterrand affecting consternation and outrage at the intrusion of money into politics, and managing to get the better of Jacques Chirac. Anticipating the reactions of the press, public opinion and his political opponents, Mitterrand called for the reform of party and campaign financing as a priority issue. The reform was rushed through but did nothing to avert finagling on the part of presidential candidates nor deceit in the form of two-source financing: an official fund managed by the campaign treasurers and a sizeable unofficial fund fed by corruption which was forced by circumstances to be more underhand. It required the new legislative initiatives of 1990 and their drastic and concrete measures to introduce profound reforms to the sources of financing and control over expenditure. The ensuing statute marked real progress, as was evidenced in the 1992 regional and 1993 parliamentary elections. However, the clauses that grant amnesty to criminal acts in regard to party political financing have had a disastrous effect in that they left the impression – correctly, as it happens – that politicians were above the law, a measure of how damaging the years between 1988 and 1992 were. Revelations by the press or the judiciary of the number of major and minor cases were not handled satisfactorily with a total lack of action being taken against politicians involved in the scandals.

The Socialist Party, which was principally concerned with the cases brought to light, has suffered more than any other party from public opprobrium towards political parties. Although polls have shown that faith in parties of whatever complexion has been rudely shaken and although the Front National has sought to blacken the issue with its slogan claiming that all are equally corrupt, the Socialist Party has had to bear the brunt of the wave of rejection affecting the political establishment. Witness the landslide victory of the right in the spring of 1993, an electoral Beresina for the party constituted at Epinay in 1971.

In certain respects the phase that began with the formation of the new Socialist Party has come to an end. It had no sooner been formed than the new PS and its secretary-general, François Mitterrand, set about turning it into a machine for the conquest of power, a prominent but discreet role being given to Urba, the consultancy firm which would make a powerful contribution to financing the presidential elections of 1974, 1981 and 1988, and the national activities of the PS as a whole. Corruption was at the heart of Mitterrand's strategy for political conquest. It also devastated the Socialist Party, paradoxically sparing the person by and for whom the apparatus for hidden financing had been set up. The last-ditch attempt by Pierre Bérégovoy to separate the Socialist Party image, as well as his own, from the many and diverse affairs involving corruption turned out to be a failure both personally and for the party. Its one achievement has been the reforms – not inconsiderable in themselves – affecting administrative structures and procedures, which, as experience shows had been open to corrupt practice, and the creation of a central office for the prevention of corruption set up in spring 1993.

The blow to the Socialist Party has been yet more bitter as regards both the ethical and legal solutions provided for the problem of corruption. On the legal side, and for all the denunciations made by the Party stressing the legal distinction between meddling or personal enrichment (unaffected by the 1990 amnesty legislation) and acts of corruption linked to party financing, so far the few individuals that have been brought to justice have been relatively unimportant. The feeling at large is that the Socialist Party has amnestied itself and that the courts have been, directly or indirectly, prevented from fulfilling the mission entrusted to them by law. Contrary to what is taking place in Italy where the courts have played a crucial role in exposing and prosecuting cases of corruption, justice in France has never been in a position to take advantage of a proper separation of powers because of interference by the legislature and the executive.

More fundamentally, the government, parliament and in general the political and administrative elites of the country have at no time initiated a thorough examination of the ethical implications of questions involving the relationship of money to politics, the frontier between public and private interests, means with regard to ends, settling conflicts of interest, a politician's responsibility and so on.

Finally, the political system and the political community have fairly successfully surmounted the ordeal represented by the 'affairs'. The ethical problem itself remains intact, that is to say for the most part foreign to the preoccupations of the elites.

Notes

1. *Le Monde*, 11 October 1991.
2. Quoted in *Le Matin*, 4 December 1987.
3. A. Pizzorno, introduction to D. Della Porta (1992).

2

FRANCE–AFRICA: WITHIN THE FAMILY

JEAN-FRANÇOIS MÉDARD

Franco-African relations have a particular and enduring character which, from General de Gaulle to François Mitterrand, has never failed to surprise foreign observers. Not only have the innumerable links between France and most of her former colonies remained strong since independence but these links have a specific nature. So it is that relations between France and the African countries within its sphere are the responsibility not of the Quai D'Orsay but of the Ministry for Cooperation (which has superseded the Ministry for France Overseas) under the direct control of the Elysée (except, of course, during periods of cohabitation). But more than this, the relationship – in theory, one between states – is, as has often been remarked, of a highly personalized kind (Bayart, 1984: 55–60). Mention of 'our African friends' or of the 'tightly-knit Franco-African family' takes in not only the country in question but its political leaders and, beyond them, the ruling elite. In other words, Franco-African relations are only loosely institutionalized, being based on a web of 'friendships' that bind a section of the French governing class and that of certain African countries. Naturally it is a source of some comfort to learn from a recent Minister for Cooperation, Michel Roussin, that 'talk of the Pasqua, Roussin or Foccart networks implies no more than the bonds of friendship that exist on both sides. What counts is that our African friends call us when they have a problem.' This notion of the bonds of friendship is, however, a particularly ambiguous one and serves to legitimize suspect practices and corrupt practices in which political, economic and social interchange is inextricably bound up. Whether the term corruption is taken in its wider classical sense of decomposition or in its current narrower sense, Franco-African relations are fundamentally corrupt. They constitute one of the areas in French politics most affected by corruption, so much so that Franco-African relations are frequently seen as one and the same with intrigue.

The enduring nature of Franco-African relations springs, at least in its original form, from a strategic essentially neocolonial view, namely to decolonize without decolonizing, the aim being to maintain a French presence and influence in Africa across and beyond the accession to independence. Furthermore, a number of strategic considerations were dominant at the time. The Algerian war was not over and General de Gaulle wanted France to have access to certain strategic raw materials, notably oil and uranium. The policy has been pursued unswervingly by successive heads of state, whatever they may have said or allowed to be thought. However, this continuity implies the marginalizing in the medium term both of Franco-African relations as compared with France's international relations as a whole, and of relations between France and French-speaking Africa as compared with relations between France and the rest of Africa. My contention here is that the maintenance of close links with a number of these countries rests to a large degree on the patrimonialization of Franco-African relations, which resolves itself into confusing public and private matters. That is not to say that what are considered to be the pillars of Franco-African relations – defence agreements, the franc area, Franco-African summits – are unimportant but that these institutional instruments have been in large part subverted by such patrimonialism. The interpretation of this neocolonialism in exclusively economic terms, given in a context of dependency, has always seemed simplistic to me. For all that, dependency is not a myth. But, as has often been remarked, the objective of this post-colonial strategy cannot be reduced to the economic advantages derived by France since the overall balance of these advantages is not necessarily positive. The interpretation of the economic consequences of French colonization given by Jacques Marseille can be extended to cover French neocolonialism. In a seamless continuation the neocolonial economy, just like the colonial economy before it, is rent seeking above all else (Marseille, 1984). Thus the economic interest of French firms treating with Africa should not be confused with that of France taken as a whole. The purpose of this neocolonial strategy was in the first place political, namely to set up a clientele of protected states so as to enable France to retain her status as a medium-size power (Bayart, 1993: 112). With the Gaullist era, French policy evolved on two parallel fronts: towards the third world, with an inherent dose of anti-Americanism, allowing France to pose as the champion of third-world countries in the face of American imperialism; and across a neocolonialist stance, in itself more discreet, but hard-headed to the point of cynicism and declining to draw the line at dirty tricks or systematic recourse to clientelism, corruption and, in a more general way, patrimonialism. The patrimonialism that characterizes the post-colonial African state (Médard, 1991: 323–54) extends precisely into Franco-African relations. The thrust of these relations in a complex way informs political, economic and social exchanges.

The *système Foccart*: the policy of networks

To understand Gaullist practice in Africa one has to go back to the origins of the Gaullist movement which, it needs to be remembered, cannot be reduced simply to its successive partisan incarnations (RPF under the Fourth Republic, UNR, UDR . . .) nor to the General's charismatic personality. The movement was born out of the Resistance and the clandestine fight against the Nazi occupying power and the Vichy regime. It had its origin in the Resistance and underground networks, particularly in the BCRA, General de Gaulle's intelligence arm in London, which was the distant source of the SDECE. Here was the matrix of the Gaullist networks. However, although the two structures have in part overlapped, they should not be confused. Gaullism before it became a movement, a party or a rally was in the first place a collection of more or less clandestine networks. These networks provided the movement with a structure. They could remain dormant for periods and be reactivated in a moment when the need arose; and it was Jacques Foccart who had the key role in setting up their basic structure. But the secrecy of his activity makes exact and precise information difficult to come by and has contributed to the aura of myth that surrounds him, which is unhelpful in terms of analysis. The easy way out has too often been to allow the man to remain an enigma, so giving free rein to fabrication. But Jacques Foccart was not merely a myth and, in spite of its being limited, there is enough plausibility in the information available to enable one to piece together the reasons that motivated his policy.

For 17 years Jacques Foccart was one of de Gaulle's closest collaborators, the one who served him longest. He occupied a strategic position at the Elysée in the sense that he was at the same time responsible for African policy as Secretary-General for the

Community, then Secretary for African and Madagascan Affairs, and for liaison with the secret services. In this dual capacity, he had daily meetings with Charles de Gaulle; thus his influence was considerable, since he could make use of the official secret services and of his own parallel services while being the President's official representative for African questions. In this capacity he carried out the more devious work of the regime, performing the task at the same time of fall guy and of lightning conductor for the General. A clear division of labour was established with Charles de Gaulle exercising the elevated official political role and Jacques Foccart the occult – because devious and undisclosable – role, the right hand insofar as was possible being unaware of what the left hand was up to, but reaping the benefit all the same. Charles de Gaulle and Jacques Foccart can no more be separated than can these two aspects of Gaullist strategy. When de Gaulle came to power in 1958, Foccart became his effective representative where Africa was concerned. In the first place, he continued to make use of both political contacts and business connections to further his influence in French circles, while his official responsibilities allowed him systematically to cultivate the friendship of African leaders. His department took charge of welcoming key African figures when they came to Paris (Cean/Institut Charles de Gaulle, 1980: 403) and his own availability ensured that their needs could be met. In this way a basis of trust, friendship and mutual understanding was built up between Foccart and African politicians. He was on hand to resolve personal and family as well as political problems; he behaved as a friend to them.

Gabon, in fact, was Foccart's chosen territory. Omar Bongo, who according to Pierre Marion, sometime head of the SDECE, then of the DGSE, was 'Foccart's creature', owed his position to friends and, in particular, to Colonel Maurice Robert, who headed the African section of the SDECE (Péan, 1983; Reed, 1987; Marion, 1991). Moreover, the nationalized oil company Elf-Aquitaine, all-powerful in Gabon, constituted its own intelligence service and filled it with friends (Péan, *ibid.*; Smith and Glaser, 1992: 63–82). The systematic interconnection of business and politics is stressed by several observers. Marion, for example, in referring to the question of recruiting for these influential positions, writes of 'links forged by longstanding loyalty to Gaullism and the convergent interests Foccart made it his business to foster' (Marion, *ibid.*: 101–3). Again, Alexandre de Marenches, Marion's predecessor as head of the SDECE, is quoted as saying: 'Foccart dealt in triangular operations, involving currency, and clearly embodied relations with Gabon. The only way to obtain illicit money is to take it out of France and bring it back' (Péan, *ibid.*: 418). Péan in turn remarks that 'a number of deals concluded between French firms, particularly in public works, armaments and electronics, and certain African governments, more especially those of the Côte d'Ivoire and Gabon, produced large commissions which, by various obscure channels, tended to end up in the pocket of the Gaullists.' In Péan's view it was this function of backdoor banker for the Gaullist movement that explains why de Gaulle raised no objection to Foccart's carrying on his official functions concurrently with his private activity. But Péan notes that Jacques Foccart 'was interested far less in money than in questions of power and influence' (*ibid.*: 420). It does not appear that in Foccart's case the association of business interests and politics represented a strategy for personal gain. What apparently drove him was personal loyalty to de Gaulle and his policies.

This all serves to underline the intrinsically corrupt nature of a system of relations where business is blithely mixed with politics, however personally uncorrupted the corrupters may be and however elevated are the political objectives that screen their activities. Certain means to ends may be employed which may totally corrupt the ends. The absence of transparency, which is the defining mark of secret services, means that people have to be of exceptional calibre if corruption is to be avoided. Bad habits are easily acquired under cover, where dealings between governments are concerned and at a more personal level, where links may rely on government resources and involve indiscretions that are difficult to control. None of this changed with the arrival of François Mitterrand and the socialist government.

Franco-African relations under François Mitterrand

On the subject of government aid in Africa, Sylvie Brunel remarks: 'Certainly the left broke no new ground and merely took over practices already in force, that dated from what was known as the "*système Foccart*", with the same cynicism and shady dealing, as its predecessors' (Brunel, 1993: 21).

When the left came to power in France in 1981, hope and panic prevailed in equal measure. Many hoped for or feared a change in France's African policy, involving a radical redefinition of objectives and, to a degree, a clean-up of methods. The socialist party's ideologists urged such a course but the ambivalence of the presidential discourse soon encouraged scepticism. With Africa remaining the preserve of the President, the socialist party had no real say in the definition of policy. On coming to office, François Mitterrand appointed Jean-Pierre Cot, known to be strongly in favour of a new direction in African policy, as Minister for Cooperation. But while initially appearing to gratify activists in the party, he appointed one of his friends, Guy Penne, to head the special African group at the Elysée. Penne had no knowledge of Africa but he had the confidence of the President who counted on him as a freemason to set in motion the highly effectual freemasonry network in Africa on behalf of French interests; as it has been well put: 'in Africa politics invariably leads back to the network' (Smith and Glaser, 1992: viii). Mitterrand's elder son, Jean-Christophe, who, in Pierre Marion's estimation, 'strikes one as casual and second-rate' (Marion, 1991: 113), was in no time recruited for the group, initially simply as acting librarian. He quickly became Penne's right-hand man, wielding greater power in fact, since he had the benefit of direct access to his father. In 1986, 'Daddy-told me', as he was known, was officially appointed technical adviser to the Elysée, then replacing Penne who had been somewhat smeared by the *Carrefour du développement* affair and opted for a seat in the Senate; and over a period of ten years he remained his father's chief adviser and policy-initiator where Africa was concerned. François Mitterrand foolishly relied on him on the grounds that he was acquainted with Africa, having spent 12 years as a journalist with AFP at Nouakchott and Lomé, 'Foccart country', according to Pierre Marion. He had formed relationships there, in particular with President Eyadema, which could prove useful to his father. It did not take long for inconsistencies to appear between the policy followed by Jean-Pierre Cot at the Ministry for Cooperation and that of the Elysée, with African policy increasingly lacking coherence. Tension between Jean-Pierre Cot and the African team at the Elysée soon became intolerable and Cot, markedly unpopular with African leaders who had traditional friendships with France, resigned to be replaced by Christian Nucci, a socialist deputy close to the President, who later achieved notoriety in the *Carrefour du développement* affair. Jean-François Bayart writes: 'Jean-Pierre Cot's replacement by Christian Nucci, who had no hesitation in describing himself as "African and born in Africa", magnified to the point of caricature, the priority accorded to personal relationships insofar as they then became a substitute for policy' (Bayart, 1984: 57). With the socialist defeat in 1986 an era of cohabitation began. Jacques Chirac, the new Prime Minister, appointed Michel Aurillac as Minister for

Cooperation and more significantly called upon the services of Jacques Foccart again as adviser, Foccart then re-established his contacts. François Mitterrand continued to intervene in African affairs by way of his own team. With the return of the socialists in 1988, the President recovered full charge of African affairs and Jean-Christophe Mitterrand was free to deploy his talents.

Thus under Mitterrand the same methods applied, politics combined with business, string-pulling resorted to. All that changed were the networks and the links between them. In *Ces messieurs Afrique*, Smith and Glaser provide detailed case-studies of 11 individuals with varying degrees of influence in regard to Africa. The President's son and his sometimes unsuitable friends were engaged undisturbed in dealings of many and various kinds (Smith and Glaser, 1992: 209–35), with his father intervening only in 1992 to exclude him from the Elysée team. One might cite the Sucden affair as an example. This refers to a firm, directed by Serge Vassano (Smith and Glaser: 63–82), which bought up 400,000 tons of surplus cocoa from the Côte-d'Ivoire that had been misguidedly stockpiled by Houphouet-Boigny in order to influence world prices. A sum of 400 million francs was made over from the Caisse centrale de coopération économique, at the Elysée's bidding, ostensibly to finance the excess cost of stockpiling, valued in fact at 150 million francs. Thus the French taxpayer was made to foot the bill for an occult, political and financial deal, that well illustrates the confusion of public and private interests typical of Franco-African affairs. The deal achieved a dual result: it enabled Houphouet-Boigny to be bailed out and a private French company to establish itself internationally. The loan in question was arranged by Jean-Christophe Mitterrand (Gombeaud, Moutout and Smith, 1990) in collaboration with Jean-Pierre Fleury, chairman of ADEFI International, a public relations firm serving African heads of state, public relations being understood in a wide sense to include security police and surveillance of opposition leaders (Smith and Glaser: 216–21).

Hence politicians did deals but the government also encouraged private racketeering, described as 'state racketeering' by Péan (1983: 96). Conversely, businessmen engaged in politics. They did so because it is difficult not to if you want to do business in Africa and because they are thereby doing politicians a service. A chapter in Smith and Glaser (9–28) deals with M. Prouteau, head of the CNPF Africa committee, chairman of the French African Investors Committee (CIAN) and of the Centre for the Promotion of Industry in Africa (CEPIA), and, in addition, a former Grand Master of the

Grand Orient of France and sometime State Secretary for Small- and Medium-Size Industries in the Raymond Barre government. According to Smith and Glaser, he was influential in French African policy-making as well as in joint governmental committees concerned with the application of cooperation agreements. They stress the significant role played by freemasonry in the spheres of business and politics. They also provide further instances of persons dubious on one count or another and implicated in Franco-African affairs. These are: Paul Barril, a police officer who had been moved from a former posting at the Elysée and then took up with a private security firm, who 'puts the aura of having served in presidential security to use in proposing his services to most French-speaking African presidents across his contacts with the *gendarmerie* officers' association' (*ibid*.: 93–104); Jacques Vergès (*ibid*.: 105–27), one-time counsel for the FLN, who counted Klaus Barbie as well as African dictators among his clients; Jean-Yves Ollivier, who was 'high-flying and influential' in relations between France and South Africa (*ibid*.: 149–68); and Hervé Bourges (*ibid*.: 129–48), a former left-wing journalist and director of schools of journalism in Yaoundé, Dakar and Lille, who subsequently embarked on a highly successful career in radio and television (Radio France International, Antenne 2, FR3). Bourges had been close to A. Ahidjo, former dictator of Cameroon, and had a regrettable tendency to view news bulletins as public relations exercises on behalf of African heads of state (see report on A. Ahidjo in *Jeune Afrique*, 19 March 1976). A final example was André Tarallo of the Elf-Erap group in Africa, who was deeply implicated in the politics of whichever country he was established in, Gabon, Congo or Angola. In all these cases, politics and business were so confused that it was difficult to tell which was accessory to the other.

Hence the notion of the network with all its implications dominates Franco-African relations: 'Africa is primarily a matter of relations' (Smith and Glaser: x); 'whether in its original form, readapted or newly set up, (the network) retains its cardinal virtues' (*ibid*.: ix). The 'new African godfathers', as described by Smith and Glaser, look on their address books as their principal asset. Each has his clientele with his chosen ground, country of preference and well-placed friends. The difference from when the *système Foccart* operated is that it is no longer a large single network run fairly flexibly from the top in a somewhat hierarchical tree-like structure. At present, it would be clearer to talk of a reticulated structure, at the top at least, because if 'no-one sees beyond the end of his own little network' there is still a form of interconnection at the apex though of a looser kind. The

Elysée unit thus appears to be the 'multiservices hub where the main points of Franco-African relations are determined' (*ibid.*: xiii), without its being the *deus ex machina* that it once was. Moreover, the Gaullist policy towards Africa, despite or rather because of the contradiction between discourse and practice, was in keeping with a clear strategic vision. Mitterrand's African policy which, as Jean-François Bayart reminds us, in fact marks a return to that inaugurated by the Mitterrand of the Fourth Republic (Bayart, 1984: 52), now has more of the character of day-to-day management of the heritage of a past that is outmoded. It follows a course that requires neither vision nor prognosis and is less the result of habit than of routine, calling on old and tried formulas rather than on the exercise of talent. Why has it come to this? Probably because the recourse to old clientelist formulas can hardly produce radical rethinking. Clientelism begets clientelism to a remarkable degree. By trying to piece together the reasoning that informs such methods, at once political, economic and social, it becomes easier to understand the abiding character of this political concept and the means it employs, both being inextricably linked.

The interconnection between political, economic and social relations

One feature constantly recurs in the foregoing pages and that is the importance of interpersonal networks in the relations between French and African governments, and it explains why analysis in terms of social interchange (Padioleau, 1986: 197–233; Emerson, 1976: 335–44) throws significant new light on the patrimonialism underlying these relations. The confusion of public and private that is characteristic of patrimonialism (Médard, 1982: 162–92) occurs at two levels: confusion of the public (or political) with the economic function and confusion of the public with the personal. Confusion of the political and the economic shows itself in political resources being exchanged for economic and vice versa. Power and wealth are not clearly differentiated; power enables wealth to be obtained while wealth similarly promotes the acquisition of power. If the relationship between the political and the economic function is impersonal as in the case of the market, where goods and services are exchanged for other goods and services through the medium of money, or as in the case of barter, where goods and services are exchanged directly, political exchange can then be clearly seen as pure economic exchange. Economic analysis of corruption is then directly applicable. Such economic corruption corresponds to what James Scott calls 'market corruption' and to what Jean Padioleau terms barter trading corruption (Scott, 1972 and Padioleau, 1975). In point of fact, the two concepts need to be distinguished since they represent two variants of economic exchange. In the first case, exchange is effected through the medium of money and the market; in the second it is direct. The only question from an analytical point of view is to know whether the corrupting party seeks political or economic benefit, since the party corrupted always seeks economic benefit. The private economic interest that is sought may be individual, i.e. to the advantage of an individual politician, civil servant or businessman, or it may be collective, i.e. to the advantage of a party, a private firm, or even in certain cases a public body, in which case the corrupt deal is necessarily effected through the intermediary of individuals acting as representatives for the organization. Such individuals may be said themselves to be corrupt to the extent that they derive personal advantage from the transaction. It is invariably correct to speak of corruption in respect of the illegal financing of political parties, a party being a political organization that represents private collective interests in spite of its claiming not to. Insofar as these forms of dealing, which have an undeniable economic component, are carried out, as is so often the case in Africa in the context of interpersonal and hence social dealings, the social exchange element is combined with the economic or political. Corruption may be termed relational or again social when it is based on a social relationship, in which case it has the character of a social and not a purely economic exchange and in such a context Padioleau speaks of 'social exchange corruption'. Even if the social exchange can never be entirely reduced to economic exchange, it nevertheless contains to a variable degree an economic component. In most instances economic and social elements intertwine in the same transactions, one being subordinate to the other. The social element may be subordinate to the economic or the economic (or political) element may instrumentalize social exchange to its advantage or simply disguise itself as social exchange.

The processes of patrimonialism are characterized by this intermingling of political exchange and economic exchange and of political exchange and social exchange. The question of motives arises: are they in the first place political? Or economic? The answer depends on the nature of the resources exchanged and the priority accorded them by one or other of the parties to the deal. At the outset it may be thought that where political leaders are concerned the stakes are primarily political: recourse to corruption is had towards a political objective in line with a political strategy of neocolonialism. But recourse to corruption has a tendency to contaminate political motives and rebound on them. Herein lies the problem of resorting to occult methods, more especially by making use of special services. Recourse to these methods, initially seen as exceptional, tends to become a matter of routine, helped by the fact that the element of secrecy which is inevitable makes control difficult. And the public interest shifts imperceptibly to the party interest, and the interest of the party to that of the individual politician. And how then are the interest of the politician and personal interest to be distinguished? Corruption which is systematically practised corrupts political activity itself in the end.

In Africa, in every field and at every level, relations are personalized to such an extent that they constitute an obstacle to institutionalized relations. One might go so far as to say that there is an allergy to relations that are anonymous and impersonal. Power is represented not by the state, not by an abstract concept, but by whoever controls the resources one has need of. This may have serious consequences on organizational functioning. Someone who is sick, for instance, may not be able to have access to treatment if he doesn't have the right contacts or belong to the right tribe. Indeed, administration whose smooth running depends on its being impersonal breaks down under the effect of such particularity; its driving force comes from its agents who pursue their own personal strategy.

For this state of affairs there are two interpretations – at first sight mutually exclusive ones – a culturalist interpretation and a strategic interpretation. According to the first, the personalization of Franco-African relations reflects the degree of adaptation on the part of their French associates to African culture, French culture being more readily adaptable to African culture than, for example, UK culture. Conversely, interpretation based on individual strategy tends to emphasize the universality and not the cultural specificity of this conduct.

In fact, both explanations are complementary. From the strategic point of view, the ability to adapt presupposes reckoning with the culture within which one operates. African countries are in a situation of structural dependency on northern countries and it is on this basis that the relationship between unequal partners is built up. This needs to be remembered, especially since dependency theories, in themselves too simplistic, are no longer in fashion. Such a situation has suggested a distinction be made between client-states and satellite-states (Médard, 1976: 130–1).

François Constantin and Christian Coulon have applied the

clientelist paradigm to account for the specific nature of the relationship obtaining between France and her former colonies (Constantin and Coulon, 1977), an idea that has been taken up and given a more general and systematic application by Bertrand Badie (1992). The problem in applying the clientelist model to relations between states is that the clientele relationship being one of dependency between persons seems inappropriate as a notion characterizing a dependent relationship between states (Lacam, 1993). The clientele relationship is in fact 'a relationship of personal dependency founded on an exchange of favours between two persons – patron or protector and client – who control unequal resources' (Médard, 1976: 103). Significant aspects of the clientele relationship are overlooked when the notion is given collective application, but the other characteristics of the relationship fit remarkably well, especially the specific nature of the exchange between unequal parties proper to clientelism. In particular, 'state clientelism' feeds on personal exchanges of a clientelist type between members of French and African elites. Ties of friendship between members of the respective elites are variously friendly relations between equals or clientele-type relations where there is inequality.

Furthermore, in such relations those who are assumed to be clients, the African heads of state, show so much ability in manipulating their protector that one is frequently left wondering who is protector and who is client, in other words who exactly is being duped (Péan, 1983). The *maestria* with which Omar Bongo manipulated French authorities, whether in the person of Valéry Giscard d'Estaing or of François Mitterrand, raises significant questions on this score (Péan, 1983). The patron/client relationship, apart from exceptional cases involving great disparity, presupposes not puppets but individuals whose resources are unequal and who enjoy relative autonomy. The advantage of the patron/client model, as against analyses of a more simplistic dependency kind, is that it provides an explanation for this. So we are faced with clientelism on two levels; first, 'state clientelism', which because it is impersonal is incomplete; and second, classic integral clientelism, a relationship between equals, between buddies, where the personal element is to the fore.

Analysis in terms of social exchange has the advantage of illuminating both the classic clientelist relationship (interpersonal exchange between equals) and the relationship between friends or buddies (exchange between equals), and of highlighting the ambiguous nature of social exchange insofar as it contains an economic (or political) factor. The social exchange between Jean-Baptiste Bokassa and Valéry Giscard d'Estaing affords a good illustration here (Lamothe, 1982).

The foregoing has aimed to substantiate the reproductive capacity not only of colonial patterns of behaviour, in a context of greater marginalization, but of patrimonial behaviour too within Franco-African relations, whoever the president and whatever the government. It is unlikely, however, that this state of affairs can last for very much longer, since the economic and political context of Franco-African relations is undergoing rapid change. International clientelism whether at the level of the state or relations between persons presupposes political and economic resources in order to be able to function. With the end of the cold war, the economic marginalization of the African continent and the recession whose effects are felt everywhere, resources – and particularly economic resources – are becoming scarce; France is less and less able to maintain a clientele of African states and finds itself obliged to pass over responsibilities to international financial institutions. Economic constraints have got the better of political impulses. Statements of intent on the part of politicians, from Jacques Chirac to François Mitterrand, should be taken at no more than face value; a radical realignment of Franco-African relations is of necessity under way. In any event, France needs to stabilize its African milieu, but this can only be done by making use of aid in a way that is more efficient for both partners and not by persisting in the error of neocolonial clientelism.

3

THE VICIOUS CIRCLES OF CORRUPTION IN ITALY

Donatella Della Porta

If the 1970s were marked in the collective memory of most Italians by political violence and terrorism, the 1980s and the beginning of the decade following them will be remembered as the years of political corruption. From February 1992 in particular, judicial investigations and journalistic inquiries have uncovered the mechanisms of corruption within public and government-controlled bodies, in the most varied sectors of public administration, both on the periphery and at the very centre of the political system. Corruption – or rather an intolerance of the extent to which the phenomenon had spread – has resulted in what has been termed 'the collapse of a regime' or 'the crisis of the First Republic'. Although knowledge of the historical development of the phenomenon is still limited, confessions by some politicians and entrepreneurs speak of a growth in corruption, particularly in the last two decades of the history of the republic. What explanations are there for this growth? What dynamics favour the widening spread of corruption?

On the subject of the dynamics of corruption, formal studies have suggested some of the possible directions in which the phenomenon spreads. First of all, corruption spreads *from the top to the bottom* (Werner, 1983: 150): corrupt bosses help to choose which men to place in political parties and public administration, and their choice is naturally oriented towards those persons that – because of their pragmatism or unscrupulousness – do not represent any risk for the highly corrupt system. Secondly, corruption extends *from the bottom to the top*: 'Once the incentives for petty corruption have been created – some have written – corruption tends to develop upwards, through a complicity of interests. This, in turn, creates through impunity a condition which encourages the growth of corruption' (Cadot, 1987: 239).

Thirdly, the continuous movement of political figures from elective posts in governmental organizations to party nominated positions in public bodies encourages the spreading of corrupt practices *from one institution to another*. The spread of corruption itself diminishes its costs, decreasing both the sense of guilt and the loss of reputation and increasing, on the other hand, the opportunities to find a partner for corrupt barter deals. Moreover, the spread of corruption makes it more expensive to control, since corrupt activities are often interwoven and, therefore, the number of people prepared to give information is smaller (Lui, 1985). Finally, because of the lack of honest administrators to turn to, entrepreneurs have no alternative but to pay the bribe (Rose-Ackerman, 1978). As a result of these mechanisms of expansion, corruption becomes systematized: 'A situation in which illegality has become the rule, and . . . corruption is so regular and institutionalised that the organisation rewards those who act illegally and, *de facto*, penalises those who accept the old rules' (Caiden and Caiden, 1977: 306).

These mechanisms, already observed 'in operation' in the case of Italy (Della Porta, 1992: 324–6), certainly contribute to the 'widening spread' of corruption. One can, however, proceed further in understanding the development of the phenomenon by not limiting oneself to the analysis of the so-called internal mechanisms, but by looking also at the interaction between political corruption and other phenomena – or, better, pathologies – often mentioned in sociological and political studies of Italy, in particular on clientelism, poor administration and organized crime (see also Della Porta, 1995).

Corrupt politicians and their clients. The vicious circle: clientelism–corruption–clientelism

A first observation emerging from research is the strong link between political corruption, which can be summed up as an exchange of public decisions for money, and clientelism, which instead takes the form of an exchange of favours for electoral suffrage.[1] The politicians implicated in cases of political corruption seem to have a rare capacity for *networking* – i.e. an ability to form relationships, create ties of trust, induce mutual obligations and favours – to which can be added a conception of public resources as a private asset. Both these characteristics, which are certainly useful in organizing illegal barters, allow the development of networks of personal consensus formed both by clients and by 'friends' in the local establishment. Several witnesses are, in fact, in agreement on the ability of many defendants to construct their own feudal dominions of electoral suffrage and complicity spread by way of favours to individuals, and favours guaranteed to various secondary associations and informal groups. One can say, therefore, that corrupt politicians tend to develop both traditional forms of clientelism, with localized relationships between patron and client, and a clientelistic network, linked to broad institutional contexts, i.e. both *patron brokerage* and *organizational clientelistic brokerage*, according to the definition given by Eisenstadt and Roniger (1984).

Besides creating for themselves feudal dominions of clients-electors, corrupt politicians succeed in building favoured relationships with sectors and groups which can 'reward' them more highly for their protection and connivance. To take but one example, in connection with a Sicilian hospital, studied during the course of my research, one of the interviewees had remarked on the 'corrupting power' of the president of the governing body: 'He called magistrates or magistrates' wives to teach in the specialist schools; he offered consultancies to important professionals; he formed links with professional and entrepreneurial circles in Catania; he made corruption the rule' (interview CT1).

In the management of their public offices, corrupt politicians are very active and show a certain 'managerial ability': they construct new hospital wards, assign consultancies, buy and sell public real estate, contract services, etc. In fact, it is their attempts to increase the volume of bribes which lead corrupt politicians to multiply the expenses and activities of their offices and, thereby, the possibility of distributing favours. In fact, they have to spend more public funds, at least in those sectors where illicit gains look easiest.

The networks of relationships and money made on the corruption market are reinvested in politics, making the corrupt politician more competitive compared with his political rivals, both inside and outside his party. In fact, the bribes received do not end up only in personal bank accounts in Switzerland – they are reinvested in political activities, above all with the main aim of getting the party to reconfirm an appointment. The corrupt politician, in order to reach his goal, may utilize illicit money in different ways. First, he can make donations to his party, or perhaps more often, to a leader of a faction. Secondly, he can create, by reinvesting illegal funds in normal clientelistic politics, an autonomous personal entourage (of 'packages' of membership cards and votes) which can later be negotiated with influential party members, obtaining in exchange new mandates in public bodies. As explained to the judges by the first informers in the large-scale investigation of corruption known as *Mani pulite*: 'With the proceeds from bribes, I paid for the membership cards of those enrolled in my section and, when it came to the various renewals of mandates, I controlled a package of membership cards and votes that I put at the disposal of my party, and in particular of those people whom my principal sponsor . . . pointed out to me each time . . . . My package of votes and membership cards, as well as my support for this or that candidate, I placed on the party's table when the time came for my mandate to be renewed, or for a different office to be given to me' (Carlucci, 1992: 118–19).

Furthermore, by distributing favours, the corrupt politician acquires the necessary complicity of the public administration. As observed by the jurist Sabino Cassese, recently Minister for Public Administration (1992), 'in local structures, an intermediate class has been created and has established itself, a mixture of bureaucrat-politicians, bureaucrats loyal to politicians, trade-unionists-politicians-public administrators, etc. who deal in politics, govern and administer: they exercise, therefore, three powers which should be separate . . . . This system has two effects. In the first place, no-one knows where politics end and administration begins. There are neither pure politicians, nor pure bureaucrats. There is no mobility, but accumulation of roles. Secondly, opposition to corrupt politics, from within public bodies, is almost totally absent.' The 'bureaucrat loyal to the politician' performs, in effect, an important role for the survival of the corrupt system. Not only does he often act as an inter-mediary between politicians and entrepreneurs, but, moreover, his connivance reduces the chance of anyone checking on the activities of politicians. The protection of public officials is useful to the corrupt in the course of judiciary investigations: in fact, it is not by chance that the judges from both Savona and Catania have complained about the disappearance of documents from the archives of the public administration and about the 'bureaucratic delays' and 'heel-dragging' with which many bureaucrats replied to their request to examine documents implicating politicians under investigation. In exchange for their connivance, the protected bureaucrats often obtain a share in the collection of bribes, as delegates of their political party, or in their own right (in general, bribes of a lesser nature, often linked to the collection of payment orders).

It must be added that bribes and votes are not alternatives. The entrepreneur who, thanks to the payment of a bribe, finds himself in a privileged market situation, may have an interest in forming a stable relationship with his counterpart and, therefore, votes and encourages others to vote for that administrator with whom he has a corrupt barter relationship. In some measure, corruption itself can become, therefore, an instrument for consensus even amongst people from whom a bribe is demanded while at the same time, there is a need to be protected by a powerful figure – as is shown, for example, by a story told to me by a Sicilian administrator: 'A small entrepreneur, who had supplied upholstery to the Vittorio Emanuele Hospital, had complained to me that he had had to pay a bribe. During the electoral campaign, he had hanging from his shop the poster of X (one of the administrators convicted for corruption). When I asked him "What's going on?", he answered "I have to live!" Thus, bribery, when it works, is a mechanism which brings consensus. It does not create victims, but accomplices. The entrepreneur who succeeds in entering the charmed circle takes risks but makes a fortune. He gives his agreement' (interview CT1).

As illustrated by Figure 3.1, clientelism and corruption are interwoven, therefore, in a spiral where the spread of one facilitates the other and vice versa:

clientelism → diffusion of the barter vote → need for money on the part of administrators → offer of corruption → corruption → availability of money to buy votes → tendency to buy votes → clientelism

Figure 3.1 The vicious circle: Clientelism–corruption–clientelism

First, the diffusion of the barter vote[2] – linked to the presence of clientelism – increases the costs of politics, driving politicians to look for material resources to invest in their search for power. Clientelism and the barter vote increase the tendency to look for money illegally – i.e. to become corrupted. Furthermore, they make corrupt politicians more competitive, since they are able, in effect, to reinvest bribes in the purchase, direct or otherwise, of votes. Therefore, the number of politicians prepared to 'buy' votes and consensus through strategies of individual relationships increases. However, there is also a further step. The offer of channels of privilege transforms citizens into clients. In order for this step to develop fully, another condition is necessary: i.e. citizens must be pressed to look for individual forms of protection. For an understanding of how this happens, one must look at yet another pathology of the Italian political system: poor administration.

Corrupt politicians and public administration

Although ideally more data or econometric models are necessary to measure this relationship, one can start by observing that research on the Italian case seems to indicate that corruption produces administrative inefficiency. In the first place, innumerable cases show that corruption makes the *price of public works and services rise*. Costs of bribery tend, in effect, to be recovered through various frauds against the public administration. Smaller price reductions than those normally applicable, continuous price rises, supplementary surveys and surcharges, contracts awarded without competitive tenders, subcontracts and revisions, these are all mechanisms that allow people to get round obstacles placed in their path by laws and regulations, and which allow the public administration to behave – according to a definition frequently met with in the course of this research – 'like the most destitute individual'. In effect, the discovery of corruption cases has coincided frequently with the uncovering of excessive costs paid by the public administration for goods and services.

In addition to making the price of works and services higher, corruption *lowers their quality*, and it does this in at least three ways. First, products supplied by 'protected entrepreneurs' often turn out to be of poor quality – one need only look at the state of many roads and motorways for the construction of which bribes have been paid. Secondly, corruption favours a distortion of public expenditure, by diverting expenditure towards those sectors in which the 'corruption' revenue tends to be higher, or where more discretionary procedures facilitate abuses. Thirdly, by guaranteeing privileged access to those prepared to pay for protection, corruption lengthens the average time that non-protected citizens are obliged to wait in order to avail themselves of the services provided by many public bodies.

Conversely, poor administration, in effect, produces corruption. In reality, inefficiency in public administration increases the discretionary powers of politicians, since it provides justification for seeking 'loopholes' in regulations which are at the basis of measures paid for by bribes. Various cases analysed during my research have shown that public administrators seek to widen the range of application of the most arbitrary decisional procedures by means of recourse to a series of *exceptions* provided for by law, in particular for 'urgent' cases. In other words, it is because of the awareness of widespread inefficiency, that exceptions to the law are provided for in those cases that cannot wait for the normal lengthy administrative procedures. The emergency procedures, by increasing the discretionary powers of administrators, favour corruption – as an example, just think of the proliferation of cases of corruption connected with a series of public works, in which exceptional procedures have been used, such as the World Cup in football, or the expenditure for the reconstruction of the districts destroyed by earthquake in Irpinia and the surrounding areas.

Furthermore, administrative inefficiency allows the *reduction of effective controls*. The controlling bodies of public administration have often, in effect, underlined that chronic deficiencies in Italian public administration foster 'incompetence' in the application of the regulatory controls. The practice of not drawing up a contract, for example, has been criticized on several occasions, since this hampers, *de facto*, any verification of the suitability of goods, services and works. Likewise, the inadequate provision of qualified personnel has been a cause of complaint for a long time. The resulting low level of planning capability within the public administration leads to the use of external expertise or to improvisation, both of which practices favour corruption. In a similar way to clientelism, poor administration is also interwoven with corruption and starts a vicious circle which leads to a simultaneous increase of both phenomena. The dynamics of this vicious circle are synthesized in Figure 3.2:

Poor administration → lack of confidence in the enjoyment of citizens' rights → search for privileged channels → susceptibility to bribery → demand for corruption → selective inclusion → increased (perception of) poor administration

Figure 3.2 The vicious circle: Poor administration – corruption – poor administration

Poor administration increases the lack of confidence of citizens and entrepreneurs in the public administration, and therefore, in the possibility of enjoying effectively rights granted by law. This results in a search for privileged channels of access to public decisions whether they involve the enjoyment of services of competition for contracts, work positions, etc. The need for privileged channels increases the willingness to 'buy' this access by bribery. Corruption, in effect, leads to a selective inclusion of those people who pay and to the progressive exclusion of the others. As we have seen, corruption increases administrative inefficiency, putting again in motion the vicious circle.

Corrupt politicians and the 'underworld'

Political corruption interacts, lastly, with a third pathological condition, often described as a characteristic of Italy or of part of Italy: the great spread of criminal powers and connivance between organized crime and politics. In particular, with respect to the Mafia there has been no lack of reference, even officially, to collusion between some parts of the state and *Cosa Nostra*. As the Parliamentary Anti-Mafia Commission recently observed:

> The acknowledgement of connections with the Mafia has not concerned only the 'low branches' of politics. It is unthinkable that such a vast phenomenon of collusion in the districts of the *Mezzogiorno* could develop without some involvement of political will at a higher level. Collusion tends to cross over into local environments, because the Mafia bosses who control votes, directing them to local political figures, are also prepared to support regional and national candidates, who are linked to the former by party loyalty or, more often, by group loyalty. (Parliamentary Anti-Mafia Commission, 1993: 2)

A first observation resulting from my research on corruption is that there has been an availability of resources of violence, which were 'lent' to politicians, thanks to the systematic relationships of barter with organized crime. In cases of political corruption, acts of intimidation sometimes occur: attacks against the property of individuals who do not agree to pay a bribe, or who try to negotiate on price; threats of aggression against potential incriminators in judicial trials, or against opponents of corrupt political bosses. 'Protection' by organized criminals offers politicians a resource of violence which, in addition to its actual use, intimidates political or trade union opposition and discourages denunciations to the judiciary. Intimidatory acts by organized crime can be commissioned to punish those entrepreneurs who do not want to pay a bribe.

In addition to physical protection, organized crime can offer *packages of votes* to corrupt politicians. The politico-mafioso electoral barter seems to have reached considerable magnitude, particularly in

Campania, Calabria and Sicily. It has been observed, in fact, that organized crime has different ways of controlling packages of votes:

> He (the *Mafioso*) gives the impression within the environment in which he operates, that he is in a position to control votes and, therefore, engenders in the electorate the fear of reprisals. Intimidation is widespread and so is the practice of overseeing polling stations. In many cases election rigging occurs. More often, no intimidation is necessary, advice is sufficient. The absence of tension and political passion, the belief that the only purpose of a vote is as a mark of belonging to one particular clientelistic group and not an indication of a choice of ideals, the weakening of political traditions among the different parties, lead almost naturally and effortlessly, to a respect for the orders of the 'stable' . . . (Parliamentary Anti-Mafia Commission, 1993a: 16)

In exchange for resources of violence and packages of votes, organized crime obtains what an ex-member of the *Camorra* has defined as 'small favours'. First, *impunity for crimes committed* is often requested from a politician. This impunity does not only have an instrumental value but is also particularly important from a symbolic point of view:

> For *Cosa Nostra*, impunity has a much greater importance than the hope all criminals naturally have of escaping penal responsibility for crimes committed. More importantly than safeguarding the position of individuals, it confirms the overall power of the organisation, legitimises it in the eyes of citizens, and brings into ridicule the function of the state. It constitutes, therefore, a structural need for the organisation since it bestows a blessing of 'material legality' on its operations. Impunity is the main concern of *Cosa Nostra*. (Parliamentary Anti-Mafia Commission, 1993a: 9)

According to the first judicial proceedings, the relationships between Mafia and *Camorra* members with important national political party representatives were, in fact, mainly directed at obtaining protection during investigations and acquittal at trials, through the intervention of political 'godfathers' with the forces of public order and with magistrates.

Another resource that corrupt politicians negotiate with organized crime is control over public contracts. It is indeed the channelling of criminal interests towards public contracts which makes relationships between crime and politics stable, promoting the formation of 'roped-together groups' of politicians, entrepreneurs and Mafia bosses, made strong by their reciprocal protection. To use the words of an ex-member of the *Camorra*: 'the relationship between politicians and administrators on one hand, entrepreneurs on the other and *Camorra* bosses on yet another, finds its fulfilment and fruition in the mechanism of public contracts' (Public Prosecutor's Office, Naples, 1993: 9). Finally, control over contracts reinforces *control over their territory by the criminal gangs themselves*. Referring again to the findings of the Parliamentary Anti-Mafia Commission:

> Contracts for public works constitute one of the principal meeting grounds of Mafia, entrepreneurs, politicians and administrative officials. There are three practical objectives: to profit from bribes; to place manpower in sub-contracts; to ensure that supplies are purchased from 'friendly' businesses. However, the general objective is more ambitious: with its hands on the contracts, *Cosa Nostra* succeeds in controlling essential aspects of the political and economic life of the territory, because it conditions entrepreneurs, politicians, bureaucrats, workers and professionals. This aspect serves to strengthen their hold on the territory, consolidates social consensus, empowers individual Mafia families in the territory, in society, and in political and administrative circles. *Cosa Nostra* totally controls contracts in Sicily. It has the function of guaranteeing that agreements are respected and fulfilled, of intervening where dysfunctions occur, of damaging businesses that refuse to submit and, if necessary, of killing recalcitrant entrepreneurs. (Parliamentary Anti-Mafia Commission, 1993a: 18)

The dynamics of the vicious circle involving the relationships between corruption and organized crime is illustrated in Figure 3.3:

Political protection for organized crime → **packages of votes and protection of corrupt politicians** → **increased power of corrupt politicians** → **contracts and impunity for organized crime** → **territorial controls reinforced by organized crime** → **increased possibility of protecting corrupt politicians**

Fig 3.3 The vicious circle: Organized crime–corruption–poor administration

Organized crime, by offering packages of votes and resources of violence, strengthens corrupt politicians, who, in turn, make use of their power to increase the power of the organized crime that supports them, through impunity and control of the territory. It can be added that corruption and the ensuing poor administration increases the *dependence of citizens on criminality itself.* As the Anti-Mafia Commission warned, in many areas of the *Mezzogiorno,* 'A Mafia micro-system has developed which conditions the everyday life of citizens in a particularly oppressive manner; *the decline is profound and there is no civil right of any importance which can be exercised without the mediation of the Mafia'* (Parliamentary Anti-Mafia Commission, 1993a: 18).

Conclusion

In summarizing what has been discussed so far, we can list some of the conditions which seem to have favoured the spread of political corruption in Italy. As is known, during the period of reconstruction in the 1950s, the presence of a polarized political culture, the climate of the cold war and decisions regarding economic development were not such as to provide the grounds for widespread consensus, in other words, approval for the system of government and its institutions. Consequently, widespread support was replaced by 'specific' support, i.e. support for whoever holds authority at the time (see Easton, 1975). Although a large part of the electorate was still made up of party members, specific support became more common, especially through the spread of the barter vote, favoured by clientelism and 'hidden government'.* The choice of the constituent assembly not to allow any organ of the state to prevail over the others – i.e. to create a weak parliament, a weak government and a weak head of state – has also led to political fragmentation and, therefore, to the practice, by coalition governments, of resorting frequently to apportionment (Pasquino, 1991: 49), thereby creating an opening for the creation of a class of professional politicians who find in the administration of public bodies greater chances of survival compared with the uncertainties of elective office.[3]

The spread of corruption is facilitated by what Alessandro Pizzorno (1992: 66–70) has defined as the substitution of state morality with political morality (linked to the presence of parties whose main feature is a strongly-asserted long-term political ideology) and,

*Translator's note: The term *sottogoverno* literally means '*sub-government*', and is a term used to define the practice of political parties using their power to unfair advantage, e.g. placing in office in public administration people favourable to their own party.

successively, by the ending of ideological tension, which has left a lack of ethical principles. Some of the political corruption cases analysed during his research have been linked, in effect, to the crisis in the internal life of the local sections in each party, to the loss of the social basis of their origins, and to the lack of membership-screening: in other words, to all those reasons which have reduced the opportunities for parties to offer ideological or pragmatic incentives to their active members. The weakening of ideological incentives has left openings for those people motivated by material incentives, i.e. by their own personal advantage. Scarcity of personnel qualified for (or simply interested in) a role as public administrator has been compensated for by the availability of a new class of 'opportunists', interested in what local politics could offer them in terms of access to public decisions that could be used for personal gain. There seem to be some phenomena peculiar to the Italian case which might have accelerated these tendencies: low financial remuneration for the local political class, with a consequent justification for seeking illegal earnings; over-representation in local government of certain parties, with a consequent influx to their ranks of personnel of a 'weak morality'; the pathological instability of local government councils, and their consequent inability to carry out projects of wide scope; and the decisive role within the majority party played by the more 'degenerate' sections of the *Mezzogiorno*.

It must be added that this control of society has not been transformed into a capacity for implementation; on the contrary, the system has lost out in terms of efficiency, and consequently in terms of legitimacy: in other words, in the possibility of gaining widespread consensus. The clientelistic management of recruitment in public administration and appointments by parties to public bureaucracy – even including the monitoring bodies of public administration – has greatly increased the opening for cases of fraud against the state, with the result that the community has to pay the cost of bribery, at the same time increasing inefficiency in the management of public affairs. A vicious circle has been created in which the lack of widespread consensus has increased the colonization of civic society by the political parties and this colonization, in turn, has reduced the ability of the government system to gain general consensus.

Clientelistic practices and 'hidden government' have, moreover, transformed the parties themselves, weakening their ability to channel and transmit the requests of those represented and strengthening, on the other hand, their ability to obtain advantages for their representatives.[4] As ideological tension and the ability to programme have decreased, the parties became increasingly fragmented, resulting in thousands of political tendencies, which were often nothing but the personal courts of various local bosses. This has increased the cost of politics; not so much the costs of official politics, or the expenditure needed for the parties to perform the tasks assigned to them by Article 49* of the Constitution, but those costs required in an electoral system which allow people to express preferences not only for a party, but also for a candidate to face up to the fierce competition between fellow party members.

This situation has had considerable impact on the system of monitoring. The system of 'hidden government' and apportionment of positions in public administration have offered administrators not only public funds to be managed in a privatist way, but also a decreased risk of being discovered and punished. Suffice it to say that the institutional bodies assigned to supervise the legitimacy of administrative measures – such as the provincial and regional monitoring commissions – have been composed mainly of representatives of those parties which they should be monitoring.

Given these conditions, corruption, clientelism, poor administration and the political protection of organized crime have been a feature of Italian development in the period following the Second World War, creating vicious circles, which have tended to reduce the widespread support for the system, and increased the need for specific support. This chronic lack of widespread consensus produced its most dramatic results when the collapse of the socialist regimes in Eastern Europe destroyed the cornerstone of legitimacy of those party systems which, not only in Italy, were founded on the division of the world into two blocks. If the traditional political parties appear to be in difficulty in various European countries, it is, however, in Italy that – precisely because of the lack of widespread consensus already mentioned – the crisis of the traditional parties has reached its most striking dimensions and forms. A sort of 'virtuous circle' has been created. Dissatisfaction with the growing inefficiency of public services has led to the de-legitimization of the political class, as is seen from the steady electoral losses of political parties. This process of de-legitimization of the political class has given momentum to the investigations of political corruption, the results of which have brought about a further de-legitimization of the political class, with

*Translator's note: Article 49 of the Constitution states that all citizens have the right to form or join a political party in order to help to determine national policies in a democratic way.

an ensuing ripple effect on judicial investigations of crimes committed against public administration, which have also laid bare the
buying and selling of votes, and even the organic relationships
between some politicians and organized crime. Indeed, the failure of
political protection seems to have started to weaken some of the
organized crime groups, which are losing power together with their
protectors. Their difficulties result, in turn, in a further loss of power
by the politicians whom they supported. The formation of this
'virtuous circle' is substantially altering the characteristics of the
Italian political system, making it now impossible to delay long-
overdue reforms.

Notes

1. My research on political corruption was part of a wider project on
    'illegal systems' directed by Alessandro Pizzorno in the European
    University Institute of Florence. The cases studied related to
    some political scandals which came to light in the last decade in
    three Italian towns: the first case concerned contracts and build-
    ing concessions, managed by town and provincial administra-
    tions and by the public body responsible for council housing
    (Autonomous Institute for Council Housing, or IACP) in the
    province of Savona; the second case dealt with the purchase by
    Florence City Council of two pieces of real estate (Albergo
    Nazionale and Villa Favard); and the third case concerned the
    supply of medicines and pharmaceutical materials by a Public
    Health Unit in Catania (Local Health Unit, USL 35). For the full
    results of the research, see Della Porta, 1992a; for a synthesis of
    these results, see Della Porta, 1991. The research on 'maladmin-
    istration' was carried out as part of a project on Public
    Administration directed by Sabino Cassese at the National
    Research Council. This second research study analysed about 30
    cases of poor administration. The results were published in Della
    Porta and Vannucci (1994).
2. I refer to the now classic definition of Parisi and Pasquino (1985:
    79–83), according to which the barter vote is 'a service within a
    barter relationship which presupposes/requires a service in
    exchange'; the *voto di apparenza* or membership vote is, on the
    contrary, 'not so much the expression of a choice . . . but evidence
    of belonging'; lastly, the *voto di opinione* or opinion vote is 'a choice
    which accepts, as the range of options, the terms of the

programmes proposed by the competing parties'.
3. Referring to the Italian political system, Mastropaolo (1987: 48) spoke of an excessive number of political professionals.
4. For this distinction, see Pizzorno (1971).

4

POLITICIANS AND GODFATHERS: MAFIA AND POLITICAL CORRUPTION IN ITALY

ALBERTO VANNUCCI

The Mafia does not engage willingly in political activity. Political problems are not of particular interest to them unless their sources of power or profit are directly threatened. It suffices for them to secure the election of 'friendly' administrators or politicians, and sometimes members of the Mafia organisation itself. This is both to direct the flow of public expenditure and to have laws passed which provide favourable opportunities for their profit, or to have laws blocked that could have adverse repercussions on their business turnover. (Falcone, 1991: 165)

These reflections by the well-known anti-Mafia judge, Giovanni Falcone, murdered by the Mafia in May 1992, clarify some essential aspects of this subject matter. The manner in which relationships develop between public and criminal powers is of central importance to the understanding of how strong and deeply rooted the Mafia organizations are in southern Italy. In order to understand the dynamics of political corruption in Italy, it is necessary to give attention to organized crime. Mafia groups are operating in at least four Italian regions under different names: *Cosa Nostra* (or Mafia) in Sicily; *'ndrangheta* in Calabria; *Sacra Corona Unita* in Apulia; and *Camorra* in Campania. Mafiosi have on a number of occasions shown great interest in the opportunities provided for their enrichment through public sector contracts and real estate activities. Notwithstanding some partial interactions, political corruption and the Mafia are, however, very different and separate phenomena. Each can successfully develop independently of the other.

Recently, new sources have thrown further light on this subject. One need only think, for instance, of the chain of confessions by 'informers' which have led to important successes in the struggle against the Mafia. In parallel, one has witnessed the legal involvement of Giulio Andreotti, several times prime minister, accused by the judges of Palermo of having 'created in – a regular and deliberate way – a type of behaviour that contributes positively to safeguarding the interests and objectives of *Cosa Nostra*' (Public Prosecutor's Office, Palermo, 1993: 9). The meeting ground between politicians and Mafiosi may be visualized as a hidden market within which the operators trade many different commodities: protection, public measures, classified information, use of violence and intimidation. While corruption is a phenomenon common to many Western democracies, the Mafia is an undesirably Italian peculiarity. The Mafiosi, as a result of their brutal actions and reputations, can radically modify the rules and the expectations and balance of the corruption market. They are like a violent and intrusive guest, who is, in spite of his behaviour, not always undesirable. As this chapter will attempt to demonstrate, many of the relationships that the Mafiosi form with other operators, including politicians, entrepreneurs and intermediaries, may be interpreted by reference to rational and voluntary interchange rather than simple extortion.

Mafia and politics: two separate 'industries'

In practice, the link between institutions and the Mafia has developed over many years as a relationship between two different sovereignties: neither one has assaulted the other so long as each kept within its limits. (Parliamentary Anti-Mafia Commission, 1993a: 13)

In order to try to understand how the Mafia interferes in corruption activities, one must first of all understand what is the 'specific nature' of Mafia activity. According to Gambetta, we may consider the Mafia as a true industry formed by 'firms' at times in conflict with each other: 'The Mafiosi are entrepreneurs above all, dealing with a particular commodity protection. This is what distinguishes them from simple criminals, from simple entrepreneurs or from criminal entrepreneurs' (Gambetta, 1992: 11). Protection essentially means guaranteed respect for agreements and ownership rights, solution of controversies, sanction for breach of agreement. As observed by

Gambetta: 'The principal market for Mafia "services" is to be found in the field of unstable transactions, in which the element of trust is fragile or absent. This is the case, for instance, in illegal exchanges, where intervention by a legitimate agency to ensure that the rules are respected – in other words by the state – cannot be invoked' (*ibid.*: 8). The Mafia supergrass Antonino Calderone fully confirms this situation: 'The reputation that we, the Mafia, had, was that we were impartial, that we were above suburban criminal groups that trusted us and accepted our intervention in their controversies' (Arlacchi, 1992: 153).

There is an aspect specific to the commodity 'protection' which has important consequences: once protection is offered to some individuals, others also benefit from it and it is impossible (or too costly) to prevent this from happening. For instance, with a Mafia act of protection against armed robbery, or small acts of extortion in a certain district, in exchange for protection money (the *pizzo*) paid by some shopkeepers, others who have not paid will benefit as well. It is often impossible, in fact, for the Mafia to 'brand' precisely those shopkeepers (or politicians or entrepreneurs) under their protection to distinguish them from the rest. In a situation of uncertainty, it is unlikely that a petty thief or swindler would risk his life in mistaking a protected for an unprotected shop. A similar problem exists for modern states which have solved it by offering generalized protection services in exchange for a compulsory tax. Such a response is incompatible with transforming protection into a private commodity for exchange. If everyone were automatically entitled to protection, no-one would want to buy it. The strategy used by the Mafia is to nourish mistrust and uncertainty concerning ownership rights, by, for example, also protecting criminal activities in this field. Furthermore, they tend to promote 'energetically' the purchase of protection in a general way. All traders within a certain district will then be obliged to pay protection money to avoid thefts, or to escape further extortion. There is a further element to consider: when Mafia protection is offered, mistrust and uncertainty consequently increase. As shown by Gambetta, 'the attempt to overcome mistrust through Mafia protection only perpetuates mistrust and makes it greater. Mistrust becomes, in effect, endogenous and no longer has to be imagined, to become an external prerequisite for the development of the protection market' (Gambetta, 1992: 22). Individuals protected by the Mafia, with their backs covered, will not have any qualms in swindling or carrying out other types of unscrupulous behaviour directed towards defenceless persons. Consequently, the risks and uncertainty for the latter increase and so does the incentive for them to turn to look for protection.

This situation is in contrast with a widely held view that physical coercion and extortion are the essence of the Mafia phenomenon. Violence represents rather an indispensable resource for providing efficient protection, which requires the Mafia clients and their counterparts to have a sense either of trust or of fear in the use of force by the Mafia in order to assert the 'rights' of the protected. Violence will be applied strictly according to need and sparingly if possible. As pointed out by Judge Falcone: 'In the Organisation, violence and cruelty are never gratuitous, they are always the "extreme ratio", the last resort, when all other forms of intimidation are inadequate or when the seriousness of a mistake is such as to deserve only death' (Falcone, 1991: 28). With time violence will be substituted with another commodity, 'reputation', which will allow drastic savings on production costs for a resource as elusive as protection. This can explain the richness in symbols and rituals that accompany Mafia activities. Trying to promote the authenticity of their protection 'brand' and to prevent at the same time any undue encroachment, the Mafiosi create and employ distinctive signals, symbols of their 'commercial' identity and of the good quality of the merchandise on offer (Gambetta, 1992: 216).

As in any other illegal market, in a corrupt system, problems of reciprocal mistrust are particularly extensive. Ownership rights over racket money and public benefits exchanged are often not defined precisely, nor is it possible to rely on promises made or written records. The attraction that such an illegal market can exercise on the Mafiosi is evident.

Rose-Ackerman has defined three levels of public activity, in which different models of corruption take place: (a) the offer by private individuals of goods or services required by public agencies; (b) the sale and distribution of goods and services produced by public agents and required by citizens; and (c) the imposition of public 'coercive' measures that result in costs for private individuals (Rose-Ackerman, 1978: 61–3). In each one of these fields, through public intervention, a condition of artificial scarcity results. In other words, opportunities for political rent are created. Private people are given property rights, through public provision, to certain resources for less than they would be prepared to pay in order to obtain them: 'Corruption is actually just a black market for the ownership rights over which politicians and bureaucrats have allocative power. Rather than assigning rights according to political power, rights are sold to the highest bidder'

(Benson, 1990: 159). The public agent that decides on or influences the allocation of the rights can obtain a part of the rent, in the shape of a bribe as a reward for his patronage. All other factors being equal, the opportunities for corruption increase proportionally to the size of the area of public intervention, and the revenues made available with discretional criteria multiply as a consequence. Furthermore, a corrupt exchange seems more convenient when the costs of illegal transactions are low. Thus corruption transforms the exercise of public authority into a sort of 'industry of power'; corrupt officials, in exchange for a bribe, offer decisions to allocate ownership rights on political rents, or classified information to facilitate the winning of such rights through official procedures.

Sometimes 'protection' comes into play: a share of the bribe is paid to a 'third party' who guarantees the fulfilment of corruption agreements. More generally, every time a citizen has contacts with public organizations, the problem of the protection of his rights over certain resources or services managed by bureaucrats or politicians can arise. Mistrust in the efficiency and fairness of official procedures can generate a request for 'private protection' even in the relationships between citizens and public authorities. For instance, an entrepreneur may pay a price in bribes for an invitation to participate in bidding for a contract, or to obtain within the foreseen contractual time frame payment for a contract under execution. Even if his rights are formally protected by the law, to try and obtain protection by the state may seem too costly. In Italy, some centres of political power, thanks to their ability consistently to bring influence on the political-legal authority, have been able to satisfy this requirement by offering in exchange for bribes a particular form of 'political protection' (Vannucci, 1993b).

Political protection and Mafia protection

> The ingress of the Mafia into local institutions is strongly facilitated by administrative fragility. Where public administration is inert or careless, where administrative controls do not work, a favourable environment for the interweaving of politics and the Mafia is automatically created. (Parliamentary Anti-Mafia Commission, 1993a: 18)

In considering the relationship between political corruption and the Mafia, one must make a preliminary distinction. In many cases, the

Mafiosi sell guarantees to agents that effect transactions on the illegal market of bribery. In other cases they intervene directly to corrupt public officials. To pay politicians, officials and magistrates, or to corrupt police agents so that they close their eyes to illegal trafficking, is often a necessary condition to reduce the risks of those activities and to crush competition (Rubin, 1973). In this chapter the central concern is in the primary field of exchanges in which the resource of protection plays a part.

At times, political protection offered by public agents and Mafia protection are addressed to the same 'clients'. A relationship of interchangeability develops. The consumption of one reduces the demand for the other. According to Max Weber, payments to the Mafia are similar to those given to political groups in exchange for 'extorted services': 'These services are initially intermittent, since they are formally illegal, but in practice they become "periodic payments" in exchange for given services and especially for a guarantee of security. Here is the observation of a Neapolitan builder as given to me about 20 years ago, in reply to doubts concerning the efficiency of the *Camorra* with respect to his business: "Sir, the *Camorra* charges me X Lire each month, but guarantees security – the State takes ten times as much, but does not guarantee anything"' (Weber, 1981 (1st edn 1922): 195). Competition between two 'protection firms' can also be bloodless, as far as price is concerned. The more economical one (if it is equally efficient) is bought. For instance, traders can have their properties protected by an inefficient and corrupt state, on payment of a percentage, or by the Mafia. The spokesman for a Traders' Association in Catania states that the Mafia, among other things, protects from bribery rackets: 'The citizen who cannot trust the city authorities, because politicians extort from him, asks for help and protection from the underworld. In the story given, a small amount of vigilance was asked for on the wholesale market. After a little while, the operators called: "Tell the *gazelle* [police car] not to come any longer. Why? Because it costs us more than the robbers"' (Fipe, 1992: 55). Inefficiency and arbitrariness on the part of the state take away protection from the domain of citizens' rights and transform it into a market. On the basis of market laws, the cheapest service is purchased. The description of the activities of a successful Mafioso, as given by the supergrass Calderone, is hardly different from that of a common political patron: 'Let us not forget that the Mafioso is also a kind of authority, a person to whom everyone turns for obtaining favours, for solving problems . . . . When we, the Calderone, were in great favour, there was a procession of people every day in my office.

It was a coming and going of people requesting anything and everything . . . there were people looking for a job, some had sat a public examination and wanted to pass it, some offered supplies for Costanzo's business' (Arlacchi, 1992: 149–50).

On the other hand, it is not always convenient for the Mafiosi to sell guarantees merely because they have been asked for. In certain contexts of exchange, to offer protective services is difficult, too costly and too risky. It can be imagined, therefore, that in spite of the Mafia presence, there are areas of exchange where politicians maintain a sort of monopoly. 'My idea', says a Sicilian entrepreneur, 'is that two different phases exist in the Sicilian system of contracts. *Cosa Nostra* does not enter the first phase – let us call it a phase of choice – financing and planning the work, because the Mafia might not be interested in that type of work . . . . In the second phase, though, from the bidding point on, the Mafia is well represented' (*Panorama*, 23 May 1993, transcript, page 54). On the other hand, in the case of controversies between political and Mafia protectors, generally the latter have a great enough capability of intimidation to persuade 'clients' to use them exclusively. A brutal threat, an attack, or wounding or murdering a politician would soon put an end to the dispute: 'The relationship between *Cosa Nostra* and politicians is of dominance of the first over the second; the availability of coercive methods gives *Cosa Nostra* infinite possibility of demand and persuasion' (Parliamentary Anti-Mafia Commission, 1993a: 16). We can expect then that in illegal markets, the protection offered by the 'men of honour' becomes a monopoly, whenever this is convenient for the Mafia bosses.

A similar hypothesis could find two possible responses. First, the multiplying of exchange levels between politicians and Mafiosi, which will be dealt with in the next paragraph. The second is represented instead by the 'price' paid for Mafia protection. With regard to the latter, a time lag has been observed, with a sharp reduction in the role of politicians in the cashing of bribes. On this topic, the judges of Palermo write:

Until the early '80s, politicians decided to whom the contract should be given and they pocketed directly as much as 50% of the bribes. All this has changed since *Cosa Nostra* has changed . . . the bosses of *Cosa Nostra* conducted their business directly through their emissaries, with ministers, with big entrepreneurs, with bureaucrats. From the time of Ciancimino [ex-mayor of Palermo, recently sentenced for association with the Mafia], to the time of 'the ministers' of Totó Riina [the 'boss of bosses' of *Cosa Nostra*] who decided the rules of the game, distributing bribes in a different way from before. In recent years, the largest share of the bribes went to the bosses of the '*Cupola*' [the apex of the Organization], then came the 'family' whose territory was involved in the contract, then the politicians. (*La Repubblica*, 27 May 1993: 8)

The number of politicians and officials in stable relationships of exchange with Mafia protectors has increased to the point that, by now, as observed by the Palermo judges 'certainly in every local authority office of interest to the Mafia groups, there are key officials and employees intimately linked to them'. (Public Prosecutor's Office, Palermo, 1990: 34)

In other regions of the *Mezzogiorno*, however, such as Calabria and Campania, a sort of collusive agreement between political and Mafia bosses appears to have emerged, with a consequent division of areas of influence. This could be the result, in the first instance, of greater fragmentation and weakness in the local Mafia groups. Compared to the Sicilian case, Campania shows signs of greater social rooting of political forces, and of stronger competition among groups of *Camorra*. According to the 1993 report of the Parliamentary Anti-Mafia Commission: 'Where the Organisation has a finer grained structure, as is the case, in fact, of the Campania *Camorra* or the Apulia *Santa Corona*, the relationship between Mafia and politicians tends to develop in a more visible way; where it is more concentrated and hierarchical, as is the case in Sicily, its manifestations are less evident' (1993a: 2). Violent competition shortens the 'life expectancy' of the criminals involved. It becomes more dangerous to protect permanently certain economic relationships and the propensity of the *Camorra* to adopt predatory strategies by the use of violence and extortion increases. At the same time, the importance of political support to obtain competitive advantages *vis-à-vis* other criminal groups increases.

Moreover, the existence of seats of decision-making removed from possible Mafia sanctions puts limits on the expansion of their influence. For example, relevant decisions concerning the financing of public works in Calabria are reached via discretionary powers in the capital, through secret negotiations with the leading national construction businesses, from which negotiations the local Mafia bosses are, inevitably, excluded. In Campania one can note also the opportunity offered to politicians to manage discretionally the hundreds of thousands of billions of lire poured into reconstruction after the 1980 earthquake, thus increasing their 'contractual power'. *Cosa Nostra*, on the contrary, has a more direct influence on the financial income concerning Sicily, which is an autonomous region: 'Palermo and Sicily remain the territory of *Cosa Nostra*. It is not by chance that in the island's capital, political heart of the region and fulcrum of the immense regional and governmental financial resources, *Cosa Nostra* has established and maintains a control structure of the territory not found in any other local situation' (Parliamentary Anti-Mafia Commission, 1993a: 8).

According to the informer Pasquale Galasso, politics and the *Camorra* are not separate worlds. Every *Camorra* clan has a 'prime political sponsor' and in common agreement politicians and criminal bosses would choose who should be elected to the principal political positions, who should obtain the contracts, which works should be planned and financed and which sites should be earmarked for construction. The murder of politicians or entrepreneurs, the speedy passage or indefinite delay of public acts, the rise or electoral failure of some politicians were all means of guaranteeing the respect of hidden agreements reached by a politico-criminal cartel. In a system of public contracts an equilibrium had been established between political protection of certain businesses and the guarantee by the *Camorra* of secret exchanges: 'It was evident to me', says Galasso, 'that a politician who manages the financing of contracts and hence the granting of the contract or related concessions, also acts as a mediator between large businesses, nearly always located in Northern or Central Italy, and the *Camorra*. Such mediation takes the form of a bribe from the business intended for himself, or his direct representative, and of the granting by the business of sub-contracts to firms directly controlled by the *Camorra* organizations. The relationship becomes more complex whenever, in addition to the principal firm contracted, some local firms are also contracted on equal working terms: in such cases a complex management of the operation by politicians, entrepreneurs and the *Camorra* takes place in total fusion' (Public Prosecutor's Office, Naples, 1993: 9). In exchange for such 'double protection', a bribe is paid both to the politicians and to the *Camorra*.

The protection of secret exchanges

Cosa Nostra totally controls contracts in Sicily. It has the function of guaranteeing that agreements are respected and fulfilled, to intervene where 'dysfunctions' occur, to damage the businesses that refuse to submit and, if necessary, to kill recalcitrant entrepreneurs. (Parliamentary Anti-Mafia Commission, 1993a: 18)

The offer of valid protection in corrupt transactions allows politicians to expand the market of bribery, consolidating illegal agreements and forcing individuals towards an obstinate conspiracy of silence. Infringements are often punished in a brutal way, for increased exemplary effect. The high number of murders among administrators and entrepreneurs bears witness to the ferocious efficiency with which in southern regions the Mafioso guarantees 'order' in the market of bribery. Between 1978 and 1987 in Palermo alone 34 entrepreneurs and 78 traders were murdered by the Mafia (Santino and La Fiura, 1990: 412). For 'clients' trying to acquire 'ownership rights' over political rents, Mafia protection becomes a necessary tool to avoid politicians failing to grant the favour promised after pocketing the bribe. Even public agents, through Mafia protection, reduce to a minimum the risks incurred in their illegal activities. Mafia protection allows them to widen considerably the radius of their illegal activities, with a very modest increase in costs and associated risks.

The efficiency of the services of the Mafia seems to be confirmed by the degree of stratification reached by illegal transactions. In Sicily, exchanges between businesses on the one hand and local and regional politicians on the other are articulated through the presence of mediators acting as channels of communication and in the transmission of counterpart merchandise. Often a regional councillor delegated a decision on allocating public resources to an intermediary would offer local administrators the opportunity to undertake work in a particular district. The companies selected to win the bidding paid a bribe equal to 25 per cent of the total estimated cost even before the bidding procedure began. The system was firmly based on strong reciprocal trust. The share of the bribes paid to the Mafia represents the price paid for the smooth operation of this complex market. The Mafioso supergrass, Sebastiano Messina, says: 'There is an agreement between politicians and entrepreneurs, then between entrepreneurs and *Cosa Nostra* and then between politicians and *Cosa Nostra*. The role of *Cosa Nostra* is to control the whole operation in every phase' (Parliamentary Anti-Mafia Commission, 1993b: 70).

The politician Vito Ciancimino, under the protection of the Mafia, apparently cashed bribes in exchange for construction licences, while he was a councillor for public works in Palermo: 'not only could the demands of Ciancimino not be refused, but he did not need any documentary evidence to claim, when necessary, his money, since it was unthinkable that anyone would betray his trust' (Palermo Law Courts, 1992: 194). One does not play with fire in the payment of bribes when there is Mafia protection. In exchange, the politician directed decisions taken within the city council to suit the interests of businesses protected by the Mafia, ensuring a state of non-interference by the public authority in the affairs of the Mafia, hampering officials and party members, who, by their activities, put obstacles in the way of the Organization. While councillor for public works, during the years of uncontrolled urban expansion of the city, he 'did not stop acting in a general way to promote the interests of private speculators, but in a more specific way was successful in favouring Mafia figures close to him' (Tribunale dí Palermo, 1992: 84–6).

The cumbersome, but often invisible, Mafia presence becomes clearly perceptible in these cases when quarrels may originate in collecting bribes. Michele Pantaleone, a specialist in this area, describes in the following way the solving of a 'normal' controversy in a corrupt exchange, where there is more than one Mafia protector in play:

> In the award phase of the contract procedure, the firm made a commitment to pay the 'patron saint' a bribe of 10% of the total cost of the work . . . . Unfortunately, the influential politician has died and the firm has lost its protection, with the entailing need to find 'a new patron saint' to whom to give the agreed 10%. The dead man's heirs insist on claiming the right which was acquired with the inheritance and demand continued payment of the bribe. There has already been one death and in the building yard there were two dynamite attacks which have damaged plant and machinery. (Pantaleone, 1984: 184)

Although the purchase of Mafia protection may appear desirable from an individual point of view, since competitors also resort to it, the general use of these means may produce disastrous collective consequences. Individuals end up finding themselves 'entrapped' in an environment dominated by reciprocal mistrust, fear and the impending threat of violence.

The supergrass Baldassare Di Maggio describes how the Mafia intervenes in sanctioning secret business cartels that divide contracts among themselves:

We began to make the various interested firms agree, in the sense of making offers agreed amongst themselves so as to obtain the tender with a minimum discount which would enable them to pay the appropriate bribe. Siino was the person in charge of ensuring the coordination between the firms (he was an entrepreneur nicknamed 'Minister of Public Works of *Cosa Nostra*') and I remember that in this first phase we, the men of *Cosa Nostra*, had the problem of accrediting him with individual firms and with the 'men of honour' of the areas that he visited. (*Panorama*, 11 April 1993, transcript, page 61)

Often politicians helped to meet the needs of the secret cartel either by disclosing classified information or by not inviting external firms to participate in the bidding. The Mafia also guaranteed the transaction between the latter and the cartel, cashing a part of the profits:

For works carried out by firms who had secured the contract thanks to the intervention of Angelo Siino, we kept 5% . . . . Of this 5%, 3% was for the Mafia Organisation and 2% was given to Siino to pay bribes to politicians. The rule was that the first payment after granting of the contract was indeed to the politicians. Siino who conducted the negotiations with politicians said that 'pandemonium would have broken out should there have been a delay in payment'. (*ibid.*)

Besides the exchange relationships that mature in the bribery market, there are other types of Mafia services available to politicians. These range from cases of virtual adoption, with its proper initiation ritual, to those services where the exchange deals with different resources such as consent (see Della Porta in this volume). By recourse to the market of votes, which is controlled and guaranteed by Mafiosi, politicians can increase their probability of success in elections. On the other hand, before the recent reform to a majority system in the electoral rules for local authorities, in Italy long negotiations were often necessary for the formation of a majority coalition, for the distribution of key positions and for the division of public funds. The progressive extension of spheres of competence and of powers given to local authorities has had the effect of increasing the strategic importance of these agreements from which a growing share of money and consent could be derived. At the same time, the incentives increased for those politicians who could alter the precarious balance of government in exchange for the promise of a bigger share of power.

The role of the Mafiosi, in some cases, has been that of ensuring the stability of political coalitions and of agreements in the allocation of positions and bribes which ensue, or to induce a change of the subsequent agreed distribution of political resources for the advantage of those they are protecting. By frightening their enemies or avoiding political crises, they ensure a peaceful and continuing division of public funds (Gambetta, 1988a: 99). In exchange, the Mafiosi obtained money, or an influence on that political power whose stability they had contributed to bringing about.

The *Camorrai* has also striven to guarantee alliances, by modifying the balance of strength between groups and political line-ups. Pasquale Galasso, a *Camorra* supergrass, says that following the election of the town council of Poggiomarina (near Naples), he was asked to intervene with a reluctant councillor 'to tell him, with all the weight of my *Camorra* fame, to ally himself with Antonio Gava [DC party representative, several times minister] who had promised him the position of mayor'. Galasso's reticence was overcome by the direct intervention of his chief, the boss Carmine Alfieri: 'he assured me that Gava was on our side and that I could not deny him that favour . . . . The politician was thus persuaded to side with Gava, though he had never liked him' (Public Prosecutor's Office, Naples, 1993: 13). A political representative with an efficient Mafia safeguard acquires power beyond that which he has from the institutional authorities or from his party role. The position of the Christian Democrat ex-mayor of Palermo, Vito Ciancimino, reflected his status as a political sponsor of the Mafia. By unanimous agreement, even when he ceased to be on the town council, 'no mayor could keep his position without his agreement' (Palermo Law Courts, 1992: 17). Another ex-mayor of the city, Giuseppe Insalaco, said: 'I have been ousted from my position as mayor because of my firm position on the question of the renewal of the contracts for city lighting, road maintenance and sewage. In this situation, the presence of Ciancimino has played an essential role . . . . In essence, therefore, Ciancimino has continued to manage events in Palermo, not because he had any official position, but because of his very strong group of allies who backed him and whom he represented' (Tribunale dí Palermo, 1992: 149—50). The power of intimidation of the Mafia was directed against politicians who opposed the interests protected by Ciancimino. Several public administrators have been victims of grave intimidation. On 12 January 1988, Insalaco himself was murdered.

Conclusion

> It is difficult for a politician to become a 'man of honour'. There is a strong sense of mistrust in *Cosa Nostra* towards politicians because they are treacherous, they do not keep promises and they are sly. They are people who break their word and are without principles. (Confession by the Mafioso supergrass, Antonino Calderone, quoted by Arlacchi (1992: 208))

This statement, unintentionally sarcastic, touches on a very important aspect. Contrary to common belief, both in Italy and abroad, the Mafia and corruption are completely separate phenomena when considered analytically. The Mafia and corruption can be considered as discrete 'industries', dealing essentially in different commodities: private protection on the one hand, rights of ownership on political rents on the other. This explains the obsession of the Mafiosi, who often have the role of guarantors and arbitrators in illegal controversies, for respecting the given word and promises made, which is connected with a distorted principle of 'honour'. On this point, the unscrupulous attitude of politicians cannot but arouse contempt. There is only a limited ground for intersection, a common market where both Mafia and political protection can be offered simultaneously.

In corruption cases that have arisen in central and northern Italy, the presence of corrupt politicians managing illegal transactions has been disclosed. In general, according to Pizzorno, one can say that 'it is convenient, for people engaging in such transactions, to count on a steady set of connections. The collective body that emerges will be more capable than isolated individuals both to inflict sanctions . . . and to ensure continuity and a long-term relationship' (Pizzorno, 1992: 30). A share of the bribes was often directed towards centres of power external to the transactions, such as the central offices of the political parties or private secretariats of particularly influential politicians. On the contrary, in cases that have arisen so far in southern Italy, corrupt groups seem to be fewer in proportion and the role of the political parties in the division of bribes seems more limited. Bribes were given personally to individual political representatives who generally pocketed sums themselves, or divided them with a few others. On the basis of the foregoing discussion, one can put forward the hypothesis that this fact might reflect a different structure in the protection market. Where groups of Mafiosi impose respect for illegal agreements, the formation of a network of politicians to cover and guarantee these secret dealings is superfluous. Each applicant can receive the necessary guarantees for the fulfilment and secrecy of the dealings simply by paying the relevant price to the Mafia. This process has as its consequence a radical individualization of the political struggle being conducted by individuals rather than by political parties, resulting in a weakening of the parties themselves in terms of both financial strength and power.

It can also be that illegal services provided by politicians or the Mafia are requested to carry out other activities. The Mafiosi who sanction corruption agreements can in their turn acquire special public benefits and in particular gain 'impunity' from the judiciary. Because of its symbolic value, impunity is used by them to obtain direct personal advantage and to offer more efficient private protection. The co-existence of corruption and the Mafia within the same territory can therefore increase the offer for sale of both 'commodities'. By reducing the risks inherent in secret dealings, the Mafia contributes to the expansion of the bribery market. At the same time, a strong conspiracy of silence covers such activities, causing enormous obstacles for magistrates in their investigations. It is not by chance that confessions of entrepreneurs and politicians during the last two years have given legal investigations an unrelenting propelling force in some parts of Italy, but have, in other parts where Mafia protection was present, shown signs of slowing down.

In turn, the capillary diffusion of political corruption feeds mistrust among citizens in the impartiality of public procedures and decisions. These negative expectations apply also to the ability of the state to provide authentic and impartial protection of the public. Citizens will turn then to the private protection offered by Mafia groups, whose power is thus strengthened. This creates the conditions for corrupt politicians and Mafiosi to strengthen each other in a dramatic vicious circle. They interweave a cross-exchange of guarantees through which politicians gain electoral consent and violent dissuasion of their adversaries and the Mafiosi gain impunity from magistrates and an influence over public measures. Rampant corruption, a ferocious Mafia presence and a deterioration in living conditions, which can be detected in several cities in the *Mezzogiorno*, represent the inevitable results of such a process.

5

FROM DICTATORSHIP TO DEMOCRACY: CHANGING FORMS OF CORRUPTION IN SPAIN*

Paul Heywood

Introduction: of hysteria and hypocrisy

An observer of media reports on Spanish politics since the general elections of October 1989 could be forgiven for believing that the country has been in thrall to an unaccountable, self-seeking and corrupt rabble of unprincipled politicians. The Partido Socialista Obrero Español (PSOE), in particular, has been accused of distorting the democratic process in a bid to maintain a firm grip on the levers of political influence. The issue of corruption in government became an almost incessant theme of political reportage throughout the early 1990s, and dominated debate during the general election campaign of May and June 1993.

Accusations of corrupt practices had simmered in inchoate fashion since the PSOE administration first took power in 1982. They centred on the existence of what could be termed 'bureaucratic clientelism' – i.e. the handing out of favours and sinecures to party members as well as influence-trafficking. However, it was only after the 1989 elections that acusations of corruption gained significant momentum. The catalyst to this upsurge was the emergence of the 'Juan Guerra case' at the start of 1990, when it was alleged that the

---

*Some of the material and arguments in this chapter have also been used in Paul Heywood's 'Continuity and change: Analysing Political Corruption in Spain', in Walter Little and Eduardo Posada-Carbó (eds), *Political Corruption in Europe and Latin America*, London, Macmillan, 1996.

then deputy prime minister's brother had used official PSOE premises for private business purposes. An unprecedented year-long press campaign, presented as investigative journalism but often amounting to little more than vindictive personalism, culminated in the resignation from government of Alfonso Guerra (Ramírez, 1990; Cavero, 1991).

That Guerra should have been a particular focus of attack was not altogether surprising. Known for his acerbic and mordant wit, Guerra's withering contempt for political opponents had won him many enemies since his rise to a position of major political influence during the transition to democracy (Miralles and Satue, 1991). Moreover, he had emphatically denied any wrong-doing by the PSOE, emphasizing the party's historic tradition of moral rectitude as symbolized by the legacy of its ascetic founder, Pablo Iglesias. On assuming power in 1982, the PSOE had continued to emphasize the slogan 'cien años de honradez' (100 years of honesty) which had been adopted three years earlier to mark the party's centenary, although cynics took to appending the coda 'y ni un día más' (and not a single day longer). There was thus more than a little *Schadenfreude* amongst political commentators when a scandal involving one of Guerra's own brothers hit the headlines.

Guerra's resignation in early 1991 did little to stem the tide of accusations against the PSOE. Further corruption scandals emerged during the following two years, most of them centring on the issue of party financing. After months of allegations and an official investigation by a High Court judge, in early 1993 auditors produced a 500-page report on a racket whereby two elected PSOE representatives – a deputy, Carlos Navarro, and a senator, José María Sala – ran a group of front companies that paid bills for the party with money obtained by charging businesses and banks for fictitious consultancy work between 1989 and 1991. The scam bore a striking similarity to the Marseilles 'Urba case' in 1988 (Mény, 1992).

The discovery of Urba's Spanish equivalent was triggered by the revelations of a disgruntled former employee of Time Export, although the investigation centred on another company, Filesa, which gave its name to the entire scandal. The auditors' report detailed payments of nearly 1bn Ptas (some £6m) on which the front companies failed to pay tax, whilst the 'donors' offset their contribution against tax. In order to disguise the true nature of the operation, invoices and receipts were re-routed through another group of companies run by the socialists' former financial controller, Aida Alvarez. Whilst the report did not explain what was received in return, it was widely believed that several of the 'donors' subsequently won lucrative government contracts (*El País internacional*, 12 April 1993).

A further scandal involving the PSOE which emerged in early 1993 surrounded the payment of commissions for contracts to carry out work at the site of the Expo92 in Seville. The newspaper *El Mundo* alleged that, just 19 days after it had been set up, a Portuguese-based company, Rio Cocon S L, won a 3bn Ptas contract to provide prefabricated structures for the Expo site. The company – which had no experience in the field and soon transferred the contract to another firm which subsequently filed for protection from creditors after Expo92 opened – had apparently paid the PSOE a 'grant' of 150m Ptas on receiving the contract. Similarly, the German multinational, Siemens, which won the contract to build the high-speed rail link between Madrid and Sevilla, handed over large sums for 'technical and commercial advice' to firms run by former PSOE officials (*El País internacional*, 1 February 1993). In another scandal relating to the high-speed rail link, the health minister, Julián García Valverde, was obliged to resign in 1991 after it was revealed that while he had been in charge of the state railway, Renfe, speculators had been tipped off about land due for compulsory purchase.

Opposition parties – most notably the Partido Popular (PP), which harboured ambitions of displacing the PSOE from power – naturally seized upon this seemingly unending series of scandals to launch bitter attacks on the socialists' moral integrity. However, such attacks courted the charge of hypocrisy, since the PP had itself been implicated in a corruption probe in April 1990 when the PP treasurer, Rosendo Naseiro, and Salvador Palop, a local councillor and president of the Treasury Commission in the Valencian city council, were arrested. Transcripts of bugged telephone conversations between Palop, Naseiro and other leading PP officials led to allegations that they were involved in various schemes to raise money for the party, mainly through bribery over property development and local government contracts. Those involved were obliged to resign from the PP, but were acquitted when they came to trial in 1992 on the grounds that the tapes had been recorded by the police for another investigation. Further corruption scandals in the early 1990s involved nationalist parties in both Catalonia and the Basque Country, where allegations were made of extortion and collusion with gambling interests.

During the early 1990s these scandals contributed to an atmosphere of generalized mistrust in the entire political class, which was reinforced by the extraordinary revelations which had begun to emerge in Italy. The probity of politicians and parties – especially the socialists – was repeatedly called into question as the issue of corruption became virtually the only focus of political debate and analysis. Sections of the media, aided by the pronouncements of certain church leaders and other public figures, attempted to promote a sense of indignant moral outrage. Coverage of the issue at times bordered on hysteria.

The position of the media was not entirely disinterested. Relations between the printed press and the government had deteriorated sharply since 1990, with open hostility surfacing on several occasions. A widespread conviction that, whilst broadcasting remained a state monopoly (private channels were introduced only in 1989), the government regularly sought to manipulate television news output had led sections of the press to assume the self-appointed mantle of guardian of the democratic process (Cavero, 1991: 325ff.). With no libel law in Spain, the press was free to engage in unrestricted reportage and its attacks on the government were partly motivated by a desire to defend its own independence against threats of official regulation. Thus, it suited sections of the media to undermine the government's moral legitimacy, and stories about political corruption provided them with an ideal opportunity.

However, for all the fulminating outrage of leading media figures such as Pedro J. Ramírez, political corruption was neither the preserve nor the invention of the socialist government. Instead, Spain's entire political history since the monarchical restoration of 1875 has been marked by corruption in one form or another. The so-called 'turno pacífico' – a corrupt system based on clientelism by which conservatives and liberals alternated in power according to pre-arranged deals over the results of fixed elections – lasted from the 1870s until the early part of the twentieth century (Carr, 1982: 473–523; Kern, 1974). Thereafter, the dictatorship of General Miguel Primo de Rivera (1923–30) introduced dubious accounting procedures to mask massive budget deficits through the expedient of uncontrolled 'extraordinary budgets' (Ben-Ami, 1983: 272–81). During the Second Republic (1931–36), the political career of Alejandro Lerroux – premier from September 1933 to September 1935 – was effectively ended through his involvement in a series of corruption scandals. The most notorious of these, which concerned the planned introduction of a crooked roulette wheel to Spanish gaming houses, bequeathed the word 'estraperlo' (meaning black market) to the Spanish language (Preston, 1978: 165).

Yet, the most corrupt of all regimes in modern Spanish history was undoubtedly the Franco dictatorship (1939–75). In a heavily bureaucratized and – at least until the 1960s – desperately poor regime, malfeasance in office became just a normal part of politics. The regime's experiment with autarky spawned a massive black market as well as facilitating administrative corruption which continued long after Franco had been forced to abandon economic self-sufficiency. As Payne (1987: 399) has noted, 'Franco seems to have regarded corruption as a necessary lubrication for the system that had the advantage of compromising many with the regime and binding them to it.' Ultimately, the Opus Dei technocrats who had been instrumental in promoting economic liberalization and administrative modernization during the 1960s were themselves discredited by a major corruption scandal, the Matesa affair (Preston, 1993: 744–8).

Political corruption takes place at all levels, from central government to municipal councils. Many of the corruption cases (both proven and alleged) which have emerged in Spain since the early 1980s have involved local officials engaging in what might be termed 'classic' examples of pork-barrel graft. Kick-backs in return for contracts, especially in construction (urban and real estate development), would seem to be a standard feature of most modern polities. Equally, parallel financing and insider trading would also appear to be widespread phenomena in the modern industrialized world. It is probably impossible to estimate accurately whether Spain is more or less prone than other European democracies to such abuses.

However, Spanish politics does appear to be particularly prone to nepotistic corruption, as well as to clientelism. More difficult to assess is the extent of more nebulous instances of corruption, such as the exercise of influence in the communications media. Insofar as certain actions of PSOE governments since 1982 – for instance, in regard to appointments to key public posts – have fallen within the technical remit of their constitutional resources (which grant very extensive executive power), they have been unimpeachable. However, the distinction between formal constitutional propriety and the misuse of political resources is not always clear-cut. It is arguable that the appointment of people to public posts on the basis of political loyalty rather than merit, although technically within the government's remit, constitutes a form of corruption. The perceived importance of the party carnet to get ahead in socialist Spain most infuriated critics of the PSOE and led to widespread accusations of corrupt practices. Yet, such accusations inevitably rest mainly upon impressions and hearsay rather than on hard evidence, making the task of analysing political corruption fraught with difficulty.

Political corruption can be seen as part and parcel of Spain's modern history. However, such an observation explains neither the forms of, nor the reasons for, political corruption. The remainder of this chapter analyses its continued existence in contemporary Spain through four different explanatory frameworks: genetic disposition, longevity in power, the financial demands on political parties and the nature of state development. It is argued that all but the first offer some clues as to the continued existence of political corruption in Spain. However, not only has its nature changed over time, but also its contemporary scale and extent have probably been exaggerated.

Explaining political corruption in Spain

Genetic disposition

One of the most familiar, yet also one of the most easily dismissed, explanations of political corruption in Spain is one which relies on some notion of 'national character'. In essence, this culturally relativist approach amounts to little more than the assertion that Spaniards — or sometimes all Mediterranean citizens — are 'just *like* that'. Just as Germans are supposedly efficient, and the French stylish, so Spaniards are lazy and corrupt — or, to dignify such a contentious cliché with an apparently value-neutral connotation, given to engaging in 'amoral familism' (Banfield, 1967).

Such views have not been confined to outside observers. Within Spain, concern with the essential nature of '*Hispanidad*' (Spanishness) became a central feature of national philosophical preoccupations at the end of the nineteenth century (Herr, 1971). One widely favoured solution to 'the problem of Spain' — which identified its root cause in the incompetence and moral decadence of the ruling class — was to call for a programme of profound 'regeneration' of Spanish culture and institutions, taking as a model the northern and central European countries. In the famous words of José Ortega y Gasset, 'if Spain is the problem, Europe is the solution'.

A more fatalistic perspective saw Spaniards as irredeemably backward in political terms. General Franco justified the dictatorial nature of his regime on the basis that 'certain peculiarities of the Spanish temperament' made it impossible to sustain democratic institutions; democracy invariably ended up unleashing violence among Spaniards (Preston, 1993: 519–20). Such patronizing assessments ultimately depend on the notion of national character being a given, impervious to socio-economic contexts or environmental influences.

More sophisticated attempts to analyse Spain's political culture can also fall prey to reductionist stereotypes. In a recent study, Richard

Gunther (1992: 21) cites approvingly the work of López Pintor and Wert Ortega (1982: 7–26) which dismissed various clichés about the Spanish character. Several studies in the 1980s have shown that Spaniards share views and values which are fully in line with those of their European neighbours (Toharia, 1989; Times Mirror Center, 1991). As Gunther comments, we can regard Spain as a fundamentally modern and European country. However, he immediately goes on to remark that 'there are some characteristic features of [Spain's] culture which distinguish it from other European countries, and some of them have a significant influence on Spanish politics'. His list of 12 such features begins with *amiguismo*, referring to the use of contacts and intermediaries in dealings with bureaucracy, and influence-trafficking in political life. Given that such activities are typical of clientelistic networks, it is hard to see them as distinctively Spanish.

A more serious objection is that such approaches explain little. At best, they offer a description of political or social reality in any given period. A country's political culture may be of fundamental significance to the maintenance and reinforcement of a particular style of politics – including, of course, the widespread existence of clientelism – but its use as an explanatory variable is open to question. Cultural mores and habits, whether defined in a narrowly political sense or more broadly, need explaining – no matter how deep-rooted they may appear. It is the self-sustaining nature of cultural norms, passed on through myriad and complex systems of socialization, which often makes them appear as a given. The danger of relying on political culture or national character to explain particular forms of behaviour is that they are self-referential and therefore static conceptions. Like appeals to 'human nature', they are incapable of explaining changes in political habits or modes of behaviour. Thus, whilst it may be empirically correct to identify *amiguismo* as being characteristic of Spanish political life, the reasons for (rather than the fact of) its existence require investigation.

Longevity in power

Somewhat prosaic, but still valuable, are analyses which emphasize longevity in power as a key explanatory factor in regard to political corruption. Governments which enjoy uninterrupted power for long periods – especially if they have repeatedly won elections – tend to believe themselves invulnerable. This in turn breeds arrogance, usually reflected in contempt for critics and political opponents.

Indeed, the demarcation between government and state can become blurred over time, a tendency which is likely to be exacerbated if – as in Spain – there exists a high degree of executive power. It has been argued that the socialists under Felipe González effectively sought to 'become' the state, using their hold on power to extend their influence to ever more areas of public life. In particular, the practice of 'insider trading' (the transfer of privileged information from the public to the private sector for the benefit of individuals or groups) and the movement of people between public and private sectors (*pantouflage*) helped to blur the distinction between state and civil society (Tusell and Sinova, 1990; Heywood, 1992). The use of networks and channels for personal contacts has allowed the Spanish establishment to avoid open markets, meritocratic competition, and public scrutiny.

The longevity argument is not without merit: it is undoubtedly the case that unchallenged power can breed arrogance and contempt for due processes of democracy. Moreover, particularly at local level, long-term clientelistic networks can become well-established and even self-sustaining. Equally, the nature of representative electoral systems is such that holding onto power may become an end in itself: the benefits which accrue from office in terms of power and influence often serve to promote pragmatism. Politics, it is often remarked, is a 'dirty business' and the peddling of influence to achieve the ultimate end of remaining in office can come as no surprise. The longer political leaders remain in power, the more access they are likely to have to sources of patronage.

However, whilst longevity in power may contribute to an increase in corrupt practices – especially in the sense of corruption as abuse of trust – it fails to account adequately for the phenomenon. In Italy, for instance, the emergence of political corruption pre-dated the grip on power exercised by coalitions built around the Christian Democrats throughout most of the post-war period. Similarly, in Spain accusations of corruption began to be levied against the PSOE shortly after the party assumed office. Moreover, the UCD government, which was in power for just five years, was deeply implicated in a number of corruption scandals (Alonso Zaldívar and Castells, 1992: 34–7). Conversely, other governments which have remained in power for long periods – such as the social democrats in Sweden – appear to have been relatively untouched by corruption scandals.

Longevity in power may be of greater relevance in explaining reactions to corruption. It is surely not coincidental that political corruption emerged as an issue in several West European countries just as they sank into deep economic recession after several years of sustained growth. As the bullish confidence which marked moves towards European union in the latter part of the 1980s withered, voters throughout the EC demonstrated growing reservations about the schemes proposed by their political leaders. The Maastricht ratification process represented the clearest example of such apprehension: voters became angered and alienated by the economic austerity measures associated with the moves towards convergence called for in the treaty, whilst political power became ever more remote and unaccountable. In the early 1990s talk of 'democratic deficit' became widespread.

Shortcomings on the part of the political class which may have been tolerated in times of optimism and economic progress were looked upon far less favourably when the going got tough. Politicians have rarely been popular, but loss of trust (as opposed to affection) had a major impact on reactions to corruption scandals. It could be argued that voters simply became more intolerant of activities which previously provoked a degree of cynical indifference. So long as 'the system' appeared to function reasonably effectively, if not efficiently, there was little cause for complaint other than from moralists. However, such an argument should not be exaggerated. Voters' intolerance is always more likely to be provoked by perceived incompetence (especially in regard to economic management) rather than corruption: the PSOE was returned to office in June 1993 – albeit as a minority government – *in spite of* a widespread conviction that it was deeply implicated in corruption scandals. The key point here was that Felipe González, at the time, inspired greater confidence than did his main rival, José María Aznar.

Party finances: catalyst to corruption

An alternative analysis is one which emphasizes concrete factors, such as the nature and role of political parties. In broad terms, Spanish political parties are characterized by three distinctive features: low levels of membership reflecting a lack of rootedness in society, a high degree of personalism, and a tendency towards ideological imprecision. To a greater or lesser extent, all of these features are related to the legacy of the Franco regime: 40 years of dictatorship inhibited the assumption of individual responsibility, the taking of organizational initiatives, and collective action. In short, there existed neither the tradition nor the experience of associative mechanisms which are central to the functioning of a democratic party system. Not only did democracy have to be established, but the civic culture necessary to sustain it had also to be nurtured (Pérez-Díaz, 1993).

Of equal significance is the fact that Spanish political parties were legalized in an era of ever-increasing mass media influence which has changed the nature of party political activity. Since the emergence of what François-Henry de Virieu has termed 'mediacracy', in which the mass media play a critical political role, parties have seen their drive for membership subordinated to the search for votes. Whilst this is true to a greater or lesser extent of all industrialized democracies, it is of particular importance in those countries where democratic rules have only recently been established and parties do not have the historical resources of their neighbours in older democracies (Lawson and Merkl, 1988).

In post-Franco Spain political parties had both to support the establishment of a democratic culture and to forge their own identities within it. Yet, there was little time to sink roots in society: parties were legalized just months – or even weeks, in the case of the Communist Party – before the first elections of June 1977. Votes were the first objective; party structures could develop later. In practice, mass affiliation to the new parties never took place. Although falling levels of membership have been a feature of many European democracies, compared to a European average figure in the early 1980s of 15 per cent overall membership, Spain barely reached 6 per cent (Bar Cendón, 1985). When the Socialist Party took over 10 million votes (48.4 per cent) in the 1982 elections, it had a membership of just 116,514 (Tezanos, 1992: 46). It has been argued that Spanish parties went from being parties of notables (*partidos de notables*) in the early twentieth century to voters' parties (*partidos de electores*) in the late twentieth century without ever having the opportunity to become mass membership parties (*partidos de masas*) (Esteban and López Guerra, 1982; Amodia, 1990).

Alternatively, following Lawson, it could be argued that Spanish parties have offered electoral and clientelistic, rather than participatory, linkage to their supporters: party leaders dominate and offer 'favours' in return for votes (Lawson and Merkl, 1988: 13–38). An example of such practices can be found in the southern region of Andalucía, a socialist heartland which is often seen almost as the personal fiefdom of Alfonso Guerra. Under Spanish law, in towns with a large rural proletariat anyone who can document working on a farm for 60 days in any one year qualifies for community employment benefits for the whole year. Certification is easy to come by if local officials decide not to look too closely at the facts. In return for pledging support to the socialists, a very vulnerable sector of the population could be helped through hard times and the PSOE benefited from the clientelistic network thereby established (Pérez-Díaz, 1993: 48–9).

As throughout the West, political leaders in post-Franco Spain have been obliged to appeal directly to voters via television, thereby undercutting some of the traditional functions of party organizations. In a televisual age the public image of party leaders assumes an ever greater significance. It is noteworthy that Adolfo Suárez and Felipe González, the two dominant figures in post-Franco politics, were both consummate television performers. Political parties became almost exclusively identified with their leading figures, both in popular perception and media coverage. Indeed, concentration on personalities, rather than issues and party programmes, remains a marked feature of much political reportage in Spain and has helped to mask the clientelistic networks which all parties have sought to establish at local level.

With political success ever more dependent on advertising and access to the mass media, parties are faced with the burgeoning financial costs imposed by the inexorable logic of the electoral process. In an era of low party memberships, newly created political parties simply cannot rely on membership dues and donations to keep them solvent. One of the principal reasons for corrupt practices in contemporary Spain is that political parties are unable to meet ever-greater financial costs. Since the return of democracy, referenda and/or general, regional, local or European elections have taken place every year, imposing a massive burden on party resources (see Appendix). In addition, the major parties maintain local headquarters throughout Spain, staffed by paid officials, in spite of their very low memberships. Parties thus find themselves waging costly battles to maintain their profile even between elections. In short, political parties are over-extended and under-resourced, which leads to the search for funds from any available source (Esteban, 1992: 79–88). As is universally the case, those parties in power (whether at national, regional or local level) and able to peddle influence are the ones faced by both temptation and opportunity.

In theory, Spanish political parties are bound by a series of laws on funding which restrict them to the proceeds of public subsidies, members' dues and limited donations. According to the terms of the Decree-Law on electoral organization of March 1977, the state defrays expenses incurred by parties during electoral campaigns according to their results, measured primarily in terms of seats won. Such an *a posteriori* system clearly favours larger parties, as well as those with close relations with the financial world which allow them to seek credit advances (Alvarez Conde, 1990: 74–5). Subsequent legislation – the 1978 Law on Political Parties, the 1985 Electoral Law and the 1987 Law on the Financing of Political Parties – sought to ensure clearer guidelines and, above all, transparency. In particular, the 1987 Law distinguished between public and private sources of finance and charged the independent Tribunal de Cuentas (Audit Commission) with auditing party accounts.

In practice, political parties have systematically by-passed the legal restrictions on funding. In spite of the introduction of official audits – a response to concern over unexplained sources of income – parliament is ultimately responsible for enforcing the law; until the early 1990s, audits were rubber-stamped even if they indicated clear financial irregularities. It took a series of major scandals – outlined at the start of this chapter – to reveal that parties not only ran up huge debts, but increasingly engaged in what has been termed 'parallel financing'. In essence, this involves a trade-off between money and favours. The scale of its existence in Spain remains unclear: during the early months of 1993, there was intense debate over the 'Filesa' case, heightened by the prospect of a general election in which the socialist majority was clearly threatened. The investigating judge in the Filesa case, Marino Barbero, ordered several raids on PSOE offices amidst acrimonious internal struggles within the party. Felipe González's statement in early April that the PSOE executive should accept collective responsibility for the 'Filesa' scandal resulted in just two resignations. As the editor of Spain's leading newspaper, *El País*, later commented, the socialists showed a 'reluctance to accept political responsibility until magistrates have determined criminal ones' (*El País*, 16 June 1995).

State development: weak, but heavy

Perhaps the most useful general approach to the question of political corruption in Spain is one which seeks to relate it to the nature of state development. Structural accounts of the emergence of the modern Spanish state suggest that, although the state took on the *appearance* of modernity following the collapse of the *ancien régime*, in reality it maintained particularistic, personalized social structures. The crucial point is that the central state remained weak, in spite of its extensive (heavy) involvement in political life. Being both financially poor and administratively inefficient, the central state was forced to rely on 'regional brokers' to perform its functions at local level (Heiberg, 1989: 234ff.). In common with most of Mediterranean Europe where the central state was weak, these regional brokers – *caciques* in Spain, *mafiosi* in Italy, *comatarhis* in Greece – mediated between centre and periphery on the basis of patronage networks which served as an important mechanism of social order. Strong patron–client networks ensured that the flow of favours and benefits was anchored in relations between individuals, a system which was largely self-perpetuating on account of the deficiencies of the state administration.

Thus, the nature of the state's administrative structure was critical to the continued existence of clientelistic practices in Spanish politics. The modern Spanish bureaucracy was founded at the start of the nineteenth century, supposedly on the French Napoleonic model – a model which implied above all else centralization and hierarchy. However, while Spain's bureaucracy shared certain structural similarities with the French example, in terms of administrative efficiency the two systems were far removed. According to Albaladejo Campoy (1980), the historic tension in Spain's public administration has been between the schemes proposed in various major reform attempts – Bravo Murillo's 1852 Royal Decree, Maura's 1918 Statute, and the 1964 Law on Public Servants – and the practice which has derived from them. That tension has been manifested in a chaotic, inefficient administration closely linked to the political powers-that-be, and their incapacity to engage in a real administrative reform which would put the state's bureaucratic apparatus at the service of the whole society.

Despite the reforms of the nineteenth century, the political parties continued to look upon the bureaucracy as an instrument whose control had to be ensured through the ideological fidelity of its personnel. After elections, the victors replaced existing officials with their own nominees: two parallel bureaucracies existed, one in active service and the other (*los cesantes*) awaiting the turn of the wheel of political destiny. Juan Bravo Murillo's Royal Decree of 1852 sought to introduce criteria of rationality and efficiency, but failed to eradicate patronage and immobilism. Indeed, the establishment of specialized elite corps (*cuerpos*) reinforced these trends. The revolutionary stirrings of 1917 led to Antonio Maura's 1918 *Ley de Bases*, which looked to solve endemic corruption through revised structures, terms of entry, promotion procedures and job protection measures. Once more, however, the best reforming intentions found little reflection in actual practice. Narrow corporative concerns came to replace wider political ones as an ever greater number of specialized corps sought to defend their elite privileges, thereby reinforcing patronage and corruption.

Despite its lack of translation into effective practice, the Maura system underwent no fundamental alteration until 1964. The Primo de Rivera Dictatorship (1923–30) left the country's administrative structure more or less untouched. In line with the Italian corporatist model, the period did see the creation of a number of autonomous associations – which gave rise to still more elite bodies – and the establishment of some important public service companies, such as the oil monopoly, Campsa, and Telefónica. Although attempts were made to confront the problem of state administration during the short-lived, modernizing Second Republic (1931–36) – for instance through the Committee to Study State Reform (established in 1934) – no fundamental reforms were ever enacted (Subirats, 1990: 5–6).

The outbreak of civil war occasioned the effective dismantling of Spain's administrative structure. The war caused considerable loss of life amongst public officials, and this was followed after General Franco's victory in 1939 by a *depuración* (purge) of Republican sympathizers. Franco was uninterested in administrative reform; instead, there was simply a massive avalanche of new appointments to the public sector in which the key criterion for selection was loyalty to the new regime. The bureaucracy became a central linchpin of the highly centralized, backward-looking dictatorship and was accordingly well represented within the power elite of Franco's Spain (Baena de Alcázar and Pizarro, 1982; Alvarez Alvarez, 1984; Beltrán Villalva, 1990).

Under Franco, although the central state became stronger and therefore less reliant on regional brokers, it remained heavy: bureaucracy was ubiquitous. Clientelism therefore continued to flourish, albeit in an altered form. Just as in Italy, where the *raccomandazione* system was deeply-rooted ('Without saints you cannot get to heaven'), so in Spain *enchufes* (contacts or connections) came to be seen as indispensable in dealings with the state. Franco announced that his public administration would at last be 'moral', but corruption soon became endemic throughout the regime. In common with many Latin societies, the concept of *mordida* (the need to pay a functionary a form of commission in order to get anything done) was widespread. Until 1958, functionaries in Spain were allowed to charge para-fiscal rates which they kept for themselves to supplement low salaries. After 1958, the *mordida* continued, but had to be forwarded to the Treasury. In addition to straightforward financial irregularities, corrupt practices took other forms such as administrative nepotism, the adjustment of work output according to salary levels, moonlighting, favourable treatment for companies and firms offering outside work to bureaucrats, and the use of state facilities for private purposes (Nieto García, 1984: 119–23).

Nonetheless, for all the corruption, some modernization did occur. By the late 1950s, the Francoist model of economic protectionism, based on the subordination of civil society to a corporatist relationship with the state in which the bureaucracy acted as mediator, had reached the point of bankruptcy – in literal as well as metaphorical terms. A solution was proposed by 'technocrats' associated with the Opus Dei, who sought to liberalize and rationalize the functioning of the capitalist market: the role of the state was changed to one in which it served as a promoter of economic development through indicative planning rather than as a producer or administrator. This entailed the need for a free labour market and a consequent reconstitution of civil society (Casanova, 1983: 955–9; Balfour, 1989).

The commencement at the end of the 1950s of a stabilization programme, assessed by the World Bank, required far-reaching administrative reform (Beltrán Villalva, 1990: 322). The 1964 Law on Civil State Officials saw the creation of a central body with overall competence on questions of personnel, the organizational unification and reinforcement of the general corps, and the restructuring of the remuneration system. The practice of 'personal ranks', by which some civil servants were promoted to grades quite out of keeping with the actual job they performed, was scrapped – as was the payment of 'extra-budgetary' special rates for particular services. The 1964 reform attempted to correct the tendency towards corporatism, but like its predecessors, was never wholly effectively applied in practice. By 1970, the hopes engendered by the new provisions had been largely frustrated: of the 159 different bodies in the state's central administration, just four fell under the terms of the general statute (Albaladejo Campoy, 1980: 44, 46; Beltrán Villalva, 1990: 326).

When Franco died in 1975, administrative reform remained a political priority. Sufficient modernization of Spain's bureaucratic structure had nonetheless taken place to facilitate the subsequent transition from dictatorship to democracy. A more rational, modern bureaucracy had gone some considerable way towards displacing the traditional patrimonial one; the more blatant examples of administrative corruption familiar from the early years of dictatorship had become rarer. The reform process – in particular, professionalization – received further impetus during the 1980s. In 1982, a 'law of incompatibilities' prevented state employees from holding more than one post. Subsequent reform laws continued the move away from traditional *cuerpos* towards open competition for all posts. A Ministry for Public Administration was established in 1986, charged with overhauling Spain's bureaucratic structure by attempting to change administrative culture from a predominantly juridical model to a management-based model, concerned with results and serving 'the customer'. To this end, there was a shift from the rigid structures of a 'mechanical bureaucracy' towards an organizational model based on grouping functional areas into self-contained units, budgeting according to policy objectives, and using audit-based methods of control (Subirats, 1990: 19–20).

These attempts to foster administrative efficiency and accountability were bolstered by the twin policies of rationalization and privatization. In line with the EC requirements on deregulation and liberalization in the drive towards a Single Market, the socialist government followed a policy of 'privatizing' state functions (Salmon, 1991: 34). Like many of its European neighbours, Spain has sought to improve administrative efficiency whilst simultaneously reducing the financial burden on the public sector. Thus, there has been a marked increase since the mid-1980s in the number of autonomous agencies, private associations and other organizations taking charge of public activities formerly handled by the state. This development aims both at cutting through the red tape for which Spain's public administration has been notorious, and at ensuring more transparent management practices (even though it is arguable that the mushrooming of para-state agencies creates even greater potential for corrupt activity). In the 1990s, the Spanish state functions in a manner which parallels more closely than ever before that of its northern European partners.

In spite of these developments, the contemporary Spanish state remains decidedly heavy and opportunities for corruption abound. There are two main reasons for this. First, public spending has grown as a proportion of GDP (from 27 per cent in 1978 to 44 per cent in 1988), and government tasks have become increasingly complex as Spain seeks to establish the kind of welfare infrastructure which has long been in place in most of Europe. Second, and far more important, is the establishment of a system of 17 autonomous regional governments in the early 1980s which presupposed the most significant reforms of Spain's public administration since its emergence in a modern guise in the early nineteenth century. There has been a dramatic shift of resources from the centre to the regions since the return of democracy to Spain. In 1977, compared to the nine member states of the EEC, Spain had by far the lowest number of permanent local officials: 19 per cent of the total number, as against 27 per cent in France and 57 per cent in the UK (Beltrán Villalva, 1990: 317). Since the promulgation of the 1978 Constitution, there has been a centre–periphery transformation, with regional government now accounting for well over a quarter of the state's total budget expenditure. In theory the centralized civil service should have contracted as power was transferred to the regions, but in practice government departments tended to expand – usually on the basis of claims that they were needed to improve coordination between the regions.

The creation of new regional administrations during the 1980s offered extensive opportunities for the development of a new spoils system, operated by the party in power (Martín-Retortillo Baquer, 1992). Inefficient basic structures, together with jealous demarcation of areas of competence, put a premium on administrative collaboration – leading to pointless duplication of services. Moreover, elections to thousands of new municipal councils throughout Spain's 50 provinces offered an extraordinary opportunity for political parties to reward their supporters: after the 1979 local government elections, for instance, there were socialist mayors in most important cities and socialists in charge of many *diputaciones* (provincial councils), as well as over 10,000 socialist town councillors – more than the PSOE's entire membership in 1977. For thousands of socialists, entering public office became synonymous with joining the party. Given the opportunities offered by holding public office for upward social mobility, the party came to be seen as a channel for social promotion and economic advancement (Juliá, 1990: 280). The same, of course, was true for other parties which won power at local level.

Conclusion

Political corruption exists in various forms in contemporary Spain. Whilst its full extent is impossible to measure, it seems likely that it is widespread and that most of it falls within the category of 'transactive' corruption (Alatas, 1990). Clientelistic and nepotistic relationships, in particular, appear to be far-reaching. The nature of political corruption in modern Spain has changed over time: whereas clientelism and bureaucratic malpractice have a long history, parallel financing and insider trading are more recent developments, associated with the emergence of a capitalist democracy. At both national and local level, the two principal conduits for political corruption are the party system (in particular, the need of parties to finance their activities) and the relationship between the public sector and private business. Opportunity is, of course, a critical factor. The lack of effective checks on executive power in Spain, poorly developed mechanisms of bureaucratic accountability, and the scope offered by a massive increase in projects of infrastructural renewal during the 1980s are all central to the continued functioning of political corruption.

In common with other Mediterranean societies, patronage and clientelism are deep-rooted in Spain. The reasons are closely connected to the nature of state development, where a weak but heavy state was forced to rely on a system of brokerage at local level in order to function with minimal effectiveness. Behind this need lay the failure to develop rational, modern and accountable bureaucratic structures, which in turn created a self-sustaining mode of political organization based on a spoils system. Only in the latter half of the twentieth century did genuine modernization of the bureaucracy begin to take place. In the 1980s, a concerted attempt to reduce the scale of the public sector at national level, as well as to introduce effective mechanisms of accountability, began to alter the traditional picture of a hopelessly inefficient and corrupt bureaucracy. However, the emergence of old-style bureaucratic frameworks at regional level has helped undermine this development. Furthermore, with the emergence of democracy, the financial demands of electoral competition in an era of low party membership have created a new stimulus to engage in corrupt activities. Old and new forms of corruption have become intertwined as democratically-won political power conferred further opportunities to establish and refine clientelistic networks.

If transactive corruption is widespread, extortive corruption – of the kind which appears to have been endemic in Italy for most of the post-war period – appears to be virtually absent. There is no equivalent in modern Spain to the apparent links between the Christian Democrats, the Mafia and the *Camorra*, no equivalent to the 'southern question' and no regional dominance of the state administration. The closest parallel in Spain is ETA, which has successfully imposed a 'revolutionary tax' on many businesses in the Basque Country. However, there appears to be no evidence of collusion between ETA and government figures; on the contrary, the socialist government was implicated in the use of reserve funds by the Ministry of the Interior to support the activities of the GAL (Grupos Antiterroristas de Liberación), which hunted down and executed ETA activists during the mid-1980s (Preston, 1986: 75).

Spain has undergone extensive, indeed remarkable, political modernization since the death of Franco. The successful transition to and consolidation of democracy was achieved with the promulgation of the 1978 Constitution and the emergence of a general belief that liberal democracy was not under any immediate threat from violence or anti-system parties. Old and deep-rooted divisions between centralizers and separatists, between the Catholic church and a secular society, between the civilian authorities and the military, have been largely superseded. Social pluralism and the market economy have been reinforced and have undergone a dramatic process of development. In short, democracy has been internalized.

However, there remain risks which could yet threaten the continued smooth development of Spanish democracy. The tendency of political parties to engage in rhetoric which is belied by their actions could undermine their authority as representative institutions. More serious is their apparent readiness to ignore the importance of accountability in their dealings with powerful interest groups, most notably the financial establishment. In addition, the continued functioning of traditional patterns of patronage and clientelism has contributed to a blurring of the boundaries between state and civil society, a trend exacerbated by the lack of effective checks on a very powerful political executive. For all that, the degree of political corruption in Spain should not be exaggerated. The current democratic regime is the most open and accountable in Spain's modern history, and it would be absurd to talk in terms of system-threatening crisis. Political corruption threatens the moral authority and legitimacy of any democratic regime, but Spain is not Italy. Nor does Africa begin beyond the Pyrenees.

Appendix
Electoral consultations in Spain, 1976–93

Year	Referenda	General Elections	Regional Elections	Municipal Elections	European Elections
1976	*Political Reform				
1977		*			
1978	*Constitution				
1979	Autonomy Statutes: Euskadi Cataluña	*		*	
1980	Autonomy Statute: Galicia Autonomy Initiative: Andalucía		Euskadi Cataluña		
1981	Autonomy Statute: Andalucía				
1982		*	Andalucía		
1983			13 CC.AA	*	
1984			Euskadi Cataluña Galicia		
1985			Galicia		
1986	*NATO	*	Andalucía Euskadi	*	
1987			13 CC.AA	*	*
1988			Cataluña		
1989		*	Galicia		*
1990			Andalucía		
1991			Eusskadi		
1992			13 CC.AA	*	
1993		*	Cataluña		

*denotes election was nationwide

6

CORRUPTION IN THE FEDERAL REPUBLIC OF GERMANY BEFORE AND IN THE WAKE OF REUNIFICATION

WOLFGANG SEIBEL

Pondering the question of possible corruption is a well-established custom in countries with a tradition of statehood,[1] the reason being that this implies a strong administrative tradition, which in turn is evidence of a central government apparatus that has shown itself capable of resisting the often brazen encroachments of society (Krasner, 1988).

German administration[2] is not entirely free of corruption. It can sometimes occur within its regular functions, if the benefit is particularly high and the costs are low.[3] Potential gain is high when administration encounters economic interests and when those who represent such interests can expect considerable advantage if the rules are not applied. A typical case is one where town-planning administration is required to conform to a tight set of regulations. The temptation of resorting to corruption to achieve a rapid solution is particularly attractive for anyone choosing to give way to it. The construction industry is one of the main centres of corruption in Germany.

The cost of corruption to administration is not high when risks of disclosure and prosecution are minimal or when infringement of the rules meets with varying degrees of social or political approval. This is particularly the case in city administration where close cooperation between the authorities and social and economic forces reduces political polarization of a partisan kind, which characterizes 'high politics' in Germany, and where competitive democracy gives way largely to proportional democracy. The direction taken by administration then becomes subject to trading between political parties and monitoring of collusion of interests is weakened.[4] Low-level corruption (affecting public administration)[5] can be reliably said to culminate when political practices of *proporz* (proportional distribution of benefits) coincide with major economic interests. This was the case when Berlin was divided and there is some evidence[6] for there having been a high degree of administrative corruption, in particular in the area of construction.

During the 1980s one might have had the feeling that 'Berlin's name was everywhere'. Germany endured a wave of scandals which led to anxious public questioning about the administration's propensity to give way to corruption. A magazine quoted a public prosecutor as saying that corruption had metastazied in Germany, blighting all levels of administration.[7] Such generalizations, however, fail to get to the root of the problem. Germans don't believe that their administration displays a general tendency to be corrupt. *Der Spiegel* wrote that only 28 per cent of German management considered corruption among administrative officials to be commonplace (as against 17 per cent in the UK, 50 per cent in France and 90 per cent in Italy).[8] Ordinary citizens are slightly more sceptical, although there is evidence that their confidence in administrative incorruptibility has risen, at least over the early part of the Federal Republic's existence: whereas in 1950 59 per cent of those questioned still considered officials to be corruptible, the figure in 1978 had dropped to 42 per cent[9] (more recent figures are not available). Likewise, crime statistics reveal that the mean number of convictions on counts of corruption showed no increase in the 1980s.[10] On the other hand, at the height of the Flick affair in 1984, survey results showed that 75 per cent believed politicians allowed economic interests to influence their decisions (Landfried, 1990: 236).

The view that German administration is incorruptible may be in the main accurate and not a myth. Its past reputation for accuracy, dependability, efficiency and professionalism is only a little tarnished. No citizen need feel apprehensive about being treated any differently from any other. That is to say that the problem in Germany is more to do with high-level than with low-level corruption. Corruption has to do not so much with officials as with politicians. It is no accident that the worst scandals in the Federal Republic have been linked to party funding. Political parties and their most distinguished representatives appear to have acted on the view that corruption offered the greatest benefits and, taking *'così fan tutte'* as a motto, a very small risk of disclosure. This at least holds true for the Federal Republic until 1989. Since then we are faced with corruption of a different sort, that one might interpret as a form of political hysteria linked to the unforeseen outcome and disenchantment of reunification.

A chronicle of scandals

The first major scandals involving corruption in Western Germany in the 1950s and 1960s were connected with the major issue of German rearmament and were to that extent specific. The scandals of the 1970s and the 1980s have to be seen against the gradual interpenetration of parties and associations, on the one hand, and divergent economic interests on the other, and hence they are more general. The incidence of corruption since reunification in 1990 concerns primarily – and unexpectedly – not so much Eastern Germany but more the West German political class.

Early scandals

During the 1950s and 1960s, irregularities occurred in connection with two major armaments projects, involving Hispano Suiza HS 30 armoured cars and Lockheed 'Starfighter' fighter bombers, the second being an element in the international Lockheed scandal which came to light in the 1970s. Both types of weaponry, in spite of grave doubts as to their reliability, were acquired through the influence of a CDU Bundestag deputy, Otto Benz, who was the representative both of Hispano-Suiza in Germany and of the then Minister of Defence, Franz-Josef Strauss (CSU). The HS 30 and Starfighter rapidly turned out to be faulty, which cast some doubt on political reputations although there was no conclusive proof of corruption. It was left to Der Spiegel[11] to uncover the two scandals.

It would seem that neither the HS 30 nor Starfighter involved a case of personal enrichment, judging by the conclusions of both journalists and historians. The politicians who were corrupt or suspected of corruption were above all lured by contributions to their parties (Landfried, 1990). The weak point in the German political system is to be found in the party set-up which lends itself to being a crucial element in corruption and an instrument to undermine institutional structures for supervision. This was shown to be the case in the most spectacular instance of corruption in the post-war process of democratization, the Flick affair.

The 1980s

At the start of the 1980s, it was discovered that the Flick consortium through its managing director, Eberhard von Brauchitsch, channelled large sums of money disguised as charitable donations to every party in Bonn.[12] Disclosure arose from the fact that payments effected by the Flick consortium were apparently directly related to a request for tax exemption made by the consortium in 1976. At that time Flick had sold its share in Daimler-Benz and would normally have had to pay 56 per cent of a total profit amounting to several billion DM in tax. This requirement was finally waived as an exceptional measure on the initiative of the then minister for the economy Friedrichs and his successor Graf Lambsdorff, both FDP. Criticism within the SPD was stifled at the last moment by the Flick consortium with several very considerable handouts amounting to a million DM, evidence of which, in spite of denials by Willy Brandt, SPD president, was borne out. Prosecution of Brandt was considered but dropped.

Entries in von Brauchitsch's private diary proved that direct payments had been secretly passed to the CDU president and future chancellor, Helmut Kohl. When asked whether the secret or indirect financing of the CDU had not been exempt from tax, Kohl replied in the negative. Documents found later in Kohl's handwriting clearly showed that the contrary was the case. An investigation of Kohl for giving false evidence was not proceeded with because it could not be established whether Kohl had knowingly lied.

In the SPD/FDP coalition at the time, the FDP, which was particularly involved, tried unsuccessfully to obtain an amnesty in the case of offences relating to party-financing. It was later asserted that one of the reasons why the coalition came apart in 1982 was the SPD's refusal to countenance such an amnesty. The subsequent coalition between CDU/CSU and FDP made another attempt in 1984 to pass an amnesty, but there was fierce opposition on the part of the public and from the left wing of both CDU and FDP and it got nowhere. Hence in 1987 only the former minister for the economy Graf Lambsdorff, who had in the meantime become FDP president, was convicted of being an accomplice in tax fraud. But there was little resolve behind the accusations made and Lambsdorff remained federal president of the FDP until 1993. Tax fraud was the worst indictable offence that the Flick personnel and politicians could be charged with; corrupting members of parliament is not a punishable offence in Germany.

Retrospectively, the Flick affair marks the beginning of a series of scandals in the 1980s, one affair after the other in the period preceding the historical event of German reunification. It is typified by the collapse of the trade-union-controlled housing consortium, Neue Heimat, following a succession of cases of corruption among union presidents.[13] At the same time, more and more low-level corruption came to light, particularly in the area of building administration.

Corruption following reunification in 1990

Corruption might have been expected to spread with the massive political and economic liberalization process undertaken in East Germany as in other former socialist countries. In fact this did not occur. Curiously, corruption became more a feature of the West following reunification. Once the great occasion was past, euphoria gave way to disenchantment and West Germany experienced a deluge of cases of political corruption:

- in January 1991, the CDU prime minister of Baden-Würtemberg, Lothar Späth, was discovered to have made regular trips abroad, alone or with his family, that were paid for by private firms, many of which had already received financial aid or other forms of subsidy from the regional government or counted on doing so. He resigned on the spot;
- in April 1992, it was learnt that Oskar Lafontaine, prime minister of the Saar and then vice-president of the SPD, had for years enjoyed a hefty pension for his past services as mayor of Saarbrucken (Lafontaine was 49 at the time of this disclosure). Lafontaine sought to justify himself on the grounds that his position as prime minister afforded him a lower pension than he would have received as mayor, while preferring not to mention that he was obliged to pay alimony to wives from two previous marriages that had been dissolved. He repaid the pension wrongfully obtained and remained in office;
- in December 1992, it was revealed in the press that the federal minister for the economy, Jürgen Mölleman (FDP), had used his position (and official paper) to publicize a cousin's invention. He resigned in January 1993;
- in January 1993, it was discovered that the prime minister of Bavaria, Max Streibl (CSU), had also had several trips paid for by private firms, among them an aviation firm which relied on Bundeswehr orders. A little later, the Bavarian minister for the

interior, Edmund Stoiber (CSU), admitted to having accepted similar invitations and further to having made free and regular use of luxury hire cars (Audi, BMW and Mercedes). Prime Minister Streibl resigned in June 1993 and was succeeded by . . . Stoiber;

- in February 1993, Hans Eichel, the SPD prime minister of Hesse, was accused of having assigned an expensive refurbishment of his official residence in Wiesbaden to an architect friend of his wife's, without its being put up for tender. This, however, did not affect his position;

- in April 1993, it was learnt that a member of Eichel's cabinet, Hesse minister for women, Heide Pfarr (SPD), had made use of public funds to renovate her apartment. As minister she was entitled to an official apartment but none was available, and officials in her department had given her permission 'officially' to refurbish her own apartment. She resigned in May 1993.

The most striking exception in Eastern Germany is the case of the transport minister, Günther Krause, a protégé of the Chancellor. While still secretary of state to the last prime minister of the DDR, de Maizière, and a matter of days before reunification came into effect on 3 October 1990, he put through a hasty order granting 41 concessions for East German motorway restaurants, which were recognized as being particularly lucrative, without putting them out to tender. It was established that those awarded the contract were unreliable and the leaseholds granted were so unfavourable to the state that they were subsequently declared 'irregular' by the government accounting office. Early in 1993 it was revealed that the council in Krause's home town in East Germany had been pressurized to make over farming land for building, which realized a considerable profit. What finally brought about Krause's downfall was the disclosure that his wife and son had accompanied him free on business trips and that the fees for a domestic servant he employed were almost entirely paid for by the local Labour authority. Krause resigned in March 1993.

Corruption and German political culture

How is one to explain the phenomenology of corruption in Germany? The answer is to be sought in the history of German government institutions and in the way Germans relate to these institutions — hence in the political culture. Institutions apportion risks and chances in the way that costs and benefits are distributed. Political culture determines how these 'risks' and 'benefits' are assessed.

Government institutions and political culture

What characterizes the shaping of institutions in Germany since the modern state is that the modernization of the political and administrative systems was not a simultaneous process.[14] It is true to say that in both the UK and France the modernization of the political and the administrative system involved a considerable time-lag, but nevertheless they occurred in the course of one and the same period. In France the centralization of the administration under the absolutism of the monarchy was followed by the 1789 Revolution. In the UK after the Glorious Revolution of 1688 there followed the setting up of a two-tier administrative system of centralized parliamentary power, royal and urbanized. In both instances, social evolution, the emergence of a bourgeoisie and the political order were reconciliable: in England following a long civil war in terms of a fruitful compromise between the provincial nobility, the nascent bourgeoisie and the throne; in France by the violent suppression of the dominant aristocracy.

In Germany, tension between the social 'base' and the 'superstructure' of the state (to use Marxian terminology) persisted. Prussian absolutism established a strong state administrative system, just as French absolutism did, at the expense of the provincial aristocracy. However, economic change in Germany was slow compared with France or the UK. What was lacking for there to have been a political revolution in the eighteenth century was the social base of an emancipated bourgeoisie. By the time this social class began to develop in the course of the nineteenth century, the old order had learnt the lessons of the revolutions of its neighbours. The apparatus of the state as such, the administrative system, became an instrument for compromise. The defeat of Prussia by Napoleon in 1806 provided the impetus for energetic reforms on the part of government: the establishment of an infrastructure for an expanding capitalist economy and incorporation of the bourgeoisie. This was effected through educational reforms and the construction of 'administrative autonomy', characteristic of German administrative law, implying participation by the middle class in administrative questions (initially locally in the towns) but not in questions relating to politics. The system lasted until 1918. In addition to this there was the German model of their *Rechtsstaat*, set up in the nineteenth century, which unlike the 'rule of law' in Anglo-Saxon-type democracies, does not designate parliamentary law as supreme, but rather highlights the need to modernize the administrative apparatus.

This pattern has had serious implications for German political culture, in that Germans lack the historical experience of acquiring democratic institutions by their own efforts. Historically, they have acquired the experience of democracy as the result of military defeat (1918, 1945–9) and as a gift on the part of friendly forces (1949, 1989).[15] Besides, democracy has proved to be unstable. The trauma of two hyperinflationary periods and the failure of the Weimar democratic model contributed to the value put upon the *Sozialstaat* (welfare state) as a guarantee of democratic stability.[16] But despite the considerable disruptions caused by recession and unemployment, democracy in Western Germany has since the 1950s given satisfaction.[17]

When Germans are asked for views on what constitutes 'sound democracy', they in general choose the 'norms and values of democracy' such as liberty, equality and justice, and almost never the 'authorities and institutions'.[18] One might conclude that the value of democracy resides first and foremost in material benefits provided by the state for social welfare and in ideological norms, while democratic institutions which translate these norms into practice have little or no significance for Germans. So the intrinsic value of democratic institutions and the separation of the individual from the mandate have relatively little impact on public opinion. The Anglo-Saxon notion of the 'mandate' as the expression of a temporary transfer of trust is foreign to German understanding of democracy. Germans are more inclined to identify the political factor with politicians themselves than with the institutional process of settling conflicts and seeking compromise. They possess no reliable measure whereby to judge political behaviour.[19] The monitoring of breaches in political conduct by public opinion is more subject to chance than to ingrained attitudes as to what is or is not done in politics. It may well be that one politician has to resign over a trifling matter while another remains in office even though he may have perpetrated a political act that is criminal.[20]

The administrative system is a different matter. The administrative system has survived every change of government since the time of the Congress of Vienna. With functions that are increasingly indispensable in everyday life, it has come to represent all that is dependable in state institutions, what the democratic constitution was unable to offer the Germans (Eschenburg, 1974). There are no survey findings available on the question, but the assumption that the stability of government apparatus and its practical value in terms of effectiveness for the common good is deeply engraved in the collective memory of Germans is more than plausible. The continuity of the notion of *Rechtsstaat* as guaranteeing the predictability of government in its concrete form, that is to say the administration, goes back to the beginning of the nineteenth century. *Rechtsstaat*, a term equivalent now with 'democracy', represents for the Germans the one reliable doctrine of government, although it is an institution that precedes democracy.

The relative weakness of government institutions requires that in a modern – that is to say, open and pluralist – society there is compensation in the form of social institutions. In Germany since the second half of the nineteenth century parties and associations have provided this compensating element; indeed German democrats recognized in these non-governmental institutions, following the failure of the 1848 revolution, the 'authentic' localization of democracy, precisely because the state was not democratic. The consequence of this delusion was that the task of organizing the institutions of the state on democratic principles was forsaken, thus making the effective compromise between government and the dominant aristocratic caste a lot easier. Towards the end of the nineteenth century, the institution of the party system, which represents the single structural and political constant to have surmounted every change of regime in Germany, evolved from the associations that were an expression of society. Under both the Nazis and the communists, institutionalized political parties not only remained intact but became central to the organization of the dictatorships.

In this context, one needs to take account of the fact that the importance of the party system is also an expression of a reaction to the territorial division of the apparatus of government. Administration in Germany is the domain of the *Länder*, whereas the *Bund* – the federation – only in a very few instances has its own administrative base. The parties are the guarantee of political uniformity in spite of the diversity of administration. Unlike France, where plurality of office is the most important prop to relations between the centre and the periphery, in Germany the parties as institutions guarantee that the expression of political will remains compatible at every territorial level of government organization and that political careers can unfold in a continuous manner from the local to the federal level. However, the party system combines structural uniformity with a polarization of content (Lehmbruch, 1976). Competition between parties is in critical situations the essential and decisive mechanism ensuring control and democratic responsibility.

The benefit, cost and social appreciation of corruption

That being the case, institutions and political culture in Germany can be considered as independent variables determining how the benefits and costs of corruption are distributed, including the decisive factor of how they are evaluated by the public. The notion of *Rechtsstaat* awakens in Germans the vague expectation that government – whether in the shape of politicians or public officials – carries out its functions in an acceptable manner. Nevertheless, there are in this respect significant differences between the world of politics and the world of administration.

Thanks to the training of its personnel, which ensures a high degree of professionalism, the administration is entirely at the service of the notion of *Rechtsstaat* and, in its effectiveness, is highly valued by Germans. The public official in Germany is not very well paid but, unlike a politician, his post is stable and he can draw considerable benefit from his professional identity, one of its components being incorruptibility. In general administration, where the client is the individual citizen, corruption holds precious few advantages for the public official. This helps to explain why administrative corruption in Germany only really appears where a monopolizable benefit, in the form of a considerable sum of money or significant privileges, more than counterbalances the risks.

The calculation made by German politicians is of a different kind. First, inasmuch as they are parliamentary deputies, they are immune from punishment for corruption, not that they are protected by a general immunity but because – and this is difficult to credit – deputies cannot be convicted of corruption in Germany. If political corruption is still relatively uncommon in Germany, it is because social disapproval may, but not necessarily, lead to a corrupt politician's career ending abruptly. Added to this is the fact that Constitution-wise, the political responsibility of government and, in particular, of ministers has undergone only slight constitutional re-inforcement. Only the Federal Chancellor is elected by parliament; ministers are not so elected and have no direct responsibility to parliament, which is not empowered to dismiss them. This pre-eminence of the executive can be accounted for by the experiences and traumas of the first experience of democracy in Germany under the Weimar Republic.

In these circumstances, the parties and internal power structures decide whether a minister remain in office or not, the grounds for which decision do not, of course, relate only to scandals. Even so, the party system in the long run weakens the political monitoring of corruption while reinforcing it in other respects on account of party rivalry. The greater the relative power of the politician, the feebler party rivalry, the greater the chance of evading punishment. In turn the two factors are influenced by a knowledge of corruptible offences which is of crucial importance in public monitoring.

This implies that a politician's image within his party has more importance than with the public at large and that in deriving favours for himself he seeks to favour his party. So the most flagrant case of political corruption in West Germany, the Flick scandal, was concerned not with the personal enrichment of politicians but with the illegal funding of their parties.

A politician's power within his party, intensity of party rivalry and communicability of corruptible offences may in Germany combine to make corruption remain politically 'gratuitous', hence unpunished. The Flick affair provides the most striking instance of this. It may well be unique in the annals of Western democracy that three party presidents – Brandt (SPD), Kohl (CDU) and Lambsdorff (FDP) – were involved in corruption, suspected of perjury (Brandt and Kohl) and guilty of tax evasion (Lambsdorff), without one of them being obliged to resign. In this case the politicians were too powerful, their resignation would have had too many implications.

Besides, party rivalry had no role at all in the Flick scandal given that every party, except the 'Greens', was involved. Elections for the Bundestag took place at the height of the scandal in January 1983, yet the scandal played no part in the campaign. As one observer noted, a 'coalition of silence' was formed between the parties (Staudhammer, 1985). The strategy might well have failed had the substance of the scandal been easily communicable; but the inter-twining of political and economic relations, pay-outs and compensation was too complex. The question of determining what this or that politician might have done exactly could only be unravelled by a highly attentive reader of reports on the case.

As was the Spiegel affair in 1962, the Flick scandal at the start of the 1980s was the result of vigilance on the part of the public. But unlike the Spiegel affair, the effect on the political system was minimal (apart from the fact that the arcane system of party-funding by

gifts took on some transparency in the mid-1980s and a limit of
100,000 DM was set for tax-exempt gifts from industry). The Spiegel
affair triggered off a serious government crisis, signalling the end of
the Adenauer era and of the phase when the Bonn democracy was constructed. The affair itself and the protests it gave rise to, in particular
among West German intellectuals, prepared the ground for the 1968
protest movement, the social democrats entering government in
1966 and power passing from the CDU to the SPD in 1969. The
whole movement for change contributed to the myth of the Spiegel
affair. Of course, political change and the immediate consequences of
the affair cannot be imputed to that alone. The change of government
which was, so to speak, in the air simply hastened the outcome.

With the Flick affair, there was no real 'changing of the guard', no
sense of purging (the coalition changed at the time the scandal
emerged in 1982 but the parties which attained power and remained
in power were the ones at the time most evidently implicated in the
scandal). The affair affected the entire political class. But why should
the scandal have been examined in detail and those responsible
excluded from political office? This is the kind of pragmatic response
expected of Germans . . . in the opinion of the political class at least.

The Flick affair sent shock waves through the Bonn democracy but
left the foundations intact. The negative point was made that for the
first time the parties in Bonn had provided clear evidence that they
considered themselves above the law. Party presidents and treasurers,
who were suspected of violating the law, blamed existing legislation
on party-funding for favouring corruption (legislation which had
long been open to modification, had the will been there). A feeling of
impotence in regard to party dominance also played a part in the way
the public reacted. As compared with the 1960s when there was a real
possibility of reform and party competition was alive and well, the
Flick affair failed to ignite a storm of indignation. The great
eminence of leftist intellectuals in Germany, Hans Magnus Enzens-
berger, remarked resignedly on the 'leaden placidness' with which
Germans responded to the Flick scandal.

To explain this attitude of abdication a fresh historical digression
may not be inappropriate. 'Leaden placidness' has long formed part of
the repertoire of political attitude among Germans, forced as they
were on many occasions to face the fact that they were not masters of
their destiny. In the Thirty Years' War (1618–1648), for instance,
when foreign armies devastated Germany, the German states were at
war with one another and the German empire, militarily as well as
politically, remained in the background. Then in 1871, the German

bourgeoisie which, like its counterparts in the UK and France, had been called upon to form the governing class were obliged to accept that not they but the nobility achieved the great objective of national unity, not through bourgeois political reform but through the aristocratic and archaic expedient of exercising military might. 'Leaden placidness' became the façade adopted to conceal the traumas dealt by history.

Corruption and pseudo-scandals: the relativity of historical studies

The experience of impotence in external affairs and the lack of opportunity to become involved in politics at home have prevented the Germans from developing that blend of pragmatism and firm principles in political behaviour that characterizes Anglo-Saxon democracy. German pragmatism is 'leaden' to a point of abnegation. Toleration reaches to the intolerable. And firmness of principle is frequently as far removed from reality as it is pitiless.

This ambiguity is externalized in another distinctively German attitude – hysteria. In the way that someone critically ill may seek a miracle cure, Germans traumatized by their history have always fallen for 'solutions' with roots elsewhere than in their own history.[21] The very fact that a state so young and initially so small as the Duchy of Brandenburg, which became Prussia, could in so short a time rise to dominate Germany finds explanation in the nostalgia for security and a stable powerbase. The chauvinism and the veneration of the emperor on the part of the bourgeoisie after 1871 who had suffered humiliation for so long explain this need for compensation. The totally unexpected shock of the German military defeat in November 1918, produced by unrealistic war aims and concealment of the true military situation, brought into being new needs for compensation with the consequences that are well known. Moderation, restraint, pragmatism, in short political steadiness, are not characteristics that Germans have shown in the course of their history. Germans are militaristic or pacifist, exterminators of Jews or protectors of trees, leadenly placid or hysterically indignant. Suggestibleness and the undeveloped ability to distinguish substance from appearance are part of the picture. Since the German bourgeoisie had little real impact on the social situation during the period of their ascent, they were soon forced to substitute the realm of ideas for that of reality.[22] Even today, Germans love ideological debate and they are inclined to accord greater importance to convictions than to actions. In instances where foreigners are threatened with violence, Germans form *Lichterketten** instead of making effective use of their police. 'Sterile nervous excitement'[23] is an archetype of the German attitude to politics.

To return to the 1990s. The scandals involving corruption which took on endemic proportions after reunification are in all appearances an aspect of German hysteria. Once again in 1989 and 1990 Germans underwent the experience of being alien to their own history. Reunification burst upon Germans as an absolutely unexpected reversal of their destiny. The indispensable psychological energy for reunification had to be mobilized without delay and effectively without notice, and this could only be done at the price of nurturing illusions: illusions as to the cost of economic transformation in East Germany, illusions as to the cultural correspondence of the two Germanies, East and West, and illusions as to the effectiveness of the institutions of government (Seibel, 1992). Disillusion materialized for the East Germans in the shape of a dramatic economic recession, in the course of which nearly 40 per cent of previously existing jobs were lost, and for West Germans – and in spite of electoral promises made in 1990 – in a reasonable fear of being hard hit by the financial costs of reunification.

In this context, revelation of cases of corruption apparently acts as a valve. Positive cases have less to do with their actual scale than with the judgment put on them by the public. On examination, it is without any doubt in comparison with the Flick affair an instance of the 'pettiness' alluded to by Bjorn Engholm at the time he was accused of corruption.[24]

The distance between ordinary citizens and those readily and understandably referred to in Germany as the 'political class' (hence as a separate caste)[25] widened during the scandals of the 1980s. The Federal President, Richard von Weizäcker, placed himself at the forefront of this criticism in the spring of 1992. Behind the 'leaden placidness' with which Germans followed the scandals of the 1980s there lay concealed an evident decline in political mobilization.[26] At this distance in relation to the 'political class' there was the added fear of being directly affected by political decisions being taken by 'those in Bonn' who were not thought up to it. The string of misdemeanours that have since come to light seem to afford manifest proof of this being the case. These misdemeanours – journeys undertaken at public expense, mindless nepotism, lucrative speculation, domestic service

*Trans. note: candlelight vigils.

paid for by taxpayers, and so on – have the advantage of being easily given prominence, they are directed less at the capacity for political judgment than at the public's voyeurism. There follow the psychological and media effect of the band-wagon: once the appetite for scandal is whetted, it requires to be constantly satisfied.

Germans observe political scandals like a crowd of voyeurs on a huge platform, as if the phenomenon had no connection with them, which explains why the wave of scandals since 1900 is peculiar to West Germany. West Germans are still on the look out for a crisis and are consequently apprehensive. They have time and leisure to find things to worry about and to search for distractions. For East Germans, catastrophe has already struck, they have other worries.

The negligible value that Germans attribute to democratic institutions and their rules of conduct, the fact that they possess only one formula to define their form of government – *Rechtsstaat* – which has been at the disposal of every regime, yet no formulas that refer to democratic responsibility and political morality, sometimes produces a quite grotesque distortion of judgment. Take for instance the facts that Kohl, the present chancellor, in his role as CDU president accepted a covert and unacknowledged gift of money from Flick's representative, without being able to account for the purpose for which it was intended, and that he failed to tell the truth before the parliamentary commission, yet none of this has damaged his career and is now largely forgotten by the German public. The derisory nature of recent misdemeanours on the part of politicians who have had to resign in the climate of hysteria – derisory, that is, as compared with the misdemeanours of Kohl or of Lambsdorff – is remarked on by virtually no-one. Apparently Germans, lacking as they do reliable indicators as to what is and is not politically responsible, are uncertain as to when and to what extent breaches of the law should require them to mobilize their energies.

The hysteria surrounding scandal is a sterile form of protest, whose consequences are entirely arbitrary. A minister for the economy who has advertised equipment produced by a cousin is obliged to resign. A minister for the interior who for his personal advantage has enjoyed free use of luxury saloon cars is promoted to become prime minister. A minister for women, who has the authority of her own ministry officials for the refurbishment of her apartment, has to resign. The prime minister of the same *Länd* government, who has procured a lucrative restoration contract for an architect friend of his wife's, remains in office.

On the other hand, Germans are unconcerned about what is really scandalous. What finally forced Günther Krause, the East German Mecklenburg minister, to resign was the storm aroused by his arranging for a domestic servant in his employment to be paid for largely from funds which were intended to relieve unemployment. As against this, Berndt Seite, prime minister of Mecklenburg-Vorpommern and a fellow countryman of Krause, saw fit to justify the attitude of the Rostock police when in August 1992 they made no attempt to prevent a hostel for immigrants being attacked and set on fire by an extreme-right group, an occurrence that was reported world-wide. Not only did Seite continue to remain in office but his party – the CDU – considered him in the spring of 1993 as a possible candidate for the post of federal president.

And then there is the grotesque, if not macabre. The prime minister of Hesse, Eichel (SPD), got away with his resort to nepotism in connection with the renovation of his official residence; yet the fact that he was held politically responsible for facilitating a neo-Nazi rally in Fulda (Hesse) with police protection in August 1993, an event also given world-wide publicity, was not looked upon as scandalous. On this occasion, Eichel dismissed not his interior minister, Herbert Günther, but secretary of state Kulenkampff, who had in fact produced a memorandum on the need to contain right-wing extremism, which Eichel put away in a drawer. At Kulenkampff's instigation 100,000 DM had been made available to obtain information on neo-Nazi activity. Eichel, the prime minister, instead of appropriating the money for the Ministry of Interior's fight against right-wing extremism,[27] put it at the disposal of a tapestry museum in Kassel, his native town. Germans apparently felt that none of this gave any cause for mobilization.

Anthony Glees (1988) has expressed the opinion that Germans have difficulties following up scandalous behaviour, since it is inevitably disproportionate to the scandal of national socialism. Unfortunately, there is little to support this indulgent view. In a country which considers that a minister's promoting a commercial product constitutes a greater calamity than providing neo-Nazis with police protection, there would seem to be, just as in the past, a want of historical judgment and, finally, of democratic political culture.

Notes

1. See for France, Mény (1992b); for Germany, von Alemann (1989).

2. Unless otherwise stated, Germany is here understood as the Federal Republic before and since reunification.
3. See Becker (1976) on the rationale of criminal behaviour and Rose-Ackerman (1978) on the micro-economics of corruption.
4. The study by Erwin and Scheuch (1992) of the situation in Cologne enjoyed a degree of success unusual in Germany for a piece of serious sociological research.
5. For the distinction between low-level and high-level corruption, see Rose-Ackerman (1978: 60–88).
6. Michael Sontheimer, 'Das ist der Berliner Sumpf', *Die Zeit*, 31 January 1986, at 12–16.
7. *Stern*, 6 February 1992, at 18.
8. *Der Spiegel*, no. 32, 9 August 1993, at 73.
9. Paul Noack, '*Die andere Seite der Macht*', Munich, 1985, at 135, quoted by Wewer (1992).
10. See Wewer (1992: 296).
11. *Der Spiegel* unquestionably deserves the title of West German democratic institution where the monitoring of government and administration by public opinion is concerned. The magazine was founded in 1947 under British licence by the journalist Rudolf Augstein. The 'Spiegel affair' in 1962 enabled the magazine to find a place as a monitoring organ. In the autumn of 1962 it reported grave defects in the *Bundeswehr* as a fighting force, which came to light during simulation of an atom bomb attack. The government led by Chancellor Adenauer accused Spiegel of divulging military secrets and the defence minister, Franz-Josef Strauss, flouted legal and political barriers by having the journalist responsible, who was in Spain, arrested by Franco's police. Strauss declined to comment on the matter when asked to do so in parliament and was obliged to resign his post. The affair showed there to be serious differences of opinion within the West German political elite over the strategy to be employed with the still-young Bundeswehr. See Schwarz (1983: 261–72).
12. The Flick family consortium was until the 1970s the largest industrial empire in the Federal Republic with interests in a huge number of firms, including Daimler Benz and Dynamit Nobel AG. Friedrich Flick, the consortium's founder, had made significant contributions to the Nazi party from 1932 onwards and was one of Heinrich Himmler's circle of friends. Flick had been a *Wehrwirtschaftführer*. This was an honorary title conferred by the Nazi regime on industrialists who showed particular

commitment to the German armaments build-up. The Flick consortium employed as workers hundreds of thousands of prisoners undergoing forced labour and in concentration camps. See Wistrich (1987: 90–1).

13. Bundestag printed report 10/50/79, 21 February 1986. See also Glees (1987: 111–26) and Landfried (1990: 188–234).

14. See here and for what follows, Dahrendorf (1965: 225–42) and Elias (1992).

15. Which certainly requires considerable qualification insofar as the change of regime in the DDR in 1989 and 1990 is concerned.

16. Elisabeth Noelle-Neumann, 'Der Zeitgeist ist das Kapital der Sozialdemokratie. Die Deutschen und ihr Sozialstaat', *Frankfurter Allgemeine Zeitung*, 19 February 1992, at 5.

17. Indications from the findings of Bauer (1993: 93–4).

18. *Ibid.*, at 101.

19. This weakness of judgment in Germans as to acceptable behaviour in the interests of the common good has been analysed in comparison with the Dutch by Elias (1992: 20).

20. The French word *'petitesse'* (pettiness) was introduced into the language of German politics in the spring of 1993 by the SPD president, Bjorn Engholm, who made use of it to play down accusations levelled at him. Even so, for such 'trifles' he was obliged to resign.

21. See Elias (1992: 11–29).

22. At the beginning of his book on the *Traume und Verblendungen* (Dreams and Delusions, 1987) of Germans, Fritz Stern quotes a familiar passage from Heine's poem 'Deutschland, ein Wintermarchen', 1844: 'To the French and to the Russians belongs the land/The sea belongs to the British/Yet we, in the ethereal realm of dreams, we hold/Undisputed power'.

23. The term 'sterile nervous excitement' appears in Max Weber (1958) (1st edn, 1919) in opposition to *Leidenschaft mit Augenmass* (controlled passion) as characteristic of politics based not on an ethic of conviction but on an ethic of responsibility.

24. See Note 20 above.

25. See in this connection von Beyme (1993).

26. See survey results shown in von Beyme (at 46).

27. *Der Spiegel*, 30 August 1993, at 33.

7

THE UK: CIVIC VIRTUE PUT TO THE TEST

Andrew Adonis

The UK is widely seen as the model of the non-corrupt industrial democracy. It certainly sees itself that way. The prevalence of corruption abroad, and its absence at home, has been the stock-in-trade of British politicians for more than a century. Far from waning, the refrain has become still more insistent in recent years as a large section of the ruling Conservative Party has struggled to stem the tide of European integration. In early 1994 Michael Portillo, a possible successor to John Major from the Conservative right wing, made a highly-publicized speech contrasting British 'purity' with foreign 'corruption' – not just in politics, but in business practices and educational qualifications. The tone of his remarks caused a furore, but many conservatives endorsed the sentiments. In terms of *mentalité*, little has changed in the UK since the early years after the Second World War, when the then Labour prime minister Clement Attlee could appeal to all parties, apropos a minor political corruption scandal, to join in defence of the principle that 'public administration in this country and public life in this country stand unrivalled in their high standards of service and incorruptibility' (Robinson, 1978: 249).

Not that the British political class has entirely avoided the whiff of corruption in the past century. The decade either side of the First World War saw a succession of corruption scandals, which seriously clouded the government of Liberal prime minister David Lloyd George (1916–22). In more recent decades, the 'Poulson affair' of the late 1960s and early 1970s, concerning shady dealings between building contractors and senior politicians, ruined the career of a leading Conservative minister, while corruption scandals have periodically erupted in local government. But such events have been discrete and fairly small scale. The British media and elite mostly regard corruption as exceptional, involving occasional episodes of questionable judgment by a few individuals, not a systematic process of personal and/or party gain through the misuse of state resources.

I say 'mostly' because the longevity of the Conservatives in office since 1979 has brought increasingly vocal claims from the political left that some of the perquisites of office are being put to improper uses by the governing party. The loudest charges concern the honours system, and other instruments supposedly used by the conservatives to generate party funds. In fact, the honours system has always been the one widely acknowledged black spot in Britain's clean bill of 'non-corrupt' health. Under Lloyd George, the systematic sale of honours to boost Liberal Party funds led to a simmering scandal. Since then, lesser charges on the same theme have surfaced periodically. But, again, the controversy has invariably been fairly low key. Even now, few in the media or on the left claim that the exchange of a few hundred honours for party donations in the past decade is the tip of an iceberg of favours sold or influence improperly gained. Tellingly, the Labour Party continues to nominate its own party members for honours.

The third and fourth sections of this chapter raise some question marks concerning the more rose-tinted view of the modern UK as the model non-corrupt democracy. If we move from the blacker forms of extortion and blatant trading of favours to the greyer areas of Alatas's 'transactive' corruption – mutual arrangements between donors and recipients to the advantage of both parties (Alatas, 1990) – then it has never been absent from the UK, at national or local level. Outside the central government departments of Whitehall, even the blacker forms have surfaced more frequently than the UK's reputation might lead one to expect. Indeed, it will be argued that corruption is on the increase, as government policies to contract out service-delivery functions to the private sector and to a plethora of new, quasi-autonomous agencies undermines established routines and checks on corrupt practice.

However, on any comparative scale of political corruption over the past century, the UK undoubtedly features at the lower end. At no stage since the 1840s has the political elite as a whole either attempted or succeeded in utilizing the resources of the state for large-scale personal or party enrichment. Serious malpractice by individual parties and politicians has also been comparatively rare. Accepted standards of public conduct have been high; the monitoring of them has been fairly exacting; and when identified, serious breaches of them have almost always turned out to be discrete – not systemic – affairs. For comparative purposes, therefore, one of the most significant facets of the British experience must be the impact of state development on corruption. How did the UK, whose public life was notoriously corrupt in the eighteenth century, make the transition across barely 50 years to a regime of extraordinary public probity? Whereas in some societies the growth of modern government has been held to foster – even to depend upon – corruption of one degree or another, (Banfield, 1981; Huntington, 1968, 1989) in the UK the opposite was the case. Modernization systematically rooted out corrupt practices previously prevalent. Even if the rhetoric to some extent belies the reality, the achievement was nonetheless remarkable. Accordingly, the two opening sections of this chapter analyse the nineteenth-century transformation and assess its contemporary legacy.

Old corruption

Most writers on political corruption in states subject to the rule of law locate it particularly in a grey area of public morality where practices of extortion and/or illicit private gain enjoy a fair degree of social tolerance. Eighteenth-century England certainly fits this model. The buying and selling of favours could be legal or illegal depending upon the office and the circumstance. Contemporaries talked in terms of 'legitimate influence' and 'illegitimate influence'. Degree and tradition were, essentially, the criteria dividing the two. For instance, most classes of parliamentary seat were regarded as property to be bought, sold or granted by a patron at will, but the wholesale purchase of seats by the *nouveaux riches* – particularly those enriched by colonial spoils – was widely regarded as 'illegitimate' and corrupt, although it was not illegal. Even flagrant extortion by state officials was generally tolerated within the ruling classes, until the 1770s at least, provided it was practised in India, not England.

Behind the Hanoverian era's endemic corruption lay a chaotic, premodern administrative system. At the highest level of the state, the monarchy, the chaos was compounded by the rudimentary nature of the division between public and private spheres. As Sir Jack Plumb writes of the ascendancy in the 1720s and 1730s of Sir Robert Walpole, Britain's first 'prime minister':

The entire administration of the country was carried out by the Royal Household, which, like the constitution, had grown up haphazardly over the centuries; when new problems had arisen they had been met either by increasing the duties of a minor official or by the creation of a minor office. Old ones were never abolished. Many offices became sinecures with no duties; if the office had duties, more often than not they could easily be discharged by a deputy, so that the Royal Household became the haven for the needy placeman. Walpole's strength as a minister arose from the fact that nine times out of ten the King accepted his advice on appointments. Naturally Walpole used this power to secure himself in the House of Commons, and all places great or small were made to pay political dividends. (Plumb, 1973: 65)

What was true of the Royal Household applied, *mutatis mutandis*, to the army, the navy, the Church of England (the state Church), and the learned professions. Within this system, the borderline between acceptable practice and malfeasance was often arbitrary. However, contemporaries were well able to distinguish between the 'grey' and the 'black'. The latter included extortion, if it became public blatant trading in favours and gross personal enrichment through the misuse of an official position. As the eighteenth century progressed, susceptibilities about corruption heightened. Significantly, they did so at a time when, in Britain's colonial empire, grosser forms of corruption were being practised on an unprecedented scale. In 1757 the British East India Company became effective ruler of most of India, on behalf of the British Crown. By the 1770s, tales of brutal extortion and fantastic enrichment by agents of the East India Company were common currency in England. The unfolding of great scandals of Indian corruption in the 1770s and 1780s, at the hands of Edmund Burke among others, led to a thoroughgoing assault on corruption as a system, in the process redefining accepted standards of conduct at home as much as in the colonies.

The details of the Indian scandals need not concern us. In essence it was the problem at home writ large: a poor division between public and private powers, with the East India Company both sole trader and the governing power. Public codes of conduct were lax, and virtually no machinery existed, until imposed from outside, to ensure that even that code was observed. Successive East India Company governors procured huge 'voluntary presents' from native rulers, supporting rival rulers on the basis of open payments and allowing their subordinates to exploit the native population with an array of fees, commissions and taxes for private benefit. 'Every man now, who is permitted to make a bill, makes a fortune', remarked Robert Clive, the governor who consolidated British rule. In a celebrated parliamentary report of 1782, Burke alleged that Bengal was being 'ravaged by an annual plunder' at the hands of British traders and officials. Burke's campaign forced the recall and impeachment of the serving governor of India, Warren Hastings.

The impeachment of Hastings ultimately collapsed, but the spirit of reform had been implanted. Indian government and administration was overhauled. Indian corruption remained rife, but it was on nothing like the scale previously practised. In the process, attitudes to personal enrichment from office changed throughout the aristocratic governing class. Whereas Walpole in the 1730s could boast openly 'every man his price', William Pitt, prime minister from 1783 until 1806 (with one break), was dubbed 'The Incorruptible' and died in office heavily indebted. Indeed, no British prime minister since Pitt has left office markedly richer than he or she entered it, with the exception of Lloyd George.

Modernization

The grosser forms of enrichment and extortion were thus on the wane by the 1780s, thanks largely to the efforts of the Whig Party in the House of Commons, a parliamentary grouping which came to constitute a 'modern' Opposition party for the first time in the 1770s. However, antiquated state structures and electoral processes continued to make corrupt and dubious practices a way of institutional life. The eradication of those practices required thoroughgoing institutional reform at home; and that had to wait on the end of the protracted wars against France in 1815, and on the rise of new middle-class commercial and financial elites – largely excluded from the governing class and increasingly resenting the exclusion – who made themselves politically awkward in succeeding decades.

From the 1820s onwards, two forces were at work in undermining the remnants of systemic corruption. First came public hostility from the rising elites to aristocratic 'abuses' and demands for admittance to governing institutions. The second, complementary, force was the radical press, exposing corruption and electoral malpractice as never before, and applying to it codes of conduct far more stringent than those previously accepted. By 1830, the pressure for political reform eliminating abuses and extending the social basis of support for state institutions was irresistible – or, at any rate, could have been resisted only at the probable cost of a revolution which Britain's comparatively liberal-inclined aristocratic elite was not prepared to countenance.[1] The result was the governments of Grey and Melbourne (1830–41), which extended the vote to the urban middle class, granted elected local government to the municipalities, eradicated the worst abuses in the Church, and further modernized administrative structures. By now, the Royal Household was firmly separated from the national government, salaries were replacing fees, and practices of audit control were taking root.

Taken together, the Grey/Melbourne reforms substantially reduced 'illegitimate' influence. But they did not eliminate it. Indeed, by conceding the principle of reform on Benthamite efficiency principles, they served only to highlight the incongruity of what remained – the 'legitimate influence' which the governing class had hitherto insisted, to general consent, was non-corrupt. The mid-century novels of Charles Dickens and Anthony Trollope testify to the rapid change in public perceptions of corruption. At one extreme – such as Dickens' famous account of the 'Eatonswill' election in *Pickwick Papers* – the condemnation was unambiguous; at the other end of the spectrum – typified by Trollope's *The Warden* (1855) – the tension between long-accepted practices and the 'spirit of the age' is treated with sympathy, but it is still not condoned.

The following 40 years, particularly the successive liberal governments of W. E. Gladstone (four times prime minister between 1868 and 1894), saw a wholesale assault on what only a generation before had been considered 'legitimate influence'. Two forces were at work. First, the inefficiency of the old aristocratic system came under further attack. This owed something to flagrant exhibitions of inefficiency, notably in the Crimean War (1853–5), but as much to the activities of a flourishing press combined with the post-1832 operation of the two-party parliamentary system, which ensured both a strong Opposition and the alternation of the major parties in government. (In Burke's day there had been the Opposition but not the alternation.) The results: a string of measures to abolish practices such as payment for commissions in the army, to define and outlaw corrupt practices by state officials, to introduce competitive examination for admission to a non-partisan civil service, to replace fees by salaries in public offices, and to set up systems of financial scrutiny by Parliament. These reforms had largely been enacted by the mid-1870s.

The second, complementary force was democratization at the level of elections. The late-nineteenth century saw a succession of statutes to extend the vote (in 1867 and 1884), further to democratize local government (in 1888 and 1894), to introduce the secret ballot for elections (1872), and so on. Each step increased pressure for the next; and with each step, more exacting definitions of what was and was not 'corrupt' came to be accepted by the political class. The old aristocracy continued to dominate the political system until the early years of this century, but increasingly it did so through its status and exertions, not by virtue of institutionalized corruption. The ability of the old elite to retain control of many of the levers of power made the reforms more palatable to the aristocratic mass: and that, in turn, owed much to the wealth, political skills and deep social roots of the English aristocracy (Adonis, 1993), a combination of strengths matched by few of its continental counterparts.

Two other factors in the transition from 'old corruption', must be mentioned. First, the reforms outlined above pre-dated by more than a generation the large-scale expansion of the social state in Britain. Gladstone's watchwords were peace, retrenchment, and reform. By the time the wholesale expansion of state welfare responsibilities began, under the aegis of the 1906 Liberal government, Gladstonian practices were a way of political life, and they came to be grafted onto new state institutions established to undertake the huge expansion of state responsibilities which took place in succeeding decades. The chronology is significant, and has implications for the Huntington/ Banfield thesis linking corruption with development. Given the experience of Lloyd George's government and ministerial career between 1906 and 1922, had the Gladstonian canons not been firmly in place already, modernization might have had very different ramifications for corruption. But they were in place, and they set the institutional framework and public tone for subsequent reforms.

The second factor relates to aristocratic wealth. However rich, no dominant class ever believes its wealth is secure, particularly in times of economic stress. The post-1875 agricultural depression was a time of acute economic stress for Britain's aristocratic governing class. One of its effects was to animate the aristocracy with a determination to diminish the spending required to exercise 'legitimate influence', particularly very high election spending. That motivation, for a kind of multilateral electoral disarmament between the two main political parties (both of them aristocratic-led), working in tandem with the Gladstonian redefinition of malpractice, led to arguably the most far-reaching of all the late-Victorian electoral reforms: the 1883 Corrupt and Illegal Practices Act. The 1883 Act defined electoral corruption more closely than ever before, outlawing all forms of treating and most variants of gifts or services 'in kind'; it also set tight limits on the amount that could be spent in election contests in individual parliamentary constitutencies, and it instituted a stringent system of election returns to independent public officials, and ultimately to the courts, which for the first time took the policing of the system out of the hands of the politicians themselves.[2] Both provisions have remained in force ever since. Indeed, in real terms spending limits have got tighter still: in 1994, the upper limit on constituency election spending was only about £5,000 per candidate per parliamentary constituency (of which there are 651 in the UK).

Incentives for electoral corruption are greatly reduced if the objects on which money can be spent are effectively controlled. In this respect the 1883 Act was an undoubted triumph. As democratic elections became the norm in Britain, two principles became firmly established in the political and public mind: that individual and party spending on elections should be comparatively small scale; and that the state has a duty to restrict election spending tightly in the interests of fair competition. In other democracies, notably the USA, neither principle is recognized; indeed in the USA the second principle is generally regarded as undemocratic.

To appreciate the impact, one need look no further than partisan television advertising. In the UK such advertising is illegal, and was made so by the broadcasting authorities after the First World War in the spirit of the 1883 Act. With little debate and virtually no public dissent, duties of political impartiality were placed on broadcasters, and in elections each party was – and still is – given a number of free 'party political broadcasts' to put forward its message. At one fell swoop the major object of party election spending in the USA – and in some European countries – was eliminated. Although there remains some controversy in the UK about the absence of controls on other aspects of national election spending by parties, the control on TV advertising means that the sums spent by parties in elections are tiny by international standards. In the 1992 general election the three main parties in the UK spent less than £20 million between them in national campaigning; in the 1988 US presidential election, about £100m was spent by the two parties on television advertising alone, and that excludes the sums spent in the preceding primary election within the parties.[3]

The cadre nature of the UK's parties, and the absence of primary elections, acts further to reduce the objects available for personal and party expenditure. And not just in comparison with the USA: a

number of institutional facets, mostly dating back to – or surviving
from – the late-Victorian period, serve to limit spending by political
parties more tightly than in most comparable democracies. The survival of a constitutional monarchy obviates the need for two sets of
national elections. The absence of sub-national or regional government gives the UK one tier of government fewer than virtually every
other democracy of its size. The UK's electoral system – first-past-
the-post in single-member constituencies, a system created by
Gladstone in 1885 – militates against the proliferation of parties,
ensuring that at no time in the past century have more than three parties been in serious electoral competition. In periods of realignment
there have been more than three 'serious' parties; but there have never
been more than three groupings in electoral contention, and the
pressure generated by the electoral system for parties within groupings to coalesce has invariably proved irresistible.

Two other aspects of the UK's modern state formation need to be
emphasized. First, the development of a non-partisan administration
– deriving from the tradition that officials are servants of the Crown,
not of the ministers of the day – has greatly restricted the scope of
party-political patronage and the incentives for corrupt practice by
governments.

Second, the constitutional position of local government has served
to contain – if not totally to curb, as we shall see – corruption of a
kind clearly unacceptable in national government. In the UK,
democratization was not accompanied by any increase in the autonomy of local authorities: on the contrary, at every stage strict central
controls have been maintained, particularly in the financial sphere.
There has, moreover, been a fairly sharp political divide in the
modern UK between national and local politics: although national
politicians have often served apprenticeships in local councils, they
sever such connections on election to Parliament. No system akin to
the French *cumul de mandats* has developed, partly, perhaps, due to the
absence of executive mayors in UK local government. That very
absence – the committee system has reigned supreme in UK town
halls since the 1830s – has helped to limit the concentration of local
authority power in the hands of a few local party bosses, a prime
source of corruption in other systems. Professional officers have been
accordingly powerful in most authorities; and although they have not
always been immune from corruption, the dispersal of power between
committees has militated against strong 'chief executives' within the
local bureaucracy.

Spots of black

Thus far, the UK appears as a state which succeeded in using modernization virtually to abolish corruption. Certainly, the constitutional
and political factors described above have eliminated all but inci-
dental occurrences of 'extortive' forms of political corruption.

That, however, is not to downplay the exceptional incidents which
have occurred. Two recent local government scandals reveal the
capacity of the UK system to foster corruption on a scale to match any
other. In 1993 Lambeth borough council, a long-time left-wing
Labour-controlled authority which covers a swathe of impoverished
inner London, was exposed by its chief executive for siphoning off
more than £10m in 'unprecedented' corruption, with work done
without proper authority, unauthorized redundancy payments,
managers subject to undue pressure to make payments, and over-
charging by the council's direct-labour organization and by former
employees. A subsequent investigation by the district auditor – a
nationally-appointed official – into highways contracts issued by the
borough found unlawful expenditure of £20m, including the
'deliberate manipulation' of contract terms to the advantage of the
council's own in-house workforce (*Financial Times*, 23 January 1993
and 22 May 1993). A year later, neighbouring Westminster was
found by the district auditor to have been engaging in an equally
expensive scam: its ruling Conservative group were found to have
been manipulating sales of vacant municipal housing in the late
1980s to coincide with electoral wards the party hoped to gain or
hold in the subsequent elections.[4]

At any one time, there are only a few Lambeths and Westminsters
among the UK's 500 local authorities, and similar instances in central
government and government agencies are equally rare. However, in
Alatas's field of 'transactive' corruption – mutual arrangements
between donors and recipients which offend against accepted notions
of trust and public morality – the UK cannot be excluded so com-
prehensively (Alatas, 1990).

On one reading, party government in democratic societies is
nothing but an organized, quasi-legal, exercise in transactive corruption. Whether the UK is more or less implicated than others is a matter of fine judgment. Governments in the UK claim to serve
something called the 'national interest', not individual or sectional
interests. But the major parties overtly associate that interest with
policies favouring different societal groups, and in government their
policies invariably favour those groups to a degree that they are rarely

prepared to justify in public on *a priori* ideological grounds. Surveying the post-war period, Labour governments have invariably said that the granting of extraordinary legal privileges to trade unions has been in pursuit of industrial harmony and progress, but the need for the Labour leadership to maintain cordial relations with trade union bosses, the main financiers and power-brokers of the party, has invariably been a key influence. Business backing for the Conservative Party has taken less explicit forms, but its significance for the evolution of policy under Tory governments is undoubted.

At local government level, Labour councils have frequently sought to 'buy' the votes of council house tenants with rent subsidies met by payers of property rates, while the motivation of Mrs Thatcher's government in abolishing property rating, the principal form of local taxation, and replacing it with a per capita fixed-rate local tax (the 'poll tax') in 1990 was a calculated bid to transfer the burden of local taxation from Conservative to Labour voters (Butler, Adonis and Travers, 1994). By the same token, a whole host of other policies, local and national, could be condemned as 'transactive corruption'. In a few cases were/are the 'corrupt' goals explicitly stated; in even fewer cases were/are they the only goals at stake. Nor, in most cases, was/is any illegality involved – though, particularly in local government, the open avowal of such 'transactive' motives might contravene statute. Nonetheless in most cases the avowal of the 'transactive' objectives at stake would have brought general press and public condemnation for corruption. Such is the slippery nature of corruption as a concept: were we able to make windows into politicians' souls, it would often be hard to decide whether or not particular actions were corrupt in a general 'transactive' sense.

However, the UK does not escape quite so easily. For in certain areas where the motivation of the parties is crystal-clear, the existence of transactive corruption is almost undeniable. The most obvious and significant is the honours system. To understand why, we need once again to go back to the late-Victorian period, from whence originates both the system and its abuse in modern guise.

In the UK, the monarch is the fount of honour: all honours, from lowly medals to peerages giving enormous social cachet and a seat in the House of Lords, the UK's second chamber, are created by the reigning sovereign. However, since the early nineteenth century virtually all honours have been granted on the nomination of the prime minister. The honours system is one part of the pre-Gladstonian *ancien régime* emphatically not 'cleaned up' by the late Victorians. On the contrary, prime ministers – even Gladstone him-

self – resorted to the blatant sale of honours, particularly knighthoods
and peerages, to consolidate support among rising commercial and
financial elites, and to fill party coffers. We noted earlier that by comparative standards Britain succeeded in containing election expenditure. Parties had nonetheless to raise considerable sums; and the
political decline of the old aristocracy, which had previously met the
bill for both main parties, forced them into reliance on plutocrats for
the purpose (Pinto-Duschinsky, 1981; Searle, 1987).

Since both major parties needed the money and wielded the
patronage with discretion, the corruption involved in selling honours
was rarely a matter of scandal before the First World War. That
changed after 1918 because of the complete absence of such discretion
on the part of Lloyd George, particularly in his creations of knights
and peers. One upshot was the Honours (Prevention of Abuses) Act
1925, which outlawed individual trafficking in honours.
Significantly, however, only a threat to the legal status of trade-union
financing of its own activities provoked the Opposition Labour Party
into mounting an attack on Lloyd George's activities. Once the position of the unions was secure, and discretion in the award of honours
returned with the more sober premiership of Stanley Baldwin, the
furore died down. The general desire not to drag the King into
politics had in any case limited its impact, and on its own it never
came close to toppling Lloyd George.

Honours were not the only item in pre- and inter-war charges of
corruption: the business interests of senior politicians also aroused
periodic controversy. It has been highlighted because of its per-
sistence in post-war Britain. One survey of Mrs Thatcher's premiership (1979–90) estimated that of 174 private-sector industrialists
given peerages or knighthoods, 85 were connected with companies
that had given a total of £13.6m to the Conservative Party or to front
organizations laundering money for the party. 'Individual trafficking
seems to have been replaced by a system of bulk purchase', comments
Vernon Bogdanor.[5] In June 1993 the chairman of the official committee responsible for vetting nominations for honours – but which
almost never vetoes them in practice – conceded that 'honours are, in
effect, being bought'. One 1993 survey showed that industrialists
were ten times more likely to be awarded peerages or knighthoods if
their firms gave money to the Conservative Party (*Guardian*, 16 June
1993).

A number of other, less definite, variants of 'transactive' corruption
should be mentioned. The practice of former ministers taking highly
paid private sector directorships has been growing in recent years. In

a few cases, former ministers have taken jobs in companies they had played a part in privatizing. A large proportion of members of the House of Commons (MPs) act as paid consultants to companies (on the Tory side) or are formally sponsored by individual trade unions (on the Labour benches). The 1989 official register of the pecuniary interests of MPs found that one in three of all non-ministerial MPs was an 'adviser', 'consultant' or 'director' to a public relations firm, with many listing several such postings. At every level of government and administration practices like these could be cited – civil servants taking highly paid jobs in companies they were previously regulating, local government officers doing the same, and so on. The degree of transactive corruption varies, indeed its very existence is largely in the eye of the beholder. But it would be naive to dismiss its existence. The final section of the chapter highlights three areas where it appears to be steadily increasing: the growth in the number of 'quangos' (state agencies appointed by central government), the contracting-out to the private sector of state administrative functions, and the handing down of financial responsibility within the state sector.

Quangos, contracting-out and state sector reform

A fifth of public spending is now in the hands of quangos of one kind or another – including schools, colleges, health authorities and regional development agencies. Most of the appointments to their boards are made by ministers; in many cases, they are being encouraged to act in entrepreneurial ways foreign to established civil service traditions. The implications for 'transactive' corruption of one kind or another are clear enough, both in the appointment process and in the *modus operandi* of the agencies. Furthermore, the drive to contract-out the delivery of services has been extended to elected local government and the remnants of Whitehall. Contracts have ever been a prime source of local government corruption; it is too early to say whether the contract revolution of the 1980s will bear similar fruit, but it would be surprising if it did not result in a marked increase in the number of exceptional 'incidents' of a kind noted earlier.

By 1994, report after report was highlighting the dangers involved in uprooting established systems of oversight and control in the spending of public money, all based on detailed studies of practices in the new institutions established to take over functions from Whitehall departments and local government. The 1992/3 Annual

Report of the Audit Commission, a nationally-appointed watchdog, expressed concern at the inexperience of many of those appointed to senior positions in quangos, and their unfamiliarity with established codes of public conduct. The commission also raised questions about the implications of the other major contemporary trend in public sector management: the elimination of the middle manager, and the handing down of budgetary authority to 'line managers' in state institutions, notably hospital managers and school head teachers. With 'reinventing government' in vogue world-wide, the objectives of such policies – efficiency, effectiveness, responsiveness – need no recital. However, the Audit Commission found serious implications for the growth of endemic low-level corruption of kind hitherto restricted largely to the police in the UK. To take just one area, schools: with the shift to 'local management' and 'grant-maintained status' for the UK's 25,000 schools, head teachers are now in more or less control of budgets totalling more than £16bn a year. Devolution on this scale has only been in operation for less than two years, but the Audit Commission found numerous cases of the employment of head-teachers' spouses at above-average rates of pay, and short-cutting in established recruitment and financial control procedures.

The respected Public Accounts Committee of the House of Commons – established by Gladstone in 1860 – went a stage further in a 1994 report on 'the proper conduct of public business'. It high-lighted recent cases of serious misuse of funds by quangos: £20 million by Wessex Regional Health Authority, £10 million by West Midlands Regional Health Authority Pounds, £1 million by the National Rivers Authority, with widespread evidence of dubious practices including 'golden handshakes' for incompetent officials and the keeping of contracts within a narrow circle. 'These failings', the committee concluded, 'represent a departure from the standards of public conduct which have mainly been established during the past 140 years.' Yet the scope for more of the same is large. The committee noted the existence of 1,444 quangos, set to rise within five years to 2,500; by 1996 it estimated that quangos would control nearly a quarter of total government expenditure.

The reference to 'the past 140 years' takes us back to the nineteenth century. We remarked earlier on the importance of the fact that in the UK reconstruction of the corrupt state machine pre-dated the sub-stantial increase in state responsibilities necessitated by social welfare legislation. In a real sense state sector reform in the 1980s and 1990s is restoring the ministerial discretion and lax oversight deliberately abolished by Gladstone and his fellow nineteenth-century reformers.

Today's reforms have been introduced in the name of management efficiency and flexibility. But their upshot could be a larger incidence of public corruption than the UK has witnessed this century.

Notes

1. See Brock (1973) for an account of the most critical struggle of the reformers.
2. For the 1883 Act and its impact see Gwyn (1962).
3. For a recent analysis of UK election spending, see the 1992 report of the Hansard Society, *Election Campaigns: An Agenda for Change*. See also Pinto-Duschinsky (1981) about party finances.
4. For local government corruption see Doig (1984), especially 157–98.
5. Vernon Bogdanor, 'A wholesale traffic in dishonourable power', *Independent*, 6 April 1993.

8

RULE BY BUREAUCRACY IN RUSSIA

Marie Mendras

The fall of the communist regime brought the Soviet state down with it and the reconstruction of a system of government in Russia is a long and arduous business. Even so, public administration is holding its own with astonishing robustness. It has rapidly adapted and made use of the legal and political vacuum to play the major role in dividing the spoils from the Soviet state. Senior officials have turned into owners; the instances are many of state employees who still hold administrative power and now manage assets that they own, at least in part.

The demise of the most bureaucratic and arbitrary regime the twentieth century has seen was marked by the triumph of the bureaucrats who understood fairly early on that appropriation of state assets afforded the new guarantee of exercising power. Property and money have conquered Russia within a few years, providing a choice terrain wherein administrative corruption can thrive. The transformation of Russia has been carried out not by adventurers moving in but by the *nomenklatura*; regional governors, city mayors, major industrialists and their organizations are the ones running the country. They are laying down the rules – financial and bureaucratic – and establishing their areas of authority, and in so doing are bound less and less to others. The executive power in Moscow is no longer running the show.

From the *chinovnik* of the tsars to the communist *apparatchik*

On the eve of the 1860s reforms, Prince Peter Dolgorukov called vehemently for the *chin*, the table of ranks established under Peter the Great, to be abolished, dubbing it the 'surest guarantee of incompetence servility and corruption'. The self-propagation of *chinovniki* effectively withdrew from the tsar the right to choose his high officials. In the nineteenth century the sovereign found himself a prisoner of those who ought by rights to have been his servants, the *dvoriane* (landowners) and the *chinovniki* (government officials) (Pipes, 1974: 136–7). Under the reign of the last tsar, Nicolas II, powerlessness passed for absolutism. Russia was administered – more often than not, poorly administered – by civil servants and provincial governors.

And yet, bureaucrats were relatively scarce in imperial Russia, roughly 50,000 *chinovniki* in the mid-nineteenth century, '11 to 13 civil servants per 10,000 inhabitants'.[1] Bureaucratic centralization, which intensified in the later years of tsarism, only became an authentic system of government after the 1917 Revolution. The Bolshevik leaders came quickly to realize that if they wanted to reconquer and control the vast empire the first requirement was to establish a strong structure of administrative power with each level subservient to the government in Moscow.

Under the tsars the civil service's size was not excessive but it already enjoyed great and relatively unrestricted power over the people. Waiting as they had to – given the great distances and the harsh climate – for the *revizor* from the capital, provincial officials were free to administer their subjects as they wished. Russian literature is full of portrayals of the *chinovnik*, who arouses fear though he may be a nonentity. Gogol and Saltykov-Shchedrin have satirized the harassment of *mujiks* by the self-important official, who in the course of furtive encounters manages to extract a small portion of what it was hoped to squeeze out of them.

Civil servants in Russia could only make a living through abuse of their administrative position. More often than not, they received no salary, the form being to 'live off their business dealings' (*kormiatsia ot del*). The Russian peasant provided for the state and its administration, who failed to provide for themselves. Thus, bribes or supplementary taxes taken by administrative officials were not in general looked upon as marks of corruption but simply as 'the way things are'. Once the administration had been paid and the government – whether central, regional or local – received its due, the peasant or community he was part of could enjoy any surplus there might be. In regard to its agriculture, the Soviet state functioned no differently. The *kolkhozes* were required to honour 'state controls' and managed what was left over as they wished. Since state controls were oppressive and productivity low, livelihood depended on the patch of land that was yours.

Russia has maintained the peasant and Oriental tradition regarding the relationship to authority. The chief, the *nachalnik*, is an object of fear, his second-in-command even more so. The aim is to mollify him and satisfy his demands yet not to give in entirely. The best that can be done is to come to an agreement since there is virtually no means of resistance nor of obtaining redress for misuse of power. Neither in the time of the tsars nor in the time of the soviets was their any virtual recourse, unless through chance or some means of persuasion one gained access to a higher authority which might countermand the administrative decision of a subordinate.

In the USSR government officials and party *apparatchiks* were paid and – far more important than payment – received significant privileges: decent housing, special shops, selective education for children, official transport and so on. They did not depend for their livelihood on the population they administered. The key to power in this system of organized shortages resided in having access to material goods and services. One did not talk of 'buying' (*kupit*) a pound of meat but of 'having access' (*dostat*) to a rare and highly-coveted delicacy. The price was unimportant since in general in the state shops it was low in relation to wages. The Soviet citizen had a sizeable nest-egg of roubles that served no purpose. Savings took the place of consumption.

Shortages and social confinement bestowed immense power on Soviet officials. There is no denying that the scarcity of consumer goods was an intended policy on the part of the authorities, especially the 'intermediate layers' of the administrative structure, to use the established term in Russia. Management of scarcity ensured power over those administered. In the absence of justice worthy of the name, in the absence of government that was representative of and responsible to those it governed, the resources of the state, in regard both to production and distribution, depended on the goodwill of a *nomenklatura*.

The *apparatchiki* caste grew considerably over 70 odd years of communist administration. The enterprise embarked on was a huge one, namely to control the whole range of economic, political and cultural activity involving 300 million people in an industralized country facing enormous technological change. Stalin had held this pyramid of *apparatchiks* in subjection in its entirety – managers of steel complexes and of kolkhozes, generals and party secretaries, minor regional officials – he had succeeded in doing so through a policy of terror. This strictly centralized construct where the *revizor* was omnipresent did not outlast the end of Stalinism. The USSR under Brezhnev saw the emergence of every sort of violation, minor as well as major, among a huge caste of officials, the *nomenklatura* of the Party-State, which no longer lived in fear of purges and punishment.

Clientelism and corruption under Brezhnev

The Soviet Union in the 1970s was, in Brezhnevian terminology, the country of 'developed socialism'. In the opinion of the Moscow writer and jurist Arkady Vaksberg, it was in the first place the golden age of the communist party mafia. Under Brezhnev, corruption was no longer limited to abuse of power on the part of the minor apparatchik or factory shop foreman. Organized networks developed everywhere, in every province and at all levels, in almost every case linked back to Moscow. All the Soviet leaders participated to a greater or lesser degree in systematic illicit activity, corruption becoming widespread as regards clientelism and economic networks which, Arkady Vaksberg stresses, were of much greater significance than a 'shadow economy' and became an 'economy of real socialism'.

> Production parallel to legal production, theft of funds allocated by the state . . . use of government supplies and factory equipment to produce merchandise that went unaccounted for, fraudulent sales, circulation of vast sums of money without official record but real nonetheless – this was all quite unknown under Stalinism. It only needed a slight relaxation of control for the 'shadow economy' to inundate the official economy. (Arkady Vaksberg, 1992: 25)

The whole system facilitated the misappropriation of national resources. Everything belonged to everyone, nothing to anyone. Theoretically, for the Soviet citizen wasting hot water or electricity did not matter since one had no incentive to economize with what was a common possession. A similar attitude prevailed in productive occupations where wastage was considerable. In particular, the system encouraged rent-seeking behaviour. Those in management positions had a free call on the wealth of the country and, from the 1960s onwards, undertook to live on what they could earn by uncontrolled exploitation of the country's riches. Arkady Vaksberg gives many instances of abuse of the Soviet system. He describes how a train carrying wheat destined for Russian flour-mills was stripped of its cargo, which was left to rot, so that it could be used for the urgent transport of a consignment of citrus fruit from Georgia, thus enabling the network concerned to realize a better profit margin. He tells of the extraordinarily labyrinthine 'cotton mafia' in Uzbekistan, that led back to the first secretary of the Party in Uzbekistan, himself protected by high party officials in Moscow. He shows how the Soviet leaders participated in misrepresenting the state of the economy by encouraging the falsification of production figures when this was deemed necessary for political reasons or for drawing income.

The absence of private property had dual consequences on corruption. On the one hand, personal enrichment did not take the form of material or monetary possessions; ambition was normally satisfied with a well-furnished apartment, a car and a *datcha*, with the exception of the party leaders naturally, who could grow rich by buying abroad (Brezhnev himself collected foreign cars). Officials did not amass much. On the other hand, an official with few scruples could readily embezzle public property being by definition answerable for such property and, at the same time, having virtually risk-free control over its 'monopolistic' use.

Moreover, the impossibility of accumulating personal wealth allowed an essential aspect of corruption − string-pulling, close contacts and network privileges − to develop. The power wielded by those in the apparatus was proportionate to the power they had over people. It was difficult to make a career without belonging to a network. One needed to be protected, and thus clientelism was the chief driving force of the soviet political and administrative apparatus. In the highest sphere of power, in the local hierarchy as in Moscow, the leaders were obliged to take on the role of protector for the numbers they 'looked after' without whom the soviet machine could not function. In other words, corruption in the *nomenklatura* of the Communist Party had become an integral part of the system.

When, following Brezhnev's death in 1982, Yuri Andropov and, later, Mikhail Gorbachev took on some of the major networks, in particular the 'Uzbek network', they were probably little prepared for the danger a purge of this sort would pose for the Soviet economic and administrative system as a whole, however reasonable their diagnosis was; by then corruption had gone beyond acceptable limits − limits, that is, that enabled the economic machine to continue to function. The authority of the leaders in Moscow was threatened by the emergence of all-powerful regional bosses and by the squandering of crucial resources such as oil, natural gas and wheat.

The USSR started to come apart less as a result of social or national demands than of the piecemeal and increasingly uncontrolled destruction wrought by those who served the Party-State. The *nomenklatura* in the regions, the republics and the major monopolies of production and distribution claimed autonomy for themselves and threw off the yoke of the central administration either by corrupting it or becoming themselves untouchables.

The situation rapidly led to administrative gridlock. In a fairly closed economy as the Soviet Union still was before the end of the 1980s and in the absence of convertibility and conditions of free trade, the economy of corruption was asphyxiated within the frontiers of the state. It became vital for the beneficiaries of the system to find ways of sending money abroad because there were no outlets for financial investment. Energy sales abroad had already provided such an opportunity, one however that really only benefited the senior party bosses in Moscow, given that the oil and gas industries were centralized and tightly controlled.

With the end of the state monopoly, privatization and the opening of frontiers, the shackles burst and government at all levels found it impossible to cope with the economic free-for-all in the absence of any legal framework. The ready recourse was to take swift advantage of Moscow's diminishing power in order to profit from economic transformation and build power for oneself.

'Get rich'

The end of the communist regime in Russia led to a number of radical changes that facilitated corruption in administration. First was the appearance and institutionalization of private property; second, the development of a money economy (as opposed to the barter system of Soviet days), its becoming open to foreign capital and the possibility of investment abroad; and third, the institutional and legal confusion that was a concomitant of the dwindling of federal government in Russia.

After 1992, the privatization of the Russian economy became virtually obligatory but in the context of 'delayed capitalism' it took unusual forms. First, it implied a winding-down of state activity. For instance, the agricultural cooperatives – *kolkhozes* – were legally bound to turn themselves into joint-stock companies. But since the means for privatization were lacking, legal changes have generally been effected without changes in administration or even any alteration in the position of those involved in the cooperative. In Novosibirsk, the agricultural cooperative 'Red October Company' made the required change and became the 'Red October' Company, its directors finding no good reason for changing its name! In the case of industrial firms, changes vary mainly with the sector concerned and the interest shown by foreign capital. In the major steel complexes, the state sells its shares which are then taken up by other public bodies or by newly-constituted legal bodies, comprising the directors of the complex. The notion of private ownership and capitalist management applies most to the creation of new firms, especially in service activities.

Privatization initially implied dismembering the state with, first, the constituent republics, then the regions acquiring their own sovereignty. In 1990, when the notion of private ownership established itself in Soviet official vocabulary and was later introduced in Soviet law, the first question to be asked was: In preparation for the share-out, who owns what? Whose is the authority for deciding that the assets of the Soviet Union should be put up for sale? So began a fierce battle between the different institutions and the different soviet *nomenklatura* that has continued for the five years or so since the formal ending of the USSR, each one claiming ownership of that part of the state under its control.

In Moscow, for example, privatization first affected the housing sector. The city of Moscow claimed the authority to oversee the distribution of ownership rights, in most cases involving sale, and hence easy revenue for the city administration. The battle naturally divided the municipal authorities, concluding with the defeat of the elected soviet and victory for the new municipality. In the face of city ambitions, the Moscow region demanded a role, the city being part of the region. Further, through the intermediary of various administrations, the Soviet Republic of Russia disputed and sought advantage from an operation that was clearly lucrative. Inevitably, the largest doll in the *matrioshka*, the Soviet state, did its best to remain master of the game. In this instance, the municipality by and large won the battle and has managed the privatization process. Literature and reports on the subject make it clear that those who carried through the operation have helped themselves in no small measure. Moreover, the right to own land has still not been fully formalized and the question of protecting property rights remains open. Lawsuits are shunted from one court or administration to another with no assurance given that a satisfactory settlement can be reached. The law often implies the law of the stronger, i.e. the administration against the private citizen, the more powerful administration against the weaker one, corruption over honesty. Put differently, Russia is a favoured ground for trading in rights of ownership that are subject to no guarantee.

The claims to sovereignty on the part of the ex-soviet republics and of the republics and regions within Russia (itself a federation) were initially strongly motivated by the nationalization or regionalization of wealth and revenue drawn from local sources. In a fast-changing landscape where the new criterion is to have ownership so as to be in a position of control, those administering the republics sought as a priority to take over assets that had been Soviet. Everything became subject to wheeler-dealing – gold, diamonds, raw materials, plant, weaponry and military infrastructure. And the battle goes on between Russia and independent republics like the Ukraine as well as inside Russia where resource-rich regions press their claims directly without reference to the Moscow bureaucracy. The new political entities institute their own legislation at republican, regional and municipal levels, often in contradiction of federal legislation which is itself confused and contradictory.

Instances of abuse in the privatization process abound. Everyday the press in Russia cite cases of misappropriation, undervaluing of assets to be privatized, and embezzlement involving the export of currency. It is not our task here to describe in detail the various forms of economic fraud that have developed in Russia over recent years. The range and diversity that prevail are considerable – drug and counterfeit currency mafias, theft in production and fraudulent appropriation, cases that sometimes involve murder – as occurs frequently in societies in which the government and judiciary are powerless to apply and enforce the law throughout the territory.

The misappropriation of public funds is what concerns us here, being at once the source and the consequence of the disintegration of government. In most cases of economic crime, administrative officials are implicated. In a country that is still administered by the 'new former *nomenklaturas*', even those engaged in legitimate business have no choice but to bribe officials. In the words of a Moscow journalist, 'the criminal milieu corrupts the officials in local government, those who represent the legal structures in the economy and even the high-ranking military'. He instances the trial of the then head of the air-force unit in the Far-East, Major-General V. Rodionov, who 'had made available transport planes from his division for the delivery of cars purchased in Japan to military airfields in the neighbourhood of

Moscow, St Petersburg, Kiev, Minsk and Kishinev. The general was arrested for accepting a baksheesh of 100,000 roubles' (Loïma, 1993: 26). In another example, in the Khabarovsk region of the Far-East, those implicated were the public office for foreign trade, the former assistant regional attorney, the chief tax inspector and some high-ranking military. The opening-up of frontiers had undeniably provided more occasions for personal enrichment and the degree of embezzlement is sometimes staggering. Official figures in Russia put the amount of oil revenue lost to corruption at nearly one third.

Corruption has found its way to the heart of administration where officials have no scruples about combining private deals with their proper functions; in addition, many with previous administrative responsibility exploit their connections for personal gain. Arkady Vaksberg writes that, since Gorbachev's time, 'changes have co-incided with the mafia's need to realise accumulated wealth and make it bear fruit – an impossibility under the soviet economy with the rouble continuing to fall in value and soviet gold, which is of poor quality, having no stable parity'.[2] Vaksberg does not say in so many words that the 'bureaucratic mafia' furthered economic change so as to grow richer, but he leaves the question open. Certainly a number of Soviet officials took advantage of the dismembering of the state to benefit themselves and were well placed for a share-out of the spoils. Why indeed should they favour the setting-up of a legal authority and see a limitation put on their activities? Yet they are no more likely to favour anarchy and unbridled capitalism since for them power is inseparable from the central control that the administration continues to wield.

Monopolistic attitudes are perpetuated. Economic rent is guaranteed by exclusive access to resources and by delivery of administrative authorizations. Here, hiccoughs in production and the hazards of distribution favour arbitrary decisions. Shortages are no longer organized but they persist in remote regions, in Siberia, for example. Products are as a rule available, their prices are often prohibitive for the average Russian.

The crisis in authority

In respect of administration, the great difference between the Soviet Union and post-communist Russia is the disappearance of the Master. Central government no longer has authority or the means to retaliate against officials of the state. It no longer holds them as before within the vast structure of a clan where diverse transactions, both legal and illegal, were carried out with the approval or forbearance of the heads of the clan. What is now absent is an 'ethical code' governing the administrative *nomenklatura*. The Soviet 'code' enabled a hierarchy of corruption to be maintained. A junior ministry official might receive a few thousand roubles a year in backhanders, but no more. His chief went for higher stakes yet without emulating the big bosses in the capitals of the republics and in Moscow. To transgress the rules and flaunt ambitions above one's station was to invite retortion. The use of the term 'mafia' was perhaps more justified then than now precisely because corruption among those who served the state was somehow regulated.

In the Russia of the 1990s, less importance is accorded to state service. The priority for those with responsibility is to first see to their own interests, whether in a locality or a region, in a firm or a corporation, and the notion of the common good, of membership of a nation-state entity, has disappeared in the course of the day-to-day struggle and the temptation of 'each for himself'.

The disintegration of public service has the effect of reinforcing mistrust of the state and government:

> Previously no one thought it a crime that an abattoir employee stole meat, or a dairy employee cheese, butter or cream . . . People robbed or cheated the state circumspectly. Now criminal acts are on the increase. A sense that anything goes has taken root at the same time as faith in help and protection forthcoming from the state has been eroded; individuals have come to feel that they can only count on themselves. And, for many at the present time, the chance of earning an honest and decent livelihood looks impossible. Wages fail to keep up with inflation; so one has to cheat and live by one's wits and the odd speculation. In so doing, there are the traditional methods, such as theft, or newer ones born of a still centralised economy existing side-by-side with uncurbed market relations in a context where police powers and the power of the law have rapidly deteriorated.[3]

This description by a Russian journalist shows how slender is the chance of a just and democratic government emerging, where service can be expected to be honest and efficient.

As regards the task of reconstructing a system of government in Russia, the most worrying tendency among the population is to turn away from the state and the common good. Disinclination to vote or to pay taxes or to invest in the future are attitudes that have become increasingly common. Insofar as it is identified with the administrative function, government continues to be seen as arbitrary and predatory; this is more so even than in the past perhaps because it is no longer the major redistributor of national resources. The soviet state was a deviant and despotic version of the welfare state. It took everything and redistributed to everyone the needs of daily living. Soviet citizens were housed and fed by the state, indifferently it is true, but in conditions of security.

With the waning of the state in its role as redistributor, the notion of 'levelling' (*uranilovka*), so deep-rooted among Russians and institutionalized in the communist system, collapsed. Boris Yeltsin is not the new tsar, the upholder of the law; no longer is the state the great redistributor. The state no longer has a monopoly of violence nor does it guarantee, as it did before, the security — security in the form of confinement — of the population. The law of the strongest prevails. Only the bureaucracy and the industrial managers continue, despite everything, to supply a form of social protection. They maintain employment by artificial means and ensure the minimal maintenance of infrastructure. The other side of the coin is self-evident. They block economic reform and, by their mafia-like practices, pervert the notion of social legitimacy.

Towards political corruption?

'If the mafia exists, then freedom exists' runs the ironic headline in a Russian newspaper.[4] Certainly, if one draws a comparison with the Soviet era, you can now corrupt and become corrupted without a party card, communist or otherwise. On the other hand, *chin* or rank in the officialdom remains no less crucial for success in the great post-communist lottery in Russia. A business person, whether Russian or Western, can get nowhere in Russia or in any other ex-Soviet republic without knowing the wheels of the administrative apparatus and the networks that surround it. Even in disarray, Russia continues to produce administrative documents, rubber-stamped and signed, as in the good old days.

The really worrying development during recent years has been the growth of embezzlement among men in uniform. If there is growing collusion between officials, private actors and the police, then the state is in danger. The gains of a democratic transformation, in particular free elections, could be lost if the corruption of the state apparatus led to its inability to properly administer Russia.

Since the end of the USSR in 1991, the principle of freely elected government is questioned by no-one. Neither the communists nor the extreme-right of Vladimir Zhirinovsky contest this new inalienable right. Nine major polls were held in the USSR and in Russia between 1989 and 1996, the results showing that the ex-Soviets have become fully fledged voters.

The holding of free elections will continue in the years ahead and marks a fundamental change in Russian public life. Russian rulers, at the central and regional levels, have had to adjust. Economic and administrative actors know that their political protectors are subject to the right of sanction and the changeover of power. The virtues of election are known, the perverse effects too. Will votes in Russia be eventually bought? The campaign financing in the elections of 1993, 1995 and 1996 aroused considerable debate over the financing of political organizations.

The vote in Russia is free but this does not imply that Russia is now a democratic country. The institutions exist but do not function well. Parliament does not know what its role is; political formations are electoral 'blocks' or nomenklaturist networks, not – except for the Communist Party – real parties; the courts lack resources, respect and the power to enforce their decisions. It is not yet essential to hold an elective office in order to wield administrative power in one's locality. But the fact of holding elective office may become a necessity in order to avoid being bothered by those who have a popular mandate. The power of money and influence might, in some regions and localities, ensure the election of leading figures in networks, whether prestigious officials or business people.

The autonomization of the bureaucracy, the criminalization of economic life and the growing influence of networks have not been a matter of indifference to the government in Moscow. Since 1992 the fight against administrative corruption has been a recurring theme of both president and government. It is present in every speech Boris Yeltsin makes.

The incompetence of the administrative apparatus is fantastic. Our Russian bureaucrat is accustomed to command, to give instructions and is always ready to 'help out a friend', while not forgetful of his own interests. The one thing he is not accustomed to is working . . . A large number of our officials harbour an intense hatred of democracy, which presupposes responsibility. Yet more serious, many officials who are paid by the government work against it without even hiding the fact . . . I am very concerned by the increase in crime in Russia, which is directly linked to political instability and which is paralysing the law and legal institutions.[5]

On the occasion of his New Year message for 1994, Yeltsin placed the fight against crime and corruption at the head of his priorities. Without a loyal administration the president and his government are unable to govern Russia. This is clear to everyone and a cause of rejoicing to many. Loyalty to the president has been constantly called into question since he was elected by universal suffrage in June 1991, and by his closest collaborators. In 1992, when Boris Yeltsin began his crusade against corruption, he put his vice-president, General Rutskoi, in charge of this aspect, and from October 1992 Rutskoi presided over the special interministerial commission for the fight against corruption and organized crime. A few months later, Alexander Rutskoi came out as a rival to the president, making use of his new responsibilities to level charges of corruption against those close to Boris Yeltsin and, in particular, some of his ministers. The president's office responded with a counterattack on Rutskoi who was accused of receiving bribes in connection with major contracts.

The attack on corruption – instead of leading to a whiter wash – eventually smeared the whole Yeltsin team and showed up the major flaw in the state and government. The fight against corruption has done little to disguise the real battle, a political battle between Moscow clans who cannot accept the division of responsibilities and, in the familiar tradition of the *boyars*, wish to make the tsar submit to their desires or bring about his dismissal. On 4 October 1993, Yeltsin gave orders for the assault on Parliament to bring an end to the rebellion of vice-president Rutskoi and the speaker, Ruslan Khasbulatov. Several hundred died in the operation. Four months later, Boris Yeltsin's two rivals were amnestied by the new state Duma. Their political clans and their networks did not desert them.

In January 1994 the conclusions of an official report were published, a report ordered by President Yeltsin, entitled 'Organised crime and the prospect of the national-socialists coming to power in Russia'. There it is alleged that 70 to 80 per cent of private firms and banks are subject to racketeering; further, corruption in the police and in local government is denounced; finally, allusion is made to the 'national-socialist' danger if the senior servants of the state fall prey to the mafias.[6] The remedies proposed are classical ones – increasing the repressiveness of the penal code, centralizing decision-making, reorganizing the tax system. But one would still need to be able to count on the integrity of the tax office, legal institutions and those responsible for the maintenance of law and order. Who today in Russia can impose rules on civil servants who no longer serve the state first? Where would the new *revizor* come from but the former *nomenklatura* which administered the USSR? Though often corrupt and ineffective, those officials and managers are what held the country together.

Notes

1. Pipes (1974: 281).
2. *Ibid.*: 253.
3. Loïma, 1993: 26.
4. *Nezavisimaia gazeta*, 2 February 1994.
5. Boris Yeltsin, *Rossiyskie*, 21 April 1993.
6. *Izvestiya*, 26 January 1994.

9

GIFTS, NETWORKS AND CLIENTELES: CORRUPTION IN JAPAN AS A REDISTRIBUTIVE SYSTEM

Jean-Marie Bouissou

The Japanese political system's reputation for corruption is well and truly established. During the long reign of the Liberal-Democratic Party (LDP), from 1955 to 1993, nine out of the fifteen prime ministers were implicated or impugned in scandals at some point or other in their careers. Over a recent five-year period, eight members of parliament received sentences, but a good half of the chamber, belonging to every party except the Communist Party, is reliably felt to have offered or taken bribes. At every election thousands of activists are arrested for corrupting voters – 24,080 between 1987 and 1991 in local elections alone. Over the same period 57 mayors had to face charges.[1] Similarly, 1,660 government officials were prosecuted between 1982 and 1991. Even the police are open to charges of corruption. After the fall of the LDP in July 1993, a further scandal removed Morihiro Hosokawa, the 'new man' set to reform political standards, after only eight months in office.

Nevertheless, this state of affairs hardly seems to affect voters. For 38 years they continued to return the LDP, which only lost power in July 1993 because of internal divisions. Politicians who are the most compromised are often triumphantly reelected.[2] Investigations since the fall of the LDP which focused on corruption in public works contracts and concluded with charges preferred against three governors and a former minister, cannot be compared with the 'clean hands' operation in Italy: the conservative political class remain firmly in control of the ongoing reconstruction, whose prime movers, Tsutomu Hata (Hosokawa's successor) and more especially his mentor, Ichiro Ozawa, have a solid reputation as apparatchiks familiar with all the techniques of extorting political funds (*kanezukuri*). Such tolerance frequently invites the conclusion that there is in Japan a special predisposition to accept corruption, born of quite different ethical standards than those prevailing in Western forms of democracy.

The most expensive political system on earth?

Estimating the amount of money going into the political system is not easy. In 1987 when the debate on political conduct started, a group of young LDP *dietmembers* known as the Society for Utopia made their annual budget public, setting it at an average of Y126.5m (a little under £1m). In 1992 one of their colleagues provided me with details of his own budget, which was in the region of Y150m, comprising an annual investment of Y2,700 (£20) for each of the 50,000 votes cast for him.[3]

But these are merely the expenses in any normal year. Every election calls for an exceptional outlay. For the 1990 parliamentary elections, public opinion, in a nicely elliptical formula, maintained that 'with five [hundred million] you win, with four you lose!' (*goto yonraku*). Knowing that a *dietmember* faces his electorate roughly every three years implies that he has to put together Y315m (well over two million pounds) on average year in year out. Counting both LDP incumbents and candidates striving to recover a seat lost or to conquer one at the next election, 400 'parliamentary machines' function permanently for a total cost of close to Y130bn (£1bn).

To this must be added 150 'senatorial machines' costing Y100m a year, 2,000 regional councillors (about Y30 million), roughly 2,300 mayors (Y50 million) and some 56,000 municipal councillors, few of whom would spend less than Y5 million.[4] Besides, the LDP itself collects money to meet its running costs: a declared figure of more than Y50 billion, combining regional federations and the central party apparatus. All in all, during the last years of LDP supremacy, the conservative political personnel needed between Y700bn and Y750bn, getting on for £5.5bn each year.

Before 1993 the Opposition comprised about 400 'parliamentary machines', 130 'senatorial machines', 700 regional councillors, 600 mayors and 10,000 municipal councillors belonging to four principal parties (socialists, *Komeito* buddhists, communists and social-democrats). On the basis of interviews conducted in 1992, their activities were roughly four times less costly, given that candidates representing the same party very rarely compete with one another, unlike conservative candidates (see below). A minimal estimate here would be Y160bn (£1.2bn), Y100bn of it being raised directly by parties at regional and national level.

Altogether, Japanese political personnel represent an annual expenditure of over Y900bn a year on average (roughly £6.5bn) – half the cost of the Channel Tunnel! Members' salaries (Y1.065m gross in 1986) barely allow them more than a comfortable living wage. Virtually their entire expenditure on political activity comes from fund-raising from firms, associations and individuals. In the knowledge that sums declared by donors as required by law amounted to Y356.9bn in 1991, one may conclude that two-thirds of the money going into the political system is laundered, *urakane* ('money from behind').

And this is a minimal estimate. In the opinion of writers whose partialities vie with the abstruseness of their sources, the average cost of an LDP parliamentary machine varies from the simple to the quadruple, from Y100m only (Hrebenar, 1986: 63) to Y400m (Van Wolferen, 1989: 137). Some consider that dissimulation reaches five times the figures declared (Sasago, 1989: 39), which would take the functioning costs of the system to Y1,800bn (£13bn). If one calculates that any public works contract involves a commission of around 3 per cent – an open secret, in fact – and in the knowledge that in 1990 they represented Y19.8bn, the building and public works sector on its own provided politicians with Y600bn in that year; hence my estimate of Y900 billion would seem to constitute an absolute minimum.

Is Japan atypical?

Whenever Japan is mentioned there is a reflex recourse to culturalist explanations, and for the problem of corruption three explanations are ready and waiting. In general, morality has no absolute value in Japan; good and evil are seen as relative. In particular, the notion of the common good is hazy, given that democracy is a fairly recent import. Lastly, citizens are passive in the face of Authority, by virtue of the celebrated 'Confucian heritage' or else of a congenital tendency towards antheap conformism. The defect of this thought process is its circularity. 'The Japanese go about in groups because they are thus inclined, and this we know because they go about in groups' . . . In the case of Japan, it is duplicated by considerable ignorance and a naive assumption of specificity. Who knows that the country unaided made the transition in the space of 35 years (1889–1924), from an absolute monarchy to a semi-parliamentary system with universal suffrage, and that democracy's performance there has been in no way unequal to its performance in many European countries? Who knows that American congressmen compromised in scandals are reelected in comparable proportions to their opposite numbers in Japan (Reed, 1987: 39)? And who can seriously maintain that the elasticity of morality and of the general good is a problem confined to Japan? It would be as well then to steer clear of culturalist explanations.

Besides we don't need them, since Japan brings together all the historical and structural factors invoked in the course of the present work to account for the development of corruption in European democracies. There is a striking parallel with Germany. In both cases, administrative modernization preceded political modernization which took the form of 'conferred democracy', one vulnerable to crisis. Hence Japanese citizens came to identify democracy with the material benefits provided by government rather than with the procedures and institutions that were supposed to infuse its values. As in Spain, one notes the exceptional length of time during which one political formation has held a monopoly of power, and the major parties have no mass base whereby to finance electoral costs. If, in regard to UK it is true (?) that corruption has tended to be uncommon because of the independence of administration, Japan provides proof to the contrary: corruption and copenetration between the conservative political elite and the bureaucracy have gone together since the start of the century. And if corrupt practice has been on the increase in France with decentralization and the reinforcement of local government, it is noticeable in fact that local government in Japan accounts for two-thirds of public expenditure and is virtually unassailable from an electoral point of view.

Thus, in common with European democracies Japan shows features which generate corruption, quite independently of any cultural particularity. But some it contains that are peculiar to itself, first and foremost the highly distinctive voting system in force between 1947 and 1994, long denounced as an essential cause of the 'structural corruption' of the political system and consequently abolished by the anti-LDP coalition under the Hosokawa government.

The *Koenkai* and social redistribution with the proceeds of corruption

In Lower House elections, each constituency elected between two and six *dietmembers* but parties present no list. Each candidate campaigned on his own account and seats were attributed after one round according to the first past the post principle. There is no transfer of votes between candidates representing the same party. The same principle applies in municipal and regional council elections and, to a limited extent, in senatorial elections.

The system gave rise to fierce infighting among conservative candidates. In most of the 130 constituencies there were more candidates than seats to be won for the LDP. Those who were not nominated stood as 'independents'. During the 1980s there were one hundred or so at each election who failed to make the grade, 10 to 20 per cent of them outgoing LDPs, almost invariably beaten by other conservatives. Use of the media for payment is forbidden and the media are legally bound to remain neutral. Victory traditionally hangs on the 'three *ban*' – notoriety acquired (*kanban*), organized clientele (*jiban*) and money to maintain it (*kaban*).

Clienteles are organized in *koenkai* (supporters' clubs). Most of the 75,000 or so elected representatives in Japan, major or minor, have a supporters' club. In the case of an ordinary conservative deputy this would number between 10,000 and 30,000 members, though there have been monster clubs with a membership of 100,000, viz. the supporters' club for the former prime minister Kakuei Tanaka in the region of Niigata. A *koenkai* comprises clubs representing city districts or small rural communities, 20 to 30 individuals led by a local worthy, to cover the area; clubs for women, young and elderly people centred on cultural or recreational pursuits; groups of small business people and shopkeepers; circles of all types; former schoolmates, local fellowships for young executives, *karaoke* or climbing fans, and so on and so on. A strong *koenkai* may well include several hundred of these small groups with widely differing interests. For the conservatives alone, membership of such groups involved some 10 or 12 million Japanese. On the basis of two watertight votes per *koenkai* member, they supply the LDP with a solid turnout on which the party has built its majority for 38 years.

These diverse networks are constantly threatened with being high-jacked by a rival candidate. Guaranteeing their loyalty requires a *diet-member* to keep a team of 10 to 15 full-time secretaries in the field, each responsible for a sector in the constituency which they 'work on' day in day out. They attend every meeting and the range of services they propose is unending. Team spirit is also fostered across countless get-togethers of a convivial and symbolic nature, picnics if you like, where they strike up the *koenkai* hymn. Above all, such events are the occasion for a drink.

Money is in constant circulation. Any group reunion, however small, takes place at a restaurant where those participating pay only a token contribution. The rest is paid for by the elected representative, as are mass excursions,[5] lady members' activities, croquet competitions for the elderly, trips abroad for the network officials and to Tokyo to enable country voters to 'visit parliament'. For every socially recognized occasion money is directly forthcoming. In the case of a marriage, a deputy may go up to Y50,000 (£350) there may be half that amount for a funeral; the annual bill may well go beyond Y10m. Equally costly in an election year are 'travel expenses' (*o-kuruma dai*), distributed by the secretaries quite openly at meetings although the law forbids this.

A *koenkai* is the means of carrying out various functions ranging from mutual aid to collusion between small business people. The access to benefits it procures is controlled by the impossibility of belonging to two rival networks in the closed world of the city district or small village. But for most of its members it is foremost a machine for distributing money and freebies. They are so unreluctant to avoid being on the receiving end that in 1989 the practice of asking a politician for money was made punishable by a fine of Y100,000.

The money needed is in theory collected under parliamentary legislation which governs the control of political financing by *seiji dantai* (political associations) set up by every politician. Individuals, associations, firms and trade unions may provide subscriptions or donations which they are obliged to declare. The *seiji dantai* in turn hand over their annual accounts to the Ministry of the Interior or (in the case of local elected officials) to the regional administration who make them public.

Legislation, dating from 1946, was seen as a 'bamboo bucket' – i.e. hole-ridden – through which illegal money poured. In theory, the law became more stringent in 1976 in the wake of the Lockheed scandal. A ceiling was set on donations – Y20m a year for individuals, Y150m for firms or unions (Y100m for parties and Y50m for individual politicians), depending on their turnover and the number of adherents. *Seiji dantai* became obliged to identify donors and no one could give more than Y1.5m to an individual politician. At the same time, any attempt to limit the number of *seiji dantai* a politician might be entitled to was studiously avoided and donations under Y1m remained anonymous. As a result there was nothing to prevent an elected representative receiving Y10m or Y20m divided between as many *seiji dantai*; some politicians had more than 300.

It was further possible to transit money via sub-contractors or a series of screen associations financing one another, or resort to the universal method of 'advertisements' in confidential publications,[6] or participate in 'fund-raising receptions' (*hagemasu kai*), borrowing American fund-raising methods with individual entries costing up to Y50,000; the best-known of these brought in Y2bn to the future prime minister Noboru Takeshita in 1988. Takings have not to be declared if they are dealt with by an *ad hoc* committee and firms can account for expenditure under overheads. Many firms transfer employees to act as secretaries to political friends. But the simplest solution is to declare nothing, a solution apparently adopted for certainly two-thirds of the money paid out and given encouragement because of its discretion and simplicity and the small risk involved.

Presents or backhanders? Legislation falls foul of social practices

In her celebrated work *The Chrysanthemum and the Sword* (1946), the anthropologist Ruth Benedict proposed the *giri* as the essential principle governing social behaviour in Japan. However, she is wrong in considering it to be a moral norm deriving from the samurai 'code of honour'. Its roots are more mundane. In concrete terms, the *giri* is the obligation to ensure an exact balance between services received and services rendered within the context of a 'closed area of obligatory social interaction' of which the prototype was the small rural community, so that no household should profit unduly from the collective labour required by rice-growing or from the collective responsibility imposed by the lord. Any breach in the engagement was punishable by exclusion from the system of solidarity. The *giri*, even if it was exalted as the highest moral imperative, the highest point of honour in political terms, especially in the Meiji era, appears to be first and foremost a market-type mechanism of social control and, as such, staunchly functional. Today the *giri* continues to operate in many 'pseudo-villages' such as small urban districts or the networks formed by a group of business people and the bureaucrats they depend on for authorizations, control and contracts. Likewise, a *koenkai* is a 'pseudo-village' whose members repay services rendered when the election falls due.[7] They act in accordance with a going social norm. In this sense, to them their reciprocating vote seems no more to stem from 'corruption' than does the way in which their *dietmember* raises funds to ensure his part of the bargain.

The *giri* moulds Japan as a 'civilization of gifts', for which there exist more than 35 different words. It serves to procure a benefit that is out of one's reach (the 'good trip present' and receive 'a souvenir' in return), to win indulgence (the 'excuses present' from the small construction firm boss to those who live on the street he breaks up), or simply as a mark of one's will to maintain relations (the little everyday gifts of a housewife to her neighbours). Refusing it constitutes an insult which disrupts the social bond. Every request is accompanied by a present in anticipation of a favour: key money to the proprietor when a lease is signed, *ohizatsuki* to the teacher who takes you as pupil, and 'present by way of introduction' (*meishigawari*) for anyone you approach on this or that matter. It is this generalized practice that provides the justification in law for the extremely generous overheads that firms are authorized to deduct – Y4,500bn in 1989 (£32bn), much of which certainly finds its way to politicians.

The frontier between *meishigawari* and corruption is indeed ill-defined. Corruption is only characterized when 'an official . . . receives, requests or negotiates a reward related to his functions' (Penal Code, Article 197) or 'exploits his functions in order for a reward to be paid to a third party' (Article 197–2). On this basis, judicial practice tends to consider that corruption only exists if the person to whom the gift is addressed is the one who takes the final decision. Further, the *meishigawari* has to have been solicited, be disproportionate in regard to the norm, and be accompanied by a particular request (Befu, 1971: 27–9), conditions which are hardly easy to establish. Accordingly, a cash-prompted intervention in the decision-making process on the part of an elected official is virtually impossible to punish. The defence invariably maintains that the sums in question are a political gift, declaration of which was overlooked by some secretary or other, and that their purpose was in no way to procure a precise decision which in any event the official concerned was not empowered to take, unless he was the minister responsible.

Two famous cases have established legal precedent. In 1976 Kakuei Tanaka was charged with having received Y500m from Lockheed Aircraft in connection with a tender put out by Japan Airlines during his premiership (1972–4). He submitted that the decision rested with the then Minister of Transport, a *dietmember* belonging to his faction, hence that the charge of corruption was not substantiated. He

was convicted and his conviction upheld on appeal (1985), but the
Supreme Court balked at finalizing a judgment that would have
gravely embarrassed his successors by deferring its verdict until his
death, which occurred in 1993. The second case concerns two members of parliament accused of sharing Y2m in order to intervene in
committee with a view to expediting payment of a subsidy promised
to the silk industry, a common enough practice which came to light
only by chance in 1985. Arguing that they had merely received a
'political contribution' while looking after the interests of those from
whom they had a mandate in a case in which they had no power of
decision, they received a conviction in 1988 but were acquitted in
1992.

Doubtless criminal practices may be indicted for crimes other than
corruption. But the sanctions for violating the law on control of
political financing (undeclared donations) are derisory. At the end of
1992, for example, Shin Kanemaru, vice-president and chief 'godfather'
of the LDP, was fined Y200,000 for 'forgetting' to declare Y500m.
Electoral law imposes strict limits on campaign-spending on pain of
invalidation; the Y15.6m authorized on average per constituency for
Lower House electioneering (Kishimoto, 1988: 135) represents only 3
per cent of the sum usually spent by an ordinary conservative candidate!
But the expenses authorized fail to allow a candidate, however virtuous,
to finance even a minimal campaign. It would seem that since all candidates are constrained to break the law, their only recourse is to con-
nive in common at the practice. The records reveal one case of
invalidation since the Second World War (1982).

But even if there were appropriate legal instruments available, the
will to prosecute would still need to be there or need to be roused by
public opinion, the media or the Opposition.

Law and opposition subjugated

In Japan prosecutors (charged with investigation into a crime) can
effectively let the accused get away at will. In the case of Shin
Kanemaru, who was linked with the huge Sagawa scandal which
threatened to reveal collusion of a highly embarrassing nature
between the LDP and gangland, they stifled the political dimension
of the investigation by letting him plead guilty to a minor charge in
accordance with Article 291–2 of the Code of Criminal Procedure, so
that he could be given a derisory 'sentence' with no further action
taken. Moreover, a prosecutor may abandon any legal proceedings on

the grounds of the 'context surrounding the offender' or 'circumstances subsequent to the offence' (Article 248), even if it implies being covered by an order from the Minister of Justice.[8] Judges can be removed, since their tenure is renewed every ten years by the government. Their careers are at the discretion of the Supreme Court secretariat, whose members are appointed by the executive and which has loyally served the LDP by relegating the independently-minded to minor posts in distant provinces (Ramseyer and McCall-Rosenbluth, 1993: 160–80). Thus the rare cases genuinely proceeded with during the LDP reign took place for reasons of internal party rivalry – in particular the Lockheed affair which enabled the traditional conservative elite to clip the wings of the overtly populist and overambitious Tanaka.

The Opposition was not well placed to denounce the scandals since it regularly exacted a price for its discretion and compliant behaviour, by threatening to block the debate on the budget or to delay measures counted on by this or that pressure group. The transfer of large sums of money to Opposition politicians, particularly under cover of mahjong matches 'arranged' between members of parliament on both sides, is a characteristic of Japanese politics. Certainly each party had its own regular sources of finance: the unions – in particular the public employees' federations – for the Socialist Party; the Sokagakkai sect for the *Komeito* Buddhist party; the motor industry and private sector unions for the small Social-Democrat Party. But even if their electors are more ideologically motivated than in the case of the conservatives, those they elect find themselves to much the same degree implicated in the costly social game of offering presents. Thus, whenever it proved impossible for a scandal to be entirely hushed up, it was not infrequent for a member on both sides to be sacrificed after some discreet bargaining – witness the Recruit affair (1988–9).

Furthermore, the Opposition had a vital interest in maintaining the electoral system in use before 1994. In a five-seat constituency, the fifth seat in practice can be taken with 11 to 13 per cent of the votes (taking into account the votes for beaten candidates and their unequal distribution). This particularity on its own enabled *dietmembers* representing small groups to get elected, which explains why the Communist Party, while being in fact the only one with clean hands, stoutly defended the voting system. But even socialist or Komeito members of parliament, backed as they are by the strong organization of their unions or the Sokagakkai, knew they stood barely a chance in single-member constituencies when confronted by the LDP machine. Hence, the immediate interest of Opposition members was to see the system maintained in spite of its having all the appearance of being a structural cause of corruption.

And the press, for its part, primarily concerned with circulation, has always shown itself capable of following up affairs with determination but only so long as it can carry public opinion. It does not systematically perform the function of denunciation, applying absolute standards. Rather its reaction is to voice a nation's indignation and only when that indignation is there to be voiced. But indignation does arise spasmodically related to contexts of disturbing social or international change, which tend to divide the LDP into factions that exploit 'affairs' against each other. So, in the early 1960s, on top of the disruption caused by ten years of phenomenal growth, the severe social reverberations of the first oil shock and the disquiet caused by the Communist victory in Vietnam helped to stir the Lockheed scandal which led to the fall of Tanaka, and the same occurred at the start of the 1990s.

Modernization as an aggravating factor

In the 1990s political life has become increasingly costly for reasons that are structural. The modernization of society has made the electorate more mobile and changeable, less a prisoner of the traditional mechanisms of exchange. Hence the *koenkai* are obliged to raise their stakes. In addition, the increase in the number of quasi-hereditary seats (a good third of conservative Lower House members are now from the second or third generation) puts the price of entry up for newcomers; as a result, the mean cost of electioneering has quadrupled over 15 years. The career of those elected within each of the power-sharing factions that make up the LDP is more and more conditioned by money because the party leaders, who are perpetually in need of funds, bestow ministerial portfolios in accordance with the money candidates can put forward. In 1989 the office of junior minister for the development of Hokkaido cost the deputy Fumio Abe Y80m, to recoup which led him to pressurize the island's firm, thus putting him at the forefront of the Kyowa scandal.

New opportunities exist for raising finance. After 1985 the 'bubble economy' (*bubble keizai*) provided increased opportunity for speculating in property or on the stock market in a country where the law ignores insider dealing and where the major shareholding institutions cover the losses of their more favoured clients. But in venturing beyond the orthodox mechanisms of trading favours, elected officials have become vulnerable to new counts of indictment. Lower House member

Toshiyuki Imamura won Y2.8bn on the stock market between 1986 and 1988 but spent three years in prison for failing to declare it. Again it was a charge of fiscal fraud that finally brought down Shin Kanemaru, arrested in March 1993 for concealing Y7.8bn in bonds and gold ingots.

More profoundly, breakneck economic modernization creates conditions for higher levies. It provides increasing opportunities for bold entrepreneurial incursion into new fields of profit, given the ability to cope with the maze of administrative authorizations that proliferate.[9] Added to this, established interests hold a monopoly of political influence, which newcomers must 'acquire' in the literal sense of the term. The two major scandals which precipitated the fall of the LDP – Recruit in 1988 and Sagawa Kyubin in 1992 – contained all these ingredients: new firms seeking to short-circuit the bureaucracy and profits in speculation systematically used to grease the palms of hundreds of politicians so as to set up networks, even when there were no precise demands. Conversely, modernization has also prompted outdated sectors to pay out to defend the regulatory system that protects them. The small local banks lobby, for instance, which has been stubbornly resisting attempts by the Ministry of Finance to facilitate their amalgamation with the major banks, rose to become the fifth most important contributor to LDP funds towards the mid-1980s (Hrebenar, 1986: 67).

Rapid modernization of an economy subjected to high-handedness on the part of bureaucracy and generating considerable demand for political mediation furthered by an underdeveloped judiciary would appear then to be an aggravating factor in structural corruption linked to the electoral system. A vicious circle has established itself. The ease and growing confusion surrounding fund-raising have fed the inflation of political expenses, leading elected representatives into increasingly hazardous methods of speculation and extortion, beyond the limits of what is tolerable for much of industry, indeed for many politicians, young ones especially; and the outcome was in part the split in the LDP in July 1993.

In addition, the appearance of ostentatious speculative wealth, the development of new social demands, such as consumer defence and the reduction in working hours, added to the media publicity surrounding the newly-acquired wealth of some politicians, lessened the effectiveness of the *koenkai* redistributive system. The terms of exchange, drawn up in a Japan that was relatively egalitarian and poor, seemed to worsen to the disadvantage of the electorate. What price a free trip offered by your local *dietmember* now when the *nouveaux riches* are savouring *sushi* wrapped in gold leaf? Public opinion has become less tolerant. Meanwhile, the ideal standards of Western democracy 'introduced' into a society that was becoming rapidly more open to the world were compounding the problem, providing the press in its onslaught on sleaze with a theme that was modern and 'international', and all the more devastating because of it. Bit by bit, the theme of 'political reform' (*seiji kaikaku*) came to crystallize the fears, frustrations and hopes of a changing society and so to dominate political debate.

The fall of the LDP and 'political reform': a façade of rehabilitation

Scenting danger, the LDP sacrificed a few scapegoats *dietmember* Imamura, for instance) and produced a number of symbolic measures, such as the obligation on the part of ministers to disclose the extent of their fortunes, extended in December 1992 to cover all members of parliament, but with a number of loopholes and no punishment for false declarations. This might perhaps have been enough had not the theme of anti-corruption been taken up within the conservative camp itself. In the provinces a number of local contenders for parliamentary seats who were unable to afford the 'entry price' found a spokesman in Morihiro Hosokawa, governor of Kumamoto, who became the champion of 'political reform' and brought them into his New Party of Japan in May 1992.

In the LDP itself a number of young *dietmembers*, overburdened with expenses, protested more and more openly. Two of their older colleagues, Ichiro Ozawa and Tsutomu Hata, who became victims of the factional infighting at the end of 1992, exploited these grievances to try their luck in forcing a split, and hence a change in the political landscape. Their defection along with 34 colleagues, who together founded the Party of Renewal, was enough to bring down the Miyazawa government in June 1993. The operation was presented as a crusade against corruption. The electorate, without overmuch enthusiasm − there was record abstentionism at 37.7 per cent − followed the new parties, who in alliance with the traditional opposition managed by a narrow margin to oust the LDP in the election of July 1993.

The new coalition in power, controlled in effect by former LDP elders, could do no less in the face of public opinion than change the electoral system, in spite of the reticence of many ex-Opposition *dietmembers* who owed their seats to it (a first draft bill was in fact thrown out of the

Senate as a result of the socialist vote). Traditional constituencies were replaced by 300 single-member constituencies with 200 further seats allotted by proportional representation. Legislation on political financing was amended, each candidate being limited to one *seiji dantai* and anonymity abolished in the case of donations over Y50,000. But radical solutions such as forbidding contributions from business and industry or centralizing fund-raising by political parties at a national level were rejected. A public system of financing was instituted with grandiose hopes, then downsized to insignificance – Y30bn – in regard to manifest expenditure. The 'political reformers' clearly showed little determination to eradicate the need and the opportunities for trading favours.

A judicial precedent in regard to political corruption could have come about after the arrest of a former minister, Kishiro Nakamura, in March 1994 for using his position as an eminent politician to stop investigation into shady public works contracts. But the charge brought against him – the outcome of which remains in doubt – was negotiated between the coalition and the LDP to put a stop to investigations into the public works sector before they went too far. It belongs to that category of purely symbolic response to public displeasure practised time and time again by the conservative elites which, though divided, remain firmly in control. So long as the forces that could crystallize discontent are lacking, Japan seems unlikely to have any Italian-type purge – especially since the LDP came back to power in July 1994.

Summary

The political system dominated by the LDP cannot escape impugnment as 'structurally corrupt' in respect of the ethical standards of democracy. Yet has this corruption been prejudicial to Japan? One cannot play down the fact that Japan under the liberal-democrats has become an economic superpower. Whatever the statistical imponderables, the distribution of wealth produced has certainly not been less equitable than in the case of France or that of the USA, where perhaps 15 per cent of the population live below the official poverty level. Starting from nothing, a general, if not greatly generous, social security system has been set up, something that the USA has not achieved. Surveys by international bodies on living standards now rank Japan in the leading group and refute the old chestnut of a 'benumbed and dump-housed workforce'.

Nevertheless, the impact and instrumentality of corruption on political and administrative decision-making, if not quantifiable, are readily identifiable. In general, consumers have had to pick up the bill by being forced to finance productive investment at too high a price because of the collusion between industry, government and administration. Yet it is a fact that the excessive profits made have been reinvested with great effectiveness in the productive apparatus and thus have led to growing wealth from which the entire community has finally benefited. Criticism at this point springs from the notion that the average Japanese might have benefited *more*. But this *more* is only subject to definition in terms of Western norms of social welfare, consumption and leisure, now called into question in the light of current economic circumstances. Hence it is far from clear that such criticism is justified.

Corruption has further resulted in a plethora of public works programming, invariably overcostly and often overdone, in favour of rural constituencies, the LDP bedrock, whereas the large urban constituencies, not having powerful political patrons, remained underprovided. Even so, benefits from this unwarranted inflation, redistributed locally via more than 500,000 small firms subcontracting for public works programmes, have provided rural areas with extra incomes, so stabilizing population. One way to regard them is as an indirect form of social welfare which elsewhere would have been financed through direct subsidies.

The temporary fall of the LDP, which was to a large extent attributable to public dissatisfaction, testifies to the limits and dysfunctioning of the system that spanned the 1980s. But the Japanese example provides clear evidence that the violation of ethical codes put forward by Western democracy, even when it is allowed to permeate the entire political system, is not incompatible with economic and social competence.

Notes

1. Figures taken from the annually published Police White Paper (Tokyo, 1992). Activists convicted during elections are regularly rehabilitated by mass amnesties (11 since the war, the latest on the occasion of the marriage of the crown prince, July 1993).
2. Kakuei Tanaka, who was the leading figure in the Lockheed scandal and imprisoned in August 1976, was reelected in December with 114,000 votes more than the second elected

candidate in Niigata-3 constituency. Noboru Takeshita, principal figure in the Sagawa scandal, increased his share of the vote in the July 1993 elections from 21.5 per cent to 21.7 per cent.

3. This passage owes a great deal to the friendship of Koga Issei, deputy for Fukuoka-3 as well as to the trust placed in me by the 40 deputies and local councillors representing all parties whom I interviewed for the purposes of my research in 1992. The exchange rate used is 100 yen=5.5 francs; but with figures that are largely clandestine, great precision is not needed.

4. These figures are averaged out. There is clearly no comparison at all between a rural mayor's budget and that of the mayor of Osaka. But since there are only 3,253 town councils for 125 million Japanese, the smallest ones number several thousand inhabitants, thus requiring rather large political investments. These estimates allow for exceptional expenditure in election years.

5. A Yamaguchi conservative deputy told me about picnics for 6,000 'to admire the cherry blossom'. An ordinary town councillor for Fukuoka provides tours of the bay for two or three thousand supporters 'to admire the summer moon' (interviews, 1992).

6. It was entirely due to these undeclared 'receipts from advertising' that the LDP managed to repay within two years the 15 billion yen borrowed for the 1990 parliamentary elections (*Asahi*, 26 February 1993).

7. The question occurs as to what certainty a politician has of being repaid in the secrecy of the polling booth, if the *giri* is not a moral imperative. In fact, repayment is effected in a way that is virtually verifiable, in country districts at least, simply by making one's activity known fairly obviously during the election campaign. Each member is concerned for the victory of his candidate because defeat would diminish his own small degree of prestige in the district, parent-teacher association, etc.

8. So it was in 1954 with Hayato Ikeda and Eisaku Sato, both compromised in a scandal involving shipyard subsidies. Both went on to become prime minister (1960–64 and 1964–72).

9. In 1992 bureaucracy created 737 new obligatory authorizations, making a total of 11,402 (*Yomiuri*, 15 December 1993).

10

THE ECONOMICS OF CORRUPTION

JEAN CARTIER-BRESSON

Following Heidenheimer (1970) it is now customary to group definitions of corruption into four categories. To the commonest definitions, focused on the duties of administration, the public interest and awareness of the incidence of corruption, are now added definitions that point to the existence of a market for corruption. The term – in my view a highly debatable one – has since the 1970s sprouted a thriving body of neoclassically-based literature whose aim is to explore the application of the concepts of micro-economics to the study of corruption, an approach which continues to dominate the subject. The object of the present contribution is to outline the range of economic concepts applied to the study of corruption in pluralist systems and demonstrate that these instruments of analysis, in their theoretical and methodological diversity, can enrich the understanding of corruption in its more recent manifestations, provided one avoids a too orthodox approach.

The economic science is doubtless a highly fragmented one. In effect, at the source of any economic comment on corruption are to be found the two most debated topics in the discipline, topics that have undergone considerable transformation in the way they are formulated over recent years. On the one hand, analysis of the nature and degree of rational calculation properly attributable to human behaviour, itself largely determining how standard models are used, is less and less generally admitted. On the other, the question of relations between the state and the market, which often boiled down to confrontation between those who stress the failures of government – neoliberals – versus those of heterodox opinion who point to the

failures of the market, is increasingly resulting in a reexamination of
the very concepts of the market and institutional bodies.

Given this analytical tool, one needs to make a distinction in terms
of conception of the market and rationality of behaviour between: (1)
Standard Neo-liberal Theory (Théorie Standard Neo-liberale (TSN) –
pure and perfect competition (PPC), substantial rationality and structural failure of state intervention); (2) *Broader Standard Theory* (imperfections in the market and limited rationality); and (3) *Non-standard
Theory* (market imperfection, organizational presence and procedural
rationality).

An intuitive and general definition of corruption would quickly
identify the existence of supply and demand in regard to corruption
susceptible to variations in price and adjustment by different
mechanisms. These terms clearly vary both in their meaning and in
their implications in line with the paradigms constructed by
economists. Whence four questions present themselves to the
economist. What are the organizational conditions that favour
corruption? What type of rationality is at work in corruption? How
is the price of the transaction determined and what are the mechanisms
of its variation? Finally, what is the economic and social cost of
corruption and how can it be fought at least expense?

Economic research into corruption is in the main traversed by the
two currents cited above. Théorie Standard Neo-libérale (*TSN*)
develops a theory of individual rational criminal behaviour acting on
a market for corruption that is more or less perfect, whereas Théorie
Standard Elargie (*TSE*) builds an analysis of the organization of illegal
transactions that is unrepresentative of the market. I propose to give
a critical account of each in turn on the basis of their definitions of
the market and the degree of rationality applied to individual behaviour before setting out principles for a meso-economic analysis.

Approaches to market corruption

I shall bring together here views based on standard assumptions
about *homo economicus*. Standard micro-economics in respect of corruption is rooted in agency models, property rights theory and rent-
seeking theory, as well as in the economics of crime.

A generic definition of corruption: divergency of interest and agency model

Banfield's seminal article (1975) identifies the variables determining the level of corruption and the means of eliminating it by recourse to a cost/benefit analysis based on an agency model. For Banfield:

> Corruption becomes possible when there exist three types of economic actor: an agent, a principal and a third party who stands to gain or lose by the action of the agent. An agent is corruptible insofar as he can *a priori* conceal his corruption from his principal. An agent becomes corrupt if he sacrifices his principal's to his own interest and thereby violates the law.

The author proposes three types of measure as tending to reduce corruption, which is assumed to be endemic given human opportunism: inducements to loyalty via an incomes policy; more stringent sanctions, so making the consequences of discovery more serious; and monitoring agents' activities by means of systematic auditing policies.

Banfield's contribution is on three levels. His reference to an agency model has enabled economists to bring their minds to bear on agency costs, i.e. the price of monitoring, incentive and sanctioning policies. According to his reasoning, betrayal of a contract which initiates corruption is specific in relation to fraud in its normally accepted sense (e.g. sale of rotting meat) because deceit necessitates an alliance of two agents against one (butcher, quality controller and consumer). A corrupt agent then sells rights that he owns *de facto*, not, however, legally (a quality-control label). Further, still relating to the notion of contract-betrayal, the agency models fall within the sphere of property rights. Hence the question of the relatively easy appropriation of property rights in line with the public or private nature of the body concerned can be raised.

Corruption as redefining and illegally appropriating a property right

The concept of property rights has extremely liberal implications. Property rights, i.e. the regulated use of goods and services and the very substance of exchange, are effective only if they are exclusive (one and the same individual bearing the positive and negative effects of their transfer) and transferable. Only freedom as regards their transfer admits of effective arbitration, which presupposes the existence of an effective market in this commodity. Therefore this theory is primarily concerned with the study of the process whereby these rights are lost, rights that may be watered down, hence be less efficacious, by legal constraints or by a prohibitive increase in their control as a result of asymmetric information (viz. separation between directors and shareholders, public officials and taxpayers).

This economic approach engenders an economic definition of corruption as a 'bureaucratic black market' (Tilman, 1968). Benson and Baden (1985) declare that 'corruption is a black market for property rights, over which public officials have been given discretionary allocative power. Hence corruption represents an illegal and flexible means of influencing how they are defined and how attributed.'

In line with this approach, since allocative and redistributive policies are equivalent to a transfer of property rights, there exists a strong incentive for economic agents to modify them. Clearly this reasoning holds the systems governing public property to be inferior to those for private property, insofar as rights are assumed to be neither exclusive (i.e. having the possibility of excluding all other agents from enjoyment of the asset) nor transferable (i.e. use not subject to the consent of other agents).

According to the view of theories of property rights and rent-seeking (see below), any large-scale organization with power delegated experiences problems of monitoring the actions of agents and hence provides occasions for appropriating rent. But, in line with this notion, opportunities and damaging economic consequences are significantly higher in the public than in the private sector, since the state is the repository *par excellence* of discretionary power. Put another way, the radical divorce between the right to make use of public resources and responsibility for the consequences of such use is a necessary, but not sufficient, condition for any act of corruption. Illegal use of discretionary power over property rights determines an act of corruption. The relative significance of transaction costs stemming from the public nature of the property rights and the tenuousness of the monitoring exercised by proprietors who are taxpayers (those who hold the property rights in regard to the product of any activity affecting a governmental organization) on the occasion of elections increases opportunities for betrayal.

The adoption of the theory of illegal appropriation of property rights as the subject of the breach of law at work in an act of corruption raises the problem of delegating power and of discretionary power, and has the virtue of simplicity. The property rights argument fails to account for some problems that give rise to corruption in a number of countries. Indeed, it is a definition which will prevent the vast majority of economists from inquiring into the historical origin of property rights and the mechanism of their allocation and redistribution which, in a case-by-case study, appears more or less just or legitimate. The origin of wealth and its initial accumulation in keeping with norms that are frequently far removed from liberal principles are thus eliminated from the field of inquiry of academic economics. Whereby as a definition it is likely to be of little use in studying societies in transition or where the system of legitimization is undergoing change. Such societies possess diverse and fluctuating value systems in that they have so far precluded the establishment of a minimum consensus. This being so, the inequality in the distribution of property rights, though in other respects clearly defined, may readily lead to breaches of loyalty on the part of economic agents which take the form of corruption. Again, the hostility towards the state contained *per se* in the definition of property rights oversimplifies choice of a policy for monitoring corruption that recommends itself 'naturally'. It must perforce imply withdrawal of governmental control, privatization and deregulation and consequent collapse of the black market concerned which will be replaced by a market for property rights that is legal and transparent.

Analyses of rent-seeking

Concomitantly, in the reasoning propounded by the neoliberal school of Public Choice, writers have drawn from studies relating to the economics of bureaucracy and the voting market to provide a model for the market for corruption. This trend in economic thinking has led to a detailed inquiry into rent-seeking in our societies and, in the main, offers an analysis of corruption as a particular form of rent-seeking.

In a Public Choice perspective, the theory of rent-seeking provides a significant addition to the analysis of the motivation for corrupt supply and demand and their social cost. The theory explicates the effects of all the situations in which arbitrary scarcity engenders rents. Such rents arising from a disturbance to competition (PPC) cannot be counted as an addition to existing wealth but take the form of a transfer that profits those who are able to appropriate them.

The state's interventionist capability, whether exercised directly through government control or indirectly through the regulations, tariffs and quotas established, gives it a special role *vis-à-vis* rent-seekers. Hence corruption is an unlawful recourse representing an expenditure of scarce resources with the aim of gaining a transfer that has been artificially created by government; so it is merely a particular form of rent-seeking (Tollison, 1982; Tullock, 1989). On the occasion of legal rent-seeking (lobbying) or illegal (corruption), 'resources which could otherwise be devoted to a value-producing activity are engaged in competition which has no aim other than redistribution' (Buchanan, Tollison and Tullock, 1980). Further, according to Buchanan, legal or illegal rent-seeking imposes three types of social loss: the efforts and expenses of candidates for monopoly; the efforts of government to obtain the outlay incurred by the corrupting agents, or indeed to respond; and the distortion imposed on the third party by monopolies and by government. The backhander then does not itself represent a social loss, it is merely a transfer borne by consumers for the benefit of corrupting monopolies. The social loss resides simply in the cost of setting up the deal and its effect – lobbying fees, wasted time and money during the posting strategies and the development of distortions such as grandiose projects, import licences granted to too many or too few firms in view of market capacity, etc.

However, the theory puts an end to debate by invariably reducing the organized body to an individual unit maximized in a coherent, homogeneous and rational way. Without question, for those of liberal persuasion, the fight against corruption, in terms of inducement and monitoring, finds a more receptive terrain in the private than in the public sector, hence the latter stands condemned. Arguments advanced take it as axiomatic that the maximization of profit is the single objective of the private firm and that the objective is a clear and straightforward one to monitor. Conversely, governmental organization is 'bogged down in a welter of uncoordinated, undirected, ambivalent, mutually antagonistic and contradictory objectives' (Buchanan, Tollison and Tullock, 1980) that make it a prey to manipulation by every lobby and corrupting agent.

The economics of crime and the control of corruption

G. S. Becker (Becker, 1976) conceives the whole of society as a continuum of markets, which has allowed him to develop a new science of rational behaviour. Viewed thus, each one of our actions is governed by a utilitarian cost/benefit calculation which is made possible by the existence of a monetary price attached to every good and service possessing an alternative use. All behaviour is thus susceptible to analysis as a form of arbitration operating over a market.

The economics of corruption therefore studies the situation in which scarcity induces individuals to adopt corrupt, rationally deviant behaviour if sufficient gain can be expected. The principle of maximizing utility therefore induces the individual (demand on the part of the corrupting agent, supply on that of the one corrupted) to make a calculation in anticipation of the advantages (gain) and costs (the sum of sanctions weighed against the risk of being caught in relation to the prospects in mind). The cost of sanction is assessed by the loss of gain imposed on the individual by the term of imprisonment and/or according to the fine ordained. The first public decision must be to verify the 'disturbing' effect of the market for corruption on the general equilibrium and inquire about the determination of tax-paying consumers in regard to the phenomenon. Then, from the point of view of public economics, if the achievement of social welfare requires it, a higher form of regulation must be implemented at as little cost as possible with a view to increasing the risk of being apprehended as well as the sanctions inflicted on those who deviate. The growth in anticipated cost then induces those who deviate (both supply of and demand for corruption) to increase the expected benefit and so in the case of corruption the price that will command the deal. Conversely, the corrupting agent will only make the deal at a lower price. Consequently, the equilibrium quantity of supply and demand at this higher price will drop. The price here is flexible since it is constantly incorporating the new situation in terms of risk and potential sanction. Nevertheless, the costs of public intervention (collective consumption) involve making inroads into individual consumption by way of taxation and are only justified if the end result is socially advantageous (pareto-optimal). As does the deviating agent, the tax-paying consumer makes a cost/benefit calculation as to the drop in his private consumption that will allow enhancement of the social order, i.e. a decrease in corruption in terms of thefts and violation of public property rights. Such reasoning may be employed by way of explicating how the choice of supplying and demanding a corrupt transaction in the face of a range of penalties is effected.[1]

The shortcoming in the constancy of references to the economics of crime is the distant image of the reality of a flexible and pareto-optimum equilibrium price in terms of which the corrupt transaction is effected. Hence the compulsion both to reduce economic agents to an individual maximizing unit and to maintain the assumption of rational calculation on the part of this unit ruin the economics of criminal corruption as projected. Certainly society is far from being a continuum of pure and perfect markets.

The fascination exercised by the analyses here set out is explained in terms of their being all-encompassing in that they take on board a political philosophy (liberalism), a methodology (methodological individualism and utilitarianism), a method of calculation (marginalism) and proposals for action (reduction in the role of government). Their richness results from their throwing light on the interpenetration of political and economic factors while laying stress on instances of betrayal of the common good by politicians and by means of a theory of bureaucratization.

So the feeling remains that while diagnosis is rich the forms of remedy, given their signal failure to appreciate the complexity of society, are likely to have perverse consequences that prove difficult to control. The positive and negative consequences that may be expected from a withdrawal by government and the watering down of 'relief groups' are so intermingled that it becomes impossible to quantify them with any degree of certainty. However, if the jaundiced look at human motivation seems exaggerated and liable to lead to a hostility to government that contains social dangers, the light thrown on deviant tendencies ensures that we are unlikely to remain blithely ingenuous and provides food for thought on what should be undertaken by way of reform and control.

A problematic source of enrichment: politicians, organizations and contracts

The authors presented here take as their purpose to enhance neoclassical theory (Broader Standard Theory) in one or other of two directions. Rose-Ackerman (1978), while retaining the behavioural context of *homo economicus*, seeks to bring together elements from the economics of bureaucracy and the political market, and to make some adjustment in application to the economics of crime. The studies which present corruption as an illegal contract do away with references to *homo economicus* and to a market for corruption and focus instead on the organizational realities of the phenomenon.

Rose-Ackerman and the integration of the economics of crime and of bureaucracy and the political market

Rose-Ackerman's book is the best-known and most quoted reference to the political economy of corruption. Its reputation has in fact transcended economic circles, a reason in itself for drawing attention to its distinctive methodology.[2]

At the outset she states as her premise the impossibility of analysing corruption by the standard methods of micro-economics. The assumption of behaviour in which rationality and self-interest are maximized, which she does not reject, holds good in institutions where the paradigm of the competitive market (PPC) is quite inadequate. Her refusal to build a normative theory she justifies by the following observations:

- in our complex societies non-market allocative processes are legitimate;
- the moral cost of transgressing norms, which is not directly seen in monetary terms, is an essential variable which is not taken into account in normative analysis;
- the normative theory of cost/benefit calculation, supported by the axiom of the maximization of the social surplus of both consumer and producer, will always be faced with the fact that the recommendations of experts are at variance with a great many political decisions in a parliamentary democracy;
- the correlation established between the expansion of government and incidence of corruption must be rejected. Corruption can develop in states that are highly-developed, underdeveloped or minimal;
- the breakdown of civic morality or administrative competence which is at the origin of many cases of corruption has nothing to do with size;
- normative analysis is immune to schemes to reform and improve non-market institutions;
- corruption can develop on a massive scale among private agents by imposing a high social cost on other private agents. Therefore a theory of the social responsibility of entrepreneurs needs to be developed.

These considerations incline Rose-Ackerman to put forward a proposal for backhanders to be treated as lawful payment through making changes in the law (lobbying activity being seen as less harmful than the hidden financing of electoral campaigns). Such a scheme for legalizing hidden transactions poses complex problems, in the author's view, in the case of redistributive policies that are targeted or in that of allocating public contracts. Indeed, even with a price that is legal and administered, public bids remain pale copies of competitive bids, and this often renders policies for quality control and pricing difficult to achieve. Allocating a subsidized apartment to the highest bidder would be clearly absurd and allocating a public works project on the basis of the least costly estimate could well involve negative consequences, viz. suspect as to quality, uncertain as to dependability, and environmentally unacceptable. In cases like this where a pricing system is inadequate or unable to provide a rational guide to a decision as to public supply and demand in relation to its objectives, schemes for effective sanctions need to be set up; and this requires a preliminary study so as to be certain that the non-market allocation is justifiable from an economic and/or social point of view and that it is not being diverted from its proper function. Unlike the Beckerian model, for Rose-Ackerman the politics of monitoring – by way of management oversight – and of sanctions – rapid and efficacious, brooking neither impunity nor immunity – will only become effective insofar as it is accompanied by structural changes. Two initiatives will in this context go to complement the real effects of threat. The first lies in bringing greater clarity and publicity to government preferences (who is entitled to subsidised housing? what are the criteria for quality in public works assignments?); the second in maintaining genuine competition between the parties contracting. These intentions offer ground for an improvement in public administration.

The scope and depth of Rose-Ackerman's study is related to her detailed knowledge of law and of cases of corruption in the USA. Her background and experience enable her to develop proposals for the reform of structures that take into account the considerable range of cases she examines. In spite of the fact that she adopts a fairly uncritical, formalized micro-economic approach and remains relatively orthodox and inclined to be cocooned in the paradigm of *homo economicus*, she manages – and this is her strength – to open up a number of paths for research, the best instance here being her conclusion where she deals with the relationship between economics, politics and morality. In this perspective she advocates going more deeply into how loyalty in regard to the law may be developed and what type of institutional structure may facilitate the process. This is the challenge that has been taken up in the economics of contracts.

Corruption as betrayal of a legal contract in the signing of an illegal contract

In Broader Standard Theory (BST) economic systems are juxtapositions of organizations and markets, both of which administer transactions, which themselves are far removed from the image of PPC. But the notion in BST goes further than this conventional observation. It provides an interpretation of the existence of organizations and their effectiveness by means of the concept of internalizing transaction costs, the term signifying that transactions occurring in a market will be administered within an organization so as to reduce the costs of market exchange resulting from asymmetric information which creates a climate of mistrust among agents. The cost of transaction itself is determined by two precepts of individual behaviour, namely bounded rationality and opportunism which together raise the risk element during the transaction. The notion of bounded rationality refers to the difficulty for the individual in stocking and processing information in a reliable manner. Hence the firm represents a structured network of effective communication and contracts with the objective of diminishing the 'moral risk' brought into play by the opportunists. A secondary effect of this reading of the firm is to introduce a conception of the economic agent as being less calculating than *homo economicus* and more open to a system of collective and qualitative value. As in the agency theory, parties contracting agree on systems of inducement, monitoring and sanctions so as to oblige each one to respect the contract.

Accordingly, it is tempting to see 'illegal transactions' and 'criminal contracts' as similar mutations. Such contracts structured by networks in corruption determine internal and external transactions that are far removed from PPC concepts. Like their twin sister, illegal organizations internalize transaction costs. Taking it further, one can even surmise that in the same way as do legal firms, they evolve systems of (illegal) internal and external contracts whose function is to increase the dependability of market exchange. The metaphor of the impersonal market, setting up a price system that informs our choice, is then to some extent replaced by that of the firm, that gives a greater role to the consciously strategic organization of economic agents. Following this reasoning one may define the object of corruption as the violation of a legal contract – a work contract, for instance, specifying the use of property rights – which operates thanks to an organizational method, i.e. the signing of an illegal contract.

Unlike assumptions made about the market for corruption, betrayal is here organized by groups or networks fostering corruption, which offer a degree of consistency and protection for the violation of contracts. Besides, the organization creates at least possible cost a supply and demand for corruption, identifies agents who are likely to be interested and organizes how the necessary information is managed.

A number of economists or socio-economists (Reuter, 1983; Arlacchi, 1986; Gambetta, 1988b), taking as their starting point concepts in new industrial economics, have set about studying criminal organizations involved in 'illegal markets' such as contraband, drugs, prostitution, gambling and corruption. In this context, corruption and the use of threats and violence, which are not always easy to dissociate, are analysed as a means of reducing the transaction cost of illegal activities. The three particular obstacles that the illegal market must overcome in order to be stable and to expand are, according to Reuter (1983), as follows: contracts are not drawn under the supervision of a neutral 'above party' authority which can be appealed to where there is conflict of interest; goods can be seized by the authorities; actors can at any time be arrested, tried and convicted.

An illegal market's activity can only develop provided a way to counteract these three obstacles is found. The resort to a combination of threats, violence and corruption − what might be termed mafioso corruption − has a priority function of evading pursuit and prosecution by the police and judiciary. But it also has a role in reducing the uncertainty which characterizes illegal transactions as a consequence of there being either asymmetric − or incomplete − information, or a significant lack of rationality on the part of agents.[3] In this underworld, which is far from a perfect market, betrayals may occur at any moment. The illegal contract must be known and abided by within the restricted circle of entrepreneurs and officials who are party to the illegality.

The studies presented here, despite their considerable diversity, all relate to what takes place when one or more of the assumptions made about PPC are relaxed. All throw a different and more penetrating light on the problem, aiming each to be more realistic, more open and explicit in studying organizations and administrations where corruption is a source of anxiety. They reject the term 'market for corruption' on the grounds that the assumptions made are unrealistic and the findings poor. Similarly, they envisage the appearance of discretionary powers other than the state − mafia or ghetto − when functions are not performed. The scope and depth of their analysis is evident, even so they still appear to be inhibited by a residue of individualistic methodology. Indeed organizations remain instruments that can be deducted from calculation, whose rationality varies in line with the complexity of choice and of private agents. The reason for this impossible breach finds explanation in upholding the assumption that society is organized on a strictly individual basis. Following this principle, it is invariably across the encounter of separate entities that socialization emerges, through contract or through market transaction. Interesting as these studies are, they need to be supplemented.

Corruption networks

Until now, but in different degrees, representations of a perfect – or imperfect – market, perfect or imperfect information, and ample or bounded rationality have been the main thrust of economic contributions under study. It is now possible to detect a transfer effected by writers between their definition of economic society and their definition of corruption. To the notion of a society conceived as a continuum of markets corresponds the image of the market in corruption. Likewise, the definition of corruption as the violation of a legal contract by an illegal one corresponds to the characterization of economic space as a network of contracts. This type of analysis leaves to one side the importance of systems of domination and legitimization and the structure-forming power of codes, routines, beliefs and ideologies in the reproduction of economic society. These definitions which are intentionally amoral and nonhistorical suffer the limits of all economic theories that are closed to other disciplines in social sciences.

In more or less conscious opposition to traditional approaches, two further ones have germinated. The first (Wade, 1982, 1985; Hirschman, 1983; Jagannathan, 1986; and Klitgaard, 1988), whose roots are more in the study of concrete problems, is characterized by the large place it gives to describing the occurrence of corruption and/or by proposals for reorganizing and overseeing administration. Therein, such studies, which are less conceptual than those so far referred to, are primarily receptive to the historical and geographical context in question. The second approach starts with a radical criticism of Standard Neoliberal Theory and a consideration of Broader Standard Theory, then proposes in outline an alternative conceptual framework. Finally, leaving aside descriptive studies and those to do with public management, I shall examine the assumptions made and problems raised by a project such as this that rests on criticisms made anew in recent years in regard to Standard Neoliberal Theory and Broader Standard Theory. I shall not provide an exception to the rule of transfer and my definition of corrupt exchange springs from my

definition of economic society. I shall find the term 'market for corruption' improper before going on to put forward an outline of networks
of corruption as an alternative concept to market for corruption.

Is it right to speak of a market?

The term market covers many different meanings. Society is, of
course, made up of individuals who are differentiated by the place
they occupy or the role they play. If individual behaviour is not
mechanically determined by its belonging to a structure, social constraints, resulting from initial unequal attributes, have a considerable
influence on it. And the question must be asked as to how a democratic society should deal with privilege and injustice by way of the
types of compromise that have been employed in the past. Since the
market does not incorporate all possible formulas for socialization,
economic non-market functions of socialization are performed by
firms and by government. In this scheme of things, economic society
proceeds from the linking of markets with the chain of socialization
which lies outside them (government, firms, family, socio-political
networks and so on). The perception of an organic link between
government and the market transforms both analysis of the origins of
corruption and proposals for measures to combat corruption.

The immediate consequence of this heterodox definition of the
market and the relationship between the market and government is
that an economic explanation of corrupt dealing is not unconnected
with the interpretation of the breakdown in loyalty in pluralist
democracy; to say which is to recognize that politico-administrative
rents are an essential element in opportunities for corruption, making
the assumption, however, that the need to betray is not consubstan-
tial with human nature. The present form that corruption has taken
bears the marks of the crisis in government, the erosion of models for
growth and citizenship, and the resulting deterioration in the sense of
community. It would appear that Hirschman's (1970) outline model
concerning the breakdown in loyalty in private firms and in regard to
the state can effectively be applied. When economic or political
agents are no longer satisfied with the response on the part of industry
or administration to their demands, i.e. when the effects of dysfunctioning are felt, they may either speak out in protest or else adopt
a strategy of exit, in which case individuals will look for a system of
alternative and justifiable codes that afford solutions to their
problems. We may well then be presented with a dual defection – one

of a socio-political kind involving citizens in respect of the parliamentary system and the state over questions of taxation and public
consumption, and one of a professional kind involving individuals *vis-
à-vis* their principals. Thus one might formulate certain propositions
about the incidence of wide-spreading political, administrative and
private corruption on the basis of these conclusions:

- corruption represents an act that is not exclusively ordered by the
  movement of prices and quantities;
- there is no permanent negotiation in regard to internal and external 'contracts' whereby they have quasi-market flexibility.
  Hence trading is continuous and relatively stable in terms of
  price;
- members of organizations dealing with corruption possess
  numerous systems of values which call on motives other than
  utilitarian (even if egoism is not absent), and these include belief,
  connivance, fidelity, obedience, imitation of others, narcissism
  and perversity. Corrupt dealing often calls for all such contradictory values;
- the multiple links of dependency and interdependency between
  agents involved are paramount;
- agents are not free subjects existing outside an historical context,
  they are indissociable from social structures;
- trading is regulated by collective cognitive devices (apprentice-
  ship and procedural rationality 'construct' transaction and
  loyalty), norms for action, traditions and routines. The price of a
  transaction is not related in this case to market state; a simple
  traditional and fairly rigid percentage serves as a reference for a
  range of operations. Consequently, a fall in public expenditure, in
  spite of increasing competition among those seeking public contracts which this entails, does not imply a rise in the percentage
  demanded;
- corruption is the expression of historical ambiguity in the
  relationship between government and the market.

*Norms, agreements, networks and the system of accumulation as offering
favourable prospects for research*

The analysis of methods of accumulating wealth and of patterns of
redistribution which in most cases accompany corruption is essential
in order to understand the structure-forming effects of corruption. If

the decision to participate in a corrupt action is a matter of personal choice and contains a self-regarding element, not to go beyond this point is to limit an understanding of the problem and of its tendency to snowball. And so it is essential to explain the links of dependency and interdependency which build up in networks of corruption. This is not to say that the study of individual motivation and behaviour can be side-stepped, rather one needs to shed light on them through an analysis of the macro-economic context.

And indeed these networks can only function if their objectives are clearly broader than mere personal enrichment. The value system that constitutes a network and determines each member's place transcends the material and monetary to incorporate strategic command and political ambition. Here political drive cannot be reduced to the lure of gain. Hence it is essential to set out the range of values that come into play in attaching an individual to a network and in his dependency on it. A complex principle of reciprocity is at work in patterns of corruption which transforms itself into a process for generating power structures.

According to this line of approach, a network forms in a clandestine way on foundations that may be multiple – family, friendship, race, clique, religion, politics or similar geographical, sectarian or corporative ties, with objectives no less so. Such objectives range from covering illegal activities of whatever scale to stifling competition in a legal market and financing political parties. A further network characteristic is that activities become entangled and that the official occupations of its members tend to proliferate. The network is an authority where political, economic and social elements merge inseparably since the accumulation of financial and political power develops out of precepts of mutual aid and solidarity. Networks are organized on the basis of systems of rights and obligations which for the individual are accorded priority over other systems and obligations – family or firm or the state. Thus each individual is defined in terms of his 'priority' network, respect for the rights and obligations of the network having precedence over his individual utilitarian interest. The network is taken to be an authority which reshapes the demarcation between private and public spheres. At the same time it represents a source of normalization and as such provides an alternative to the state.

Two types of coordination can be envisaged. In one instance, there are two structured entities, each independent of the other (political party and entrepreneur), who negotiate the transaction. Then the coordination between organizations must be looked at. In line with evidence provided by the economics of organizations, we need to explore what occurs in each of the two 'black boxes' before and at the time the transaction is realized. Each of the two entities is a sphere for collective procedures with the aim of controlling competition and evading overmuch price flexibility. In the other case, the situation is characterized by entities being incorporated in one complex of activity (interdependence of interests). Here the principles of intra-organizational coordination (freemasonry, head of nationalized firm and politician of the same persuasion) require to be studied. In this instance the image of a process of market coordination distorts the true picture of corruption even further, and has to be replaced by the principles guiding the construction of authority and the network hierarchy.

Consequently, there exist neither acts nor individuals that are perfectly autonomous and amoral, but networks and repetitions of acts constantly developing in line with tenable principles. Indeed, the more corruption becomes generalized, the less are transactions monetary, taking on as they do other forms of preferential exchange and thereby facilitating their justification considerably; the form of justification most frequently met with is that corruption compensates for a number of functional deficiencies in the official and legal structure of the system. So it comes about that rationalizing corruption develops from a situation where an individual feels free to find solutions that meet his problems. The injustice, real or imagined, of the state – the law – or of the market – forms of competition that are too strong for oneself and for others not strong enough – authorizes all transgressions. But individuals do not establish their new moral code independently of other individuals. They free themselves from adherence to the law only to claim the right to adhere to another common code, that of the network which judges differently what is lawful or unlawful. Consequently, when the state and the market are no longer capable of responding to the ecoomic and social demands of those with problems, be they wage-earners or entrepreneurs, the networks are there to help them. Hence they appear as alternative modes for the creation of wealth, for redistribution and integration.

Conclusion

This survey of the economics of corruption, in its diversity, needs a further few remarks by way of conclusion. In the course of reviewing the economic literature on corruption, Lafay (1990) observed that 'there now at least exists a general theoretical outline of the problem'. That is certainly true as far as the neoliberal viewpoint is concerned. But if, as I believe, this research programme, despite the headway made, remains hermetic or, to say the least, fragile if it is to re-introduce morality and social codes into the study of deviant be-haviour, much effort is still needed to give more rigour to discussion about the interconnection of government, organizations and markets. For it has to be emphasized that so far, unfortunately, the para-mountcy of the neoclassical model divides the vast majority of economists from others whose research has to do with corruption.

A new programme of economic research might start by quantify-ing the macro-economic effects of corruption and developing a theory of the price of transactions and their variation, supported by case studies. It will then be essential to analyse – upstream of the point of exchange, where the market can assume certain functions – the pro-ductive structures of supply and demand as well as their employment. By analysing channels of corruption associated with varied comple-mentary sectors and by drawing comparisons between sectors, apply-ing the principles and techniques of meso-economics, it should be possible to grasp to some extent how circuits of corruption perform and interact, and how they proliferate economically and socially.

Notes

1. More or less similar reasoning is used in the work of Banfield (1975), Shackleton (1978), Beenstock (1979), Lui (1985, 1986) and Nas, Price and Weber (1986).
2. For a more complete presentation of some of its models and their limitations, see J. Cartier-Bresson (1992).
3. With a view to shedding light on strategies for corruption, it is not surprising that researchers have made use of – or proposed to make use of – games theory for studying forms of cooperation and conflict between agents (Beenstock, 1979; Macrae, 1982; Cadot, 1987).

CONCLUSION: DEMOCRACY AND CORRUPTION: TOWARDS A COMPARATIVE ANALYSIS

Donatella Della Porta and Yves Mény

One of the main innovative features of this book is that it attempts to collect together in-depth analyses of political corruption in various democratic nations.[1] As mentioned in the introduction, the painful realization that the scourge of corruption is spreading has given rise to the need to compare the characteristics and evolution of the phenomenon in various democracies. Although indispensable to an understanding of any phenomenon, a comparative analysis is not an easy task. It involves, first of all, the need to create concepts that 'travel well' or, in other words, are applicable to the analysis of different nations (Sartori, 1971). For this purpose, the contributions included in this volume can serve to illustrate the diverse facets of political and administrative malpractices, ranging from out-and-out extortion to the various forms of specific and non-specific corruption, from *pantouflage* to inside trading, from conflict of interests to the barter vote, from *sottogoverno* to *criptogoverno*.[2] Starting from this broad overview, it will be possible to classify the different forms of political corruption and their related phenomena.

It also seems essential to make a systematic comparison of the contributions on different national cases, in order to attempt to understand the genesis and dynamics of political and administrative corruption. In analyses of individual national cases, in fact, one is often inclined to link corruption with any other pathology present in the political system or the public administration. A comparison of several cases can help in getting away from ethnocentrism, by constructing generalizable explanations of the phenomenon and its dynamics. Although it is not possible to construct general theories, given that our comparative analysis is at a very early stage, we would like in these concluding notes to begin discussing, in the light of information that has emerged during the compilation of this volume, some of the issues concerning political corruption found in scientific literature, political debate and the press.

Between state and market: the careers of the corrupt

The proliferation of political scandals has raised, first, questions about the main players in the corruption drama: Who are the corrupted? How do they progress in their careers? How do they succeed in occupying important places within the complex political and economic systems of industrialized democracies? On this subject, two different hypotheses can be formulated. On the one hand, political corruption is associated with the presence of career politicians, in other words, according to the well-known definition by Weber (1919), those politicians who 'live by politics', looking for extrinsic or instrumental advantages, as opposed to those politicians who 'live for politics' and do so for intrinsic or ideological satisfaction. According to a different hypothesis, however, corrupt politicians originate from an emerging political class, still inexperienced and lacking public ethics. These, for example, are interpretations found in American publications on corrupt party machinery, the development of which is linked to the fact that 'ex-plebeians', lacking both financial resources and civic values, now have access to politics (see, for example, Dahl, 1961; Banfield and Wilson, 1967: 330).

From what has emerged from the analysis of national cases, the protagonists of corrupt deals seem, in effect, to be endowed with particular characteristics, which distinguish them from career politicians in the traditional sense.

First, political careers appear to be a channel for rapid social mobility. If in the English case we have seen the moralizing role carried out by an elite of enlightened aristocrats, political corruption, on the other hand, has appeared more widespread among those described (to coin a new Italian term) as 'rampant': 'ex-plebeians' and social climbers. By their use of politics as a channel for upward mobility, corrupt politicians, as described in some of the essays included in this volume, resemble those defined as 'gain politicians' by Rogow and Lasswell (1974), in their research on American party 'bosses', whom they depict as barely interested in national politics and only motivated to enter politics as a channel for personal enrichment.

In addition to the social climbing aspect, another element appears frequently in the career of corrupt administrators: *the interweaving of public positions and financial and entrepreneurial activities.* To mention but a few examples, both in France and the UK, the opportunities for corruption are increased by the practice of large businesses of recruiting retired public administrators or distributing consultancies to those still working.[3] The widespread practice of *pantouflage* allows politicians and public bureaucrats to use information obtained by virtue of their institutional positions for their own gain and that of the businesses that employs them.

A third observation – linked to the preceding two – is that political corruption leads to a proliferation of figures who do not properly belong *either to the state or to the market,* and who, therefore, 'violate' the rules governing both. According to the most widespread theories, in the course of corrupt deals, public administrators, on the one side, and private entrepreneurs on the other – the state and the market – meet and exchange their merchandise. In general, the two protagonists should have different motivational structures: bureaucracy, according to Weber's criteria, should administer the state in a rational and impersonal way, while entrepreneurs should pursue the maximization of their own profit through market competition. Political corruption shows, however, a sort of genetic mutation in the motivational structure of both protagonists. The various contributions to this volume indicate the presence, in the corrupt deal, of figures that one would find difficult to place clearly in either one or other camp, the state or the market.

The corrupt political class, which we have observed in action in different Western democracies, is composed of different figures, many of whom are characterized by their management of a public authority which is not subject to democratic investiture or bureaucratic control: the 'public body bosses' who found their careers on the fact that they occupy party-nominated posts in public bodies; 'party cashiers' who coordinate the expenditure of various public bodies and the illicit revenue of the administrators linked to them; 'bag-carriers' who – as emissaries of the most powerful politicians – organize illicit activities in public administration; 'protected' professionals, i.e. architects, engineers, lawyers and managers – who have connections with politicians and administrators – placed by the parties, as their trusted men, in the various commissions which give out and monitor public contracts; 'bureaucrats with party membership cards', in other words, employees or executives in public administration, loyal servants to their political godfathers. These different figures have been grouped together under the definition 'business politicians', i.e. individuals who combine 'an intermediary role in business affairs, licit or illicit, and generally, involvement in their own right in financial activity, with political intermediation in the traditional sense' (Pizzorno, 1992: 24; see also Della Porta 1992a and Pizzorno and Della Porta, 1993 on 'business politicians'). As far as this type of politician is concerned, the rewards are secret and of a financial nature. Their principal function is mediation between the various protagonists in secret deals, creating contacts and facilitating negotiations between two or more parties interested in a corrupt deal. Their principal resources are knowledge and 'privileged information' which are collected and exchanged on illegal markets.

The hybridization of state and market seems also to characterize entrepreneurs who interact with corrupt politicians, whose economic successes are based not on their competitiveness in the market, but on their privileged access to the state. Amongst the entrepreneurs who enjoy a relationship with the public administration, cartels, formalized to a greater or lesser degree, include businesses which are victims of extortion, businesses 'protected' by individual politicians, or 'sponsored' by political parties, and even businesses which are actually owned directly by public administrators (albeit, in most cases, hiding behind a borrowed name). The characteristic feature of many of these businesses is that their financial fortunes are founded on privileged relationships with managers of public funds, replacing the usual professional competence and entrepreneurial skills with political 'contacts'.

Strength or weakness in the corrupt parties?

The theme of political careers is linked to that of the political parties, who should be the ones selecting the political class. As can be imagined, sociologists and political scientists have often tackled the subject of political corruption in relation to the characteristics of political parties. In his now classic explanation, the American political scientist, Samuel Huntington, has linked the development of the phenomenon to the weakness of parties in the expansion phase of political involvement. In the course of modernization, corruption spreads along certain specific paths, those where the normal growth in the people's involvement in political decisions does not go hand-in-hand with a strengthening of those institutions which – like the parties – should screen and channel the demands of the people: 'The weaker and less accepted the parties, the greater the probability of corruption' (Huntington, 1968: 71). In apparent contradiction with this hypothesis is the widespread conviction that corruption is in fact helped by the omnipresent and omnipotent nature of political parties, which are strong, well-organized machines, capable of controlling civil society and the economic system. It appears reasonable, therefore, to ask which of the two interpretations best explains the reality: is political corruption encouraged by the weakness of parties, or by their strength? An analysis of our national cases helps us to specify what measure of relative 'strength' and 'weakness' affects the dynamics of corrupt deals.

In the first place, one must make clear that strength and weakness cannot be related simply to the size of the electorate or the number of party members. In our examples, in fact, political corruption has developed both in large and in small parties, especially parties endowed with a strong 'power of coalition'. Furthermore, political corruption appears to be widespread, both in parties with few members – the parties of the influential few referred to in the contribution on France, and the parties of voters referred to in the Spanish case – and in parties with many members – the parties of the masses in Italy and Germany. If in the first case, political corruption can develop to compensate for the lack of internal channels of financing, in the second case, bribes can be seen as a means of maintaining the mammoth party bureaucracy.

Corruption appears to be linked to the motivation of the voters and party members, rather than to their number. As has been argued by Alessandro Pizzorno (1971), the 'strength' or 'weakness' of parties can be evaluated differently according to whether one is considering their power to strengthen their own mandate, thereby obtaining advantages for their representatives or for the party apparatus, or else their power to transmit the requests of those represented. As far as we have been able to observe, *the dynamics of political corruption appear to be interwoven with the power of parties to strengthen their mandate.* Thanks to the alibi of 'the political element' in administrative decisions, parties have penetrated the administrative councils of public bodies, using their power in ways that are not always directed to the public good and not always legal. The mechanisms of political control – some official, some less so – over the nomination of certain public bureaucrats – ranging from the outright *spoils system* of the USA, to the German *Proporz* or to the Italian system of 'apportionment' (*lottizzazione*) – lead to the party domination of public administration, producing fiefdoms which parties and their men can exploit for practices of corruption and clientelism. The influence of the parties has spread even outside public administration – from banks to newspapers – leading many countries to talk of an infiltration of civil society, which has had the effect of further reducing defences against political corruption and bad administration.

The use of practices of corruption in fact appears to be negatively correlated with the second type of party power, *reducing the parties' ability to draw up long-term programmes, mobilize ideological resources, distribute incentives for participation, and gain the support of a thinking electorate*. As has been seen in the Italian case, by concentrating on the organization of corrupt exchanges, the political parties favour, in effect, the decisions that are the most productive in terms of bribes, instead of those decisions which might receive more support from the electorate. Furthermore, by their very nature, corrupt deals lead to the dominance of secret politics over open politics, and of the dialectics of a small restricted group over the quest for wider participation. The evidence of waste linked to bad administration in the long term prevents corrupt politicians from attracting a thinking electorate, by putting themselves forward as the bearers of affluence and progress. The pragmatism of under-the-counter agreements replaces ideological appeals.

*Consociativismo** and secret deals

Corruption seems linked not just to the characteristics of the individual parties but to the characteristics of the whole party system. On this subject too, we can offer some hypotheses, at first sight conflicting, on the causes and dynamics of corruption. Political corruption has appeared, in some cases, to be linked to the *rise to power of new parties*. Both in France and in Spain, parties which after a long period in opposition have taken it in turns to govern, have been accused of malversation (corrupt administration). In both cases the socialist parties, immediately after gaining power, have had to face problems in financing their bureaucratic machinery, without being able to count either on the goodwill of big financial interests, as is normally

---

*Trans. note: 'The tendency to consociate' . . . In a pluralistic government such as Italy's, the tendency to involve all the major political forces, whether government or opposition, in government decisions.

the case with conservative parties, or on contributions from ideologically motivated militants, as happens with their cousins, the-
communist parties.

It must be added, however, that in other cases political corruption
seems to have been fostered by the *long stay in power of the same party*,
i.e. by absence of any alternation. In Japan as in Italy, the apparent
irremovability from power of the Liberals and Christian Democrats
respectively, seems to have given them a certainty of impunity, both
from the electoral point of view and from the legal point of view. In
both countries, the parties excluded from government, sharing a
common belief that they will never be able to gain power, have been
unable to exercise the function of a coherent opposition which, for
example in the UK case, is recognized as an effective instrument of
control over corruption.

In effect, *the lack of a real opposition* appears to be a factor common
to many corruption cases. The spread of political corruption is permitted, in fact, by a system of agreements between the majority and
opposition parties for the sharing out of certain material benefits. In
'open' politics, the interest of the parties in increasing their political
financing has resulted in increasingly generous and permissive laws
concerning public contributions as well as to the proliferation of
front-associations, like the *Stiftungen* of the German parties, the
10,000 foundations officially linked to the Japanese parties, or the
research companies (engineering studios, consultancy firms, technical
offices) unofficially linked to French parties (see also Mény, 1992a:
Ch. VII). In illicit politics, widespread *consociativismo* encourages
secret pacts of connivance over illicit income, as symbolized both by
the 'Flick case' in Germany[4] and by the so-called 'business committees' in Italy which brought together politicians from various
parties and sometimes the high-level bureaucrats responsible for the
management of local or national public bodies.

By means of 'consociating' pacts, the party system assumes the
function of acting as guarantee for illegal deals. The representatives of
parties within the public administration, in fact, perform – as one
reads in the request for authorization to take proceedings against a
senator of the Italian Republic – 'the function of acting as guarantee
in the awarding of contracts, the successful managing of contracts,
the timeliness of payments and so on' (Senate, 1992: 4–5). As a consequence of the spread of corruption in all geographical areas and in the
various bodies and sectors of the public administration, agreements
between the parties ensure a sort of corrupt 'perpetual replay', con-
tinuously 'rewarding' entrepreneurs who are prepared to pay bribes

and 'punishing' those who refuse the requests of the politicians.

Cost of politics and clientelism

'Consociationism' allows the amount of political financing to be increased illegally, but, of course, does not eliminate competition between parties, sections and political figures; some of the money obtained through bribery is spent in this competition. A variable which influences the spread of corruption seems to be, in fact, the cost of politics. The need for money, for politicians, is determined partly by institutional factors which influence both the levels of competition between the parties and within parties (e.g. whether they are single-candidate constituencies or not, use of the preference vote, etc.) and the number of elections (e.g. factors such as the levels of government, existence of primary elections, number of elective chambers, etc.). Alongside the institutional variables there are, however, variables of a cultural nature which define the models for the organization of the consensus. In particular, many cases indicate that the costs of politics increase where political integration is based on the distribution of material resources through clientelistic exchanges.

It is not new for clientelism and corruption to be considered as 'related' phenomena, almost indistinguishable even from each other. There are, however, good reasons to consider the two concepts as analytically separate. In the first place, there is a considerable difference in the medium of barter. In fact, while political corruption involves the trading of public decisions for money, clientelism, on the contrary, barters protection for consensus (Weingrod, 1968: 379). This difference leads to other differences relating both to the relationships between the protagonists and to the structure of the barter. First, although the barter is a two-way process in both cases, only in the case of clientelism is it possible to determine a vertical distinction with the subordination of clients to a patron. Furthermore, while the patron/client relationship is based on a generalized exchange relating to unspecified services, political corruption, on the other hand, is an exchange of a financial type, with an immediate and well-defined payback. This also has certain consequences for the mechanism by which such services are repaid; in the case of clientelism the repayment is guaranteed by personal obligations and gratitude (Graziano, 1980), while in the case of corruption it is linked more to a choice of instrumental rationality linked to the expectation of a replay of the 'game' (Vannucci, 1993a). Also linked to the medium – money versus consensus – is another difference between the two phenomena: the different degree of perceived illegality. In fact, whereas the protagonists in a corrupt exchange know they are committing illegal actions – and therefore tend to conceal them more – clientelistic practices (including the custom of pulling strings) have long been considered as legal and are therefore carried out in the light of day.

If, therefore, the two phenomena are to be kept separate from an analytical viewpoint, on an empirical level, in countries with histories as diverse as Spain, Italy and Japan, corruption develops *together* with political clientelism. It can be added that the co-presence of corruption and clientelism is not fortuitous, but rather is linked to certain complementary aspects of the two phenomena, and to the similarity in their causal dynamics.

In the first place, both clientelism and corruption – at least in the forms that we have analysed – entail *exchange relationships*, i.e. interaction based on extrinsic or instrumental benefits, as opposed, therefore, to those relationships of an 'ideological nature' which are based on intrinsic or expressive benefits (Graziano, 1980). As noted with reference to the Japanese case, in the clientelistic structure of consensus, the politician must guarantee his electorate a series of services which range from the organization of recreational activities to a financial contribution at the key points in their lives (weddings, funerals, etc.). To be able to offer these services, the politician must construct a very complex electoral apparatus which, with reference still to Japan, is composed of thousands of clubs and hundreds of local federations. Lastly, a proportion of the votes are bought, in Japan as in Italy, through the good offices of various mediators who hold entire 'packages' of electoral votes. We can add that both clientelism and corruption require a similar *structure of values*.

The emphasis on instrumental friendship is typical not only of corrupt exchanges, but also of clientelistic relationships where 'actions which are clearly a repayment of services given by a client to a patron are described as being given out of friendship'. In Spain *amiguismo* leads to a search for intermediaries – patrons or corrupt politicians – who can facilitate contacts with the public administration. In Japan, identification with one's own community prevents any recognition of a broader collective welfare, leading to the bartering of votes or bribes with those political mediators who can guarantee the flow of resources from the centre to the periphery. As has already been noted in other research studies, the Italian cases also show that the main players in corruption are very skilful at developing personal contacts, satisfying needs and doing favours, appearing friendly and affable, and even going as far as adopting the gift-giving strategy, as mentioned in the Japanese case.[5] Corrupt public administrators, as well as entrepreneurs who pay bribes and citizen-clients, seem to share the belief that it is fair to use public means as private resources. Clientelism and corruption appear, therefore, to be based on the vestiges of patrimonialism, visible, for instance, in the hereditary political careers of Japanese politicians, or in the personalized management of Franco-African relationships, or in the private financing of public administrators mentioned with reference to past history in Russia and Spain.

To conclude, both clientelism and corruption stand at the crossroads where two interacting demands meet. On the one hand, both corruption and clientelism imply a privatization of politics by public administrators, i.e. utilization of access to political authority as a private resource (Graziano, 1978). On the other hand, both clients and entrepreneurs involved in corruption demonstrate a pattern of preferences oriented towards individual activity. With this in mind, an antidote to corruption should therefore also be sought in a country's political culture, and particularly in the spread of those civic values referred to in the case of England.

Whereas this last solution requires the lengthy time span necessary for any cultural change, in the short term it is more feasible to manipulate another variable which affects the cost of politics: the potential outlay, particularly with reference to expenditure on electoral campaigns. In this instance, as well, the English case seems to offer a positive example, thanks to the rigorous restriction of electoral expenditure established at the end of the last century.

Public administration and corruption

With reference to the structure of values, particular mention is made, in studies on political corruption, of the culture of public bureaucrats: team spirit and ethics in public service (i.e. the belief that public service must be performed in an impersonal, impartial and efficient way) are among the elements – mentioned in the German and English cases – which discourage such officials from taking part in corrupt exchanges by increasing their moral cost. Still within the area of public administration, we can also mention other variables which certainly have an effect on the opportunities for political corruption. Here too, the hypotheses that have been formulated so far are partly contradictory.

A first variable, often used to explain political corruption, is the *growth of intervention by the state*. It has been said that, on the one hand, the growing number of rules and regulations and, on the other, the ever-increasing availability of money in the public sector, increase the opportunities for corruption, by providing incentives for private individuals and at the same time opportunities for public officials. The opportunities for corruption emanate, it is said, from the increased number of decisions now made through political rather than market mechanisms. Corruption is therefore encouraged by phenomena such as the extension of welfare programmes, an increase in the relative dimensions of the public sectors and the proliferation of laws and regulations.

The cases assembled in this volume show, in effect, that political corruption tends to be frequent in *areas where political decisions have greater weight*. The opportunities for corruption have appeared, in fact, to be particularly prevalent in those sectors where public expenditure is higher and where measures taken by the public administration have greater influence. In these sectors, the frequency of relationships between the public and private protagonists supports a sort of institutionalization of bribery.[6] It must be added, however, that the actual point of privatization and deregulation – in the new Federal Germany, or in the UK or in Russia – seems to be characterized by an increase in the opportunities for corruption.

A second characteristic in the evolution of public administration, mentioned as favouring the expansion of corruption, is *administrative decentralization*. The increase in the number of public bodies appears to lead to a similar growth in the number of potential areas for corrupt decisions – as observed, for example, with reference to the creation of 17 autonomous regions in Spain. Furthermore, local bodies seem to have a potential advantage as arenas for corrupt exchanges, given the high number of individualized regulations. As has been shown in Italy and Japan, for example, an increased capacity for expenditure at the periphery, without the possibility of raising taxes, leads to a lack of responsibility among local administrators. At the periphery, furthermore, it is easier to avoid any control by central bureaucracies – as demonstrated in English history by the scandals which affected the East India Company, involving a new bureaucratic apparatus far from any control exerted by the centre. It must be observed, however, that centralization of power can also produce opportunities for corruption, as shown both by the 'monarchic' power of the French mayors and by the personalized nature of decisions in Franco-African relationships, traditionally considered the sphere of action of the President of the Republic. In general, in fact, the smaller the number of people involved in a decision, the lower the risk of being reported.

It can be added that, in each case, the degree to which state intervention and administrative decentralization affect the development of political corruption is determined by other conditions in the organization and in the bureaucratic procedures. The information presented in the analyses of individual national cases suggests, in particular, the importance of three linked themes: the discretionary nature of the administrative powers, the control structures, and the transparency of administrative action. One can, in the first instance, observe that cases of bribery have been found in the course of contracts – entailing money payments by the public administration – awarded by different procedures.[7] As seen in the case of Italy, notwithstanding the complex rules which regulate decisions on expenditure by public bodies, businesses which are prepared to pay a bribe can be helped to win contracts through various mechanisms, according to the type of allocation procedures selected beforehand. Among these mechanisms there is the invitation to tender, the distribution of information on secret index cards relating to the minimum and maximum amounts fixed by the commissions, the distribution of information on the criteria used by the commission to evaluate 'the best offer', the distribution of information on offers already received from other competitors.

Corruption seems, therefore, *easier when the administrative decisions are more arbitrary*. Frequently, corrupt administrators try, in fact, to increase the possibilities of employing less restrictive procedures.[8] From this point of view, for example, the emergency procedures employed during national disasters – ranging from typhoons in Japan to earthquakes in Italy – clearly increase the risks of malversation. An increase in the opportunities for corruption also seems to occur with those administrative procedures which delegate public duties to private businesses – such as, in France, associations that come under the Act of 1901. In other words, corruption may be facilitated in those private businesses which manage public funds with fewer procedural constraints and controls, or in *state agencies* which are supposed to operate with entrepreneurial objectives, like the UK quangos,.

In modern bureaucracies, a complex *control structure* should punish any subversion of discretionary power into arbitrariness. With respect to controls, the Italian cases also allow us to make certain observations. A first observation, based particularly on the case of France, but also confirmed in the case of Spain (and by contrast in the case of the UK) is that the accumulation of administrative mandates increases the possibilities for corruption to the extent to which it increases the number of situations with objective conflicts of interest, reducing, furthermore, the possibilities for any cross-controls to function effectively. A second observation is that the proliferation of purely formal controls seems useless and even counterproductive. As seen with reference to both Italy and France, formal controls not only impede the discovery of cases of political corruption but they also create the need for loopholes, thereby encouraging the spread of informal procedures which favour corruption. Conversely, the possibilities of discovering cases of bad administration – thereby increasing the costs of corruption in terms of the risks of discovery and punishment – are increased by a system of substantial controls on the efficiency and effectiveness of administrative decisions.

Alongside substantial controls, an important element in reducing the opportunities for corruption is the 'transparency' of the decision-making process. On examining our national cases, we can observe, for example, that the opportunities for corruption increase where there is less control by public opinion. In the course of decision-making processes concerning military expenditures (referred to in the German case) or prison construction (examples of which can be found in the Italian case), the 'confidentiality' of the dealings, requested ostensibly for reasons of national security, appears to have facilitated the spread of bribery. In an analogous fashion, opportunities for corruption seemed to be very considerable, both in the French and Italian cases, in the aid policies for developing countries, the effects of which are not easily visible, objectively speaking, to public opinion in the investing countries.

The reference to transparency in the decision-making process in public decisions leads to the last element to emerge from our comparative analysis of the various national cases: the role played, in the growth of corruption, by various informal and often secret networks. In the discussion on political corruption in Russia, we have noticed the importance of the widespread existence of informal networks of relationships – often including criminal groups – which occupy the void left by the lack of a state power, and which manage independently the relationships between the centre and the periphery. Both studies on the Italian case underline the close interweaving, particularly in the south of the country, between corrupt politicians and criminal powers, such as *mafia, camorra* and *'ndrangheta*. With reference to Franco-African politics, mention has been made, for instance, of the influence of a network of Gaullist activists originating from the resistance and underground groups which were active during the period of Nazi occupation and the Vichy Republic. Still with reference to French politics in Africa – but also with reference to many countries in Mediterranean Europe and Latin America, including one of the most recent scandals in Italy – mention may be made of the role sometimes played by intelligence agents in the development of secret exchanges.

In both the Italian and French cases, we can highlight the role played in organizing more or less legal dealings by some masonic lodges. We can conclude, therefore, by observing that important functions in the widening spread of corruption are played by various networks of power, characterized by secrecy: 'transverse' involvement of politicians from different parties, entrepreneurs, public officials, professionals; selective membership procedures which consolidate the relationships between members.

Corruption and democracy: a final note

As already observed in the introduction to this volume, political corruption endangers the very functioning of democracy. Our comparative analysis has allowed us to specify some of the mechanisms through which corruption weakens democracy: the proliferation of 'business' politicians interested in their own personal enrichment, rather than in the preparation of general programmes; the invasion of society and of the market by political parties, which have become 'guarantors' of corrupt exchanges; the transformation of citizens into 'clients' and the increasing discrimination against those citizens not prepared to pay bribes; the partiality of the public administration; the growth of a secret, invisible, illegitimate power. However, we would like to add – and not only so that we can end on a note of optimism – that the democracies studied in this volume are far from being destroyed by increasing corruption.

If one of the strengths of democracy lies in its ability to reform itself, it seems to us that the aspect of political corruption is no exception to the rule. The degree of alarm shown by public opinion has called attention to the problem and to the legislative, administrative and judicial intervention aimed at reducing the occurrence of administrative illegalities. Those cases where political corruption has been shown to be most widespread – in Italy, above all – seem to demonstrate that a deep understanding of the dynamics of the phenomenon can bring about effective projects of reform. We hope that with this volume we shall have contributed to this understanding.

Notes

1. Useful collections of papers on political corruption, although not concentrating on Western democracies, are those edited by Heidenheimer (1970) and Heidenheimer, Johnston and Le Vine (1989). Gardiner and Olson (1974), Benson, Maaren and Heslop (1978), Gardiner and Lyman (1978) concentrate on political corruption in the United States.
2. In other words, the assembled decisions taken by subversive political forces operating underground, in contact with the secret services (Bobbio, 1987).
3. For a detailed explanation on this point, see also Mény (1992a) for France, and Pinto-Duschinsky (1981) for the UK.
4. On the German case, see also Roth, 1995. On corruption and 'consociative' democracy in Belgium, see Frognier, 1986.
5. In a research study on cases of corruption in Great Britain (Chibnall and Saunders, 1977) it has been noted that this conception of politics functions as a 'neutralizing technique' allowing corrupted and corruptors to justify their own conduct as not illegal, though not strictly orthodox.
6. Johnson (1986) has described, on this subject, some peculiar characteristics of 'routine' corruption vis-à-vis 'extraordinary' corruption.
7. Diego Gambetta (1988c) has demonstrated by a deductive process that it is possible to find mechanisms suitable for circumventing even the most complex procedures in the awarding of contracts.
8. On this point, see also Banfield (1975).

SELECT BIBLIOGRAPHY

Adonis, A., *Making Aristocracy Work: The Peerage and the Political System in Britain 1884–1914*, Oxford, Clarendon Press, 1993.

Alatas, S. H., *Corruption: Nature, Causes, Consequences and Functions*, Aldershot, Averbury Press, 1990.

Albaladejo Campoy, Miguel, 'Pasado, Presenta y Futuro de la Función española. Una propuesta de reforma', *Cuadernos Económircos de ICE*, 13, 1980.

Alemann, U. (von), 'Bureaucratic and political corruption controls: reassessing the German record' in Heidenheimer, A. J., Johnston, M. and Le Vine, V. (eds) *Political Corruption, a Handbook*, New Brunswick, Transaction Publishers, 1989, 855–69.

Alonso Zaldivar C. et Castells M., *Spain Beyond Myths*, Madrid, Espasa Calpe, 1992.

Alvarez Alvarez, Julián, *Burocracia y poder politico en el régimen franquista*, Madrid, Instituto Nacional de Administración Pública, 1984.

Alvarez Conde, E., *El régimen político español*, Madrid, Technos, 1990 (4th edn).

Amodia, J., 'Taxinomia e inestabilidad del sistema de partidos en España', *Journal of the Association of Contemporary Iberian Studies*, 3(1), 1990.

Arlacchi, P., *Mafia et compagnie, l'éthique mafiosa et l'esprit du capitalisme*, Grenoble, PUG, 1986.

—, *Gli uomini del diesonore*, Milan, Mondadori, 1992.

Badie, B., *L'État importé*, Paris, Fayard, 1992.

Baena de Alcázar, Miguel and Pizarro, Narciso, 'The structure of the

Spanish power elite, 1939–1975, Florence, *Eui Working Paper*, 55, 1982.

Balfour, S., *Dictatorship, Workers and the City*, Oxford, Oxford University Press, 1989.

Banfield, E. C., *The Moral Basis of a Backward Society*, New York, Free Press, 1967.

Banfield, E. C., 'Corruption as a feature of governmental organization', *Journal of Law and Economics*, 18(3), 587–606, 1975.

—, *Political Influence*, New York, Greenwood Press, 1981.

—, and Wilson, J. Q., *City Politics*, Cambridge (Mass.), Harvard University Press, 1967.

Bar Cendón, A., 'Normalidad o excepcionalidad? Para una tipologia del sistema de partidos español, 1977–1982', *Sistema*, 65, 1985.

Bauer, P., *Ideologie und politische Beteiligung in der Bundesrepublik Deutschland. Eine empirische Untersuchung politischer überzeugungssysteme*, Opladen, 1993.

Bayart, J.-F., *La politique africaine de François Mitterrand*, Paris, Karthala, 1984.

—, 'Fin de partie au sud du Sahara? La politique africaine de la France', in Michailof, F., *La France et l'Afrique, vade-mecum pour un nouveau voyage*, Paris, Karthala, 1993.

Becker, G. S., 'Crime and Punishment', in Becker, G. S., *The Economic Approach to Human Behavior*, Chicago and London, University of Chicago Press, 1976.

Beenstock, M. 'Corruption and Development', *World Development*, 7, 15–24, 1979.

Befu, H., *Bribery in Japan. When Law Tangles with Culture*, Berkeley, University of California Press, 1971.

Beltrán Villalva, M., 'La administración pública y los funcionarios', in Giner, S. (ed.), *España. Sociedad y Política*, Madrid, Espasa Calpe, 1990.

Ben-Ami, S., *Fascism from Above*, Oxford, Clarendon Press, 1983.

Benson, B. L., *The Enterprise of Law. Justice Without the State*, San Francisco, Pacific Research Institute for Public Policy, 1990.

—, and Baden, J., 'The political economy of governmental corruption: the logic of underground government', *Journal of Legal Studies*, 14, 391–410, 1985.

Benson, G. C., Maaren, S. A. and Heslop, A., *Political Corruption in America*, Lexington, Lexington D.C., 1978.

Beyme, K. (von), *Die politische Klasse im Parteienstaat*, Frankfurt, 1993.

Bobbio, N., 'Are they Alternatives to Representative Government?', *Telos*, 35, 1987.

Bouissou, J.-M., 'Corruption à la japonaise', *L'Histoire*, 142, 38–45, 1991.

—, 'La politique conviviale au quotidien. Une étude des machines politiques des parlementaires japonais', in Bouissou, J.-M. (ed.), *L'envers du consensus. Les conflits et leur gestion dans le Japon contemporain*, Paris, Presses de la Fondation Nationale des Sciences Politiques, 1994.

Brock, M., *The Great Reform Act*, London, Cassell 1973.

Brunel, S., *Le gaspillage de l'aide publique*, Paris, Le Seuil, 1993.

Buchanan, J., Tollison, R. D. and Tullock, G. (eds), *Toward a theory of rent-seeking society*, Texas A&M University Press, 1980.

Butler, D., Adonis, A. and Travers, T., *Government Revealed: the Politics of the Poll Tax*, Oxford, Clarendon Press, 1994.

Cadot, O., 'Corruption as a gamble', *Journal of Public Economics*, 33, 223–44, 1987.

Caiden, G. E. and Caiden, N. J., 'Administrative Corruption', *Public Administration Review*, 37, 301–8, 1977.

Carlucci, A., *Tangentomani. Storie, affari e tutti i documenti sui barbari che hanno saccheggiato Milano*, Milan, Baldini e Castoldi, 1992.

Carr, R., *Spain, 1808–1975*, Oxford, Clarendon Press, 1982 (4th edn).

Cartier-Bresson, J., 'Eléments d'analyse pour une économie de la corruption', *Revue Tiers Monde*, 131, 581—609, 1992.

—, 'Corruption, pouvoir discrétionnaire et rentes', *Le Débat*, 77, 26–32, 1993.

Casanova, J., 'Modernization and democratization: Reflections on Spain's transition to democracy', *Social Research*, 1983.

Cavero, J., *El PSOE contra la prensa*, Madrid, Temas de Hoy, 1991.

CEAN/Institut Charles de Gaulle, *La politique africaine du général de Gaulle*, Paris, Pédone, 1980.

Chibnall, S. and Saunders, P., 'Worlds apart: Notes on the social reality of corruption', *British Journal of Sociology*, 28, 138–54.

Constantin, C. and Coulon, C., 'La difficile décolonisation de la diplomatie africaine', in CEAN, *L'évolution récente du pouvoir en Afrique*, Bordeaux, 1977.

Curtis, G., *The Japanese Way of Politics*, New York, Columbia University Press, 1988.

Dahl, R., *Who Governs?*, New Haven, Yale University Press, 1961.

Dahrendorf, R., *Gesellschaft und Demokratie in Deutschland*, Munich, 1965.

Della Porta, D., 'La logica della corruzione in Italia', *Il Mulino*, 40, 902–15, 1991.

—, *Lo scambio occulto. Casi di corruzione politica in Italia*, Bologna, Il Mulino, 1992.

Della Porta, D. and Vannucci, A., *Corruzione politica e amministrasione publica. Resorse, meccassismi e Horí*, Bologna, Il Mulino, 1994.

—, 'Corruzione e carriere politiche: immagini sui "politici d'affari"', *Stato e mercato*, 34, 35–61, 1995.

Doig, A., *Corruption and Misconduct in Contemporary British Politics in Modern Britain*, Harmondsworth, Penguin, 1984.

Easton, D., 'A Reassessment of the Concept of Political Support', *British Journal of Political Science*, 26, 435–57, 1975.

Eisenstadt, S. N. and Ronigen, L., *Patrons, Clients and Friends. Interpersonal Relations and the Structure of Trust in Society*, Cambridge, Cambridge University Press, 1984.

Elias, N., *Studien über die Deutschen. Machtkämpfe und Habitusentwicklung im 19- und 20- Jahrhundert*, Frankfurt, Suhr Kamp, 335–62, 1992.

Emerson, R., 'Social exchange theory', *Annual Review of Sociology*, 1976.

Eschenburg, T., 'Der bürokratische Rückhalt', in Lowenthal, R. and Schwarz, H. P. (eds) *Die zweite Republik, 25 Jahre Bundesrepublik Deutschland – eine Bilanz*, Stuttgart, 1974.

Esteban, J. (de), *El Estado de la Constitución (Diez años de gobierno socialista)*, Madrid, Libertarias/Prodhufi, 1992.

—, and López Guerra, L., *Los partidos políticos en la España actual*, Barcelona, Planeta/Instituto de Estudios Económicos, 1982.

Falcone, G. (in collaboration with Padovani, M.), *Cose di Cosa Nostra*, Milan, Rizzoli, 1991.

FIPE (Federazione italiana pubblici esercenti), 'Malati di tangente', 1992.

Frognier, A. P., 'Corruption and consociational democracy: First thoughts on the Belgian case'. *Corruption and Reform*, 1, 143–8.

Gambetta, D., 'Apologia della proporzionale', *Biblioteca della libertà*, 101, 95–106, 1988a.

—, 'Fragments of an economic theory of the mafia', *Archives européennes de sociologie*, 29, 127–45, 1988b.

—, Anatomía della tangerite, *Mezichiana*, 4, 237–47, 1988.

—, *La mafia siciliana. Un industria della protezione privata*, Turin, Einaudi, 1992.

Gardiner, J. A. and Olson, D. J. (eds), *Theft of the City*, Bloomington, Indiana University Press, 1974.

—, and Lyman, T. R., *Decisions for Sale? Corruption and Reform in Law Use and Building Regulations*, New York, Praeger.

Glees, A., 'The Flick Affair: a hint of corruption in the Bonn Republic', *Corruption and Reform*, 111–26, 1987.

—, 'Political Scandals in West Germany', *Corruption and Reform*, 262–76, 1988.

Gombeaud, J.-L., Moutot, C. and Smith, S., *La guerre du cacao, histoire secrète d'un embargo*, Paris, Calmann-Lévy, 1990.

Graziano, L., 'Center-periphery relations and the Italian crisis. The problem of clientelism.' in Tarrow, S., Katzenstein, P. and Graziano, L. (eds), *Territorial Politics in Industrial Nations*, New York, Praeger, 290–326.

—, *Clientelismo e sistema politico. Il caso dell'Italia*, Milan, Angeli, 1980.

Gunther, R., 'Política y cultura en España', *Cuadernos y Debates*, 36, Madrid, Centro de Estudios Constitucionales, 1992.

Gwyn, W. B., *Democracy and the Cost of Politics in Britain*, Oxford, Oxford University Press, 1962.

Heiberg, M., *The Making of the Basque Nation*, Cambridge, Cambridge University Press, 1989.

Heidenheimer, A. J. (ed.), *Political Corruption: Readings in Comparative Analysis*, New Brunswick, Transaction Publishers, 1970.

—, Johnston, M. and Le Vine, V. T. (eds) *Political Corruption, a Handbook*, New Brunswick, Transaction Publishers, 1989.

Herr, R., *An Historical Essay on Modern Spain*, Berkeley, University of California Press, 1971.

Heywood, P., 'The Socialist Party in power, 1982–1992: the price of progress', *Journal of the Association of Contemporary Iberian Studies*, 5(2), 1992.

Higuchi, Y. and Sautter, C. (eds), *L'État et l'individu au Japon*, Paris, Presses de l'EHESS, 1990.

Hirschman, A. O., *Exit, Voice, and Loyalty*, Cambridge (Mass.), Harvard University Press, 1970.

—, *Bonheur privé, action publique*, Paris, Fayard, 1983.

Hrebenar, R., *The Japanese Party System*, Boulder (Colorado), Westview Press, 1986.

Huntington, S. P., *Political Order in Changing Societies*, New Haven, Yale, University Press, 1968.

—, 'Modernisation and corruption', in Heidenheimer, A. J., Johnston, M. and Le Vine, V. T. (eds), *Political Corruption, a Handbook*, New Brunswick, Transaction Publishers, 1989.

Iwai, T., *Seidji Shikin no Kenkyu*, Tokyo, Nihon Keizai, 1990.

Jagannathan, N. V., 'Corruption, delivery systems, and property rights', *World Development*, 14(1), 127–32, 1986.

Johnson, C., 'Tanaka Kakuei, Structural Corruption and the Advent of Machine Politics in Japan', *Journal of Japanese Studies*, 12, 1–28, 1986.

Julia, S., 'The ideological conversion of the leaders of the PSOE, 1976–1979', in Lannon, F. and Preston, P. (eds), *Elites and Powers in Twentieth Century Spain: Essays in Honour of Sir Raymond Carr*, Oxford, Clarendon Press, 1990.

Kern, R., *Liberals, Reformers and Caciques in Restoration Spain 1875–1909*, Albuquerque, University of New Mexico Press, 1974.

Kishimoto, K., *Politics in Modern Japan. Development and Organization*, Tokyo, Japan Echo, 1988.

Klitgaard, R., *Controlling Corruption*, University of California Press, 1988.

—, 'Incentive myopia', *World Development*, 17(4), 447–59, 1989.

Kohno, M. and Nishizawa, Y. 'A Study of Electoral Business Cycle in Japan. Elections and Government Spending on Public Construction', *Comparative Politics*, 151–66, 1990.

Krasner, S. 'Sovereignty, an institutional perspective', *Comparative Political Studies*, 21, 66–94, 1988.

Lacam, J.-P., 'De la relation de clientèle au clientélisme: les théories revistées', thesis, Bordeaux I, 1993.

Lafay, J. D., 'L'économie de la corruption', *Analyses de la SEDEIS*, 74, 62–6, 1990.

Lamothe, Ph., 'Le Centrafrique de Bokassa: un pouvoir néo-patrimonial', mémoire de DEA, CEAN-IEP, Bordeaux, 1982.

Landfried, C., *Parteifinanzen und politische Macht. Eine vergleichende Studie zur Bundesrepublik Deutschland, zu Italien und den USA*, Baden-Baden, Nomos, 1990.

Lawson, K. and Merkl, P. (eds), *When Parties Fail*, Princeton, Princeton University Press, 1988.

Lehmbruch, G., *Parteienwettbewerb im Bundesstaat*, Stuttgart, Kohlhammer, 1976.

Loïma, A., 'Les embûches de la transition en Russie: corruption et pratiques mafieuses', *Le Courrier des pays de l'Est*, 381, 20–36, 1993.

Lopez Pintor, R. and Wert Ortega, J. I., 'La otra España: insolidaridad e intolerencias en la tradicion', *Revista Española de Investigaciones Sociologicas*, 19, 1982.

Lui, F. T., 'An equilibrium queuing model of bribery', *Journal of Political Economy*, 93(4), 760–81, 1985.

—, 'A dynamic model of corruption deterrence', *Journal of Public Economics*, 31, 215–36, 1986.

Macrae, J., 'Underdevelopment and the economics of corruption: a game theory approach', *World Development*, 10(8), 677-87, 1982.

Marion, P., *La mission impossible, à la tête des services secrets*, Paris, Calmann-Lévy, 1991.

Marseille, J., *Empire colonial et capitalisme français, histoire d'un divorce*, Paris, Albin Michel, 1984.

Martin, C. and Stronach, B., *Politics East and West. A Comparison of Japanese and British Political Culture*, New York, M. E. Sharpe, 1992.

Martin-Retortillo Baquer, L., 'Pervivencias del "spoil system" en la España actual', *Anuario de Derecho Constitucional y Parlamentario*, 4, 1992.

Mastropaolo, A., 'Scambio politico e ceto politico', *Democrazia e diritto*, 27, 27–62, 1987.

Médard, J.-F., 'Le changement dans la continuité, la conférence des chefs d'État de France et d'Afrique', *Politique Africaine*, (5), 1976.

—, 'The underdeveloped state in tropical Africa; political clientelism or neo-patrimonialism?', in Clapham, C. (ed.), *Private Power and Public Policy*, London, Pinter, 1982.

—, 'L'État néo-patrimonial en Afrique', in Médard, J.-F., *États d'Afrique*, Paris, Karthala, 1991.

Mendras, M., *Un État pour la Russie*, Bruxelles, Complexe, 1992.

Mény, Y., *La corruption de la République*, Paris, Fayard, 1992a.

—, 'Corruption et politique', *Esprit*, 186, 68–75, 1992b.

Miralles, M. and Satue, F., *Alfonso Guerra: El Conspirador*, Madrid, Temas de Hoy, 1991.

Nas, T. F., Price, A. C. and Weber, C. T., 'A policy-oriented theory of corruption', *American Political Science Review*, 80(1), 107–119, 1986.

Nieto Garcia, A., *La organización del desgobierno*, Barcelona, Ariel, 1984.

Nye, J. S. 'Corruption and political development: a cost-benefit analysis', *American Political Science Review*, 61(2), 417–27, 1967.

Padioleau, J., 'De la corruption dans les oligarchies pluralistes', *Revue Française de Sociologie*, 16(1), 33–58, 1975.

—, *L'ordre social*, Paris, L'Harmattan, 1986.

Pantaleone, M., *L'industria del potere*, Bologna, Cappelli editore, 1984.

Parisi, A. and Pasquino, G., 'Relazioni partiti-elettori e tipi di voto', in Pasquino, G. (ed.) *Il sistema politico italiano*, Bari, Laterza, 74–97, 1985.

Parliamentary Anti-Mafia Commission, *Testo integrafe della relasione sui rapportitra Cose Nostra e le politica*, approved 6 April 1993, supplement in *la Repubblica*, 10 April 1993, 1993a.

Parliamentary Anti-Mafia Commission, report of court hearings of

Tommasso Buscetta, Leonardo Messina and Gaspare Mutolo, 'Mafia e Potere', supplement in *l'Unita*, 15 April 1993, 1993b.

Pasquino, G., *La Repubblica e cittadini ombra*, Milan, Garzanti, 1991.

Payne, S., *The Franco Regime, 1936–1975*, Madison, University of Wisconsin Press, 1987.

Péan, P., *Affaires africaines*, Paris, Fayard, 1983.

—, *L'homme de l'ombre*, Paris, Stock, 1990.

Pérez-Días, V., *The Return of Civil Society*, Cambridge (Mass.), Harvard University Press, 1993.

Pinto-Duschinsky, M., *British Political Finance 1830–1980*, London, Macmillan, 1981.

Pipes, R., *Russia under the Old Regime*, London, Penguin Books, 1974.

Pizzorno, A., 'I due poteri dei partiti', *Politica del diritto*, 2, 197–209, 1971.

—, 'La corruzione nel sistema politico', in Della Porta, D., *Lo scambio occulto*, Bologna, Il Mulino, 1992.

—, and Della Porta, D., 'Geschäftspolitiker in Italien Uberlegungen im Anschluß an eine Studie über politische Korruption', *Kölner Zeitschrift für Soziologie und Sozialpsychologie*, 45(3), 1993.

Plumb, J. H., *Walpole*, London, Macmillan, 1973.

Preston, P., *The Coming of the Spanish Civil War*, London, Macmillan, 1978.

—, *The Triumph of Democracy in Spain*, London, Methuen, 1986.

—, *Franco: A Biography*, London, HarperCollins, 1993.

Public Prosecutor's Office, Naples, 'Richiesta di autorizzazione a procedere pervenuta alla camera il 7 aprile 1993', supplement in *la Repubblica*, 15 April 1993, 1993.

—, Palermo, 'Richiesta per l'applicazione di misure cautelari, no. 2789/90 NC, 1990.

—, Palermo, 'Domanda di autorizzazione a procedere contro il senatore Giulio Andreotti, 27 March 1993', *Panorama*, 11 April 1993.

Ramirez, P., *La rosa y el capullo*, Barcelona, Planeta, 1990.

Ramseyer, M. and McCall-Rosenbluth, F., *Japan's Political Marketplace*, Cambridge (Mass.), Harvard University Press, 1993.

Reed, M., 'Gabon: a neo-colonial enclave of enduring French interest', *Journal of Modern African Studies*, 25(2), 1987.

Reed, S., *Making Common Sense of Japan*, Pittsburgh, Pittsburgh University Press, 1993.

Reuter, P., *Disorganized Crime, the Economics of Visible Hand*, Cambridge (Mass.), MIT Press, 1983.

Robinson, M. R., 'The British method of dealing with political corruption', in Heidenheimer, A. J. (ed.), *Political Corruption: Readings in Comparative Analysis*, London, Transaction Books, 1978.

Rogow, A. A. and Lasswell, H. D., 'Game politicians and gain politicians', in Gardiner, J. A. and Olson, D. J. (eds), *Theft of the City*, Bloomington, Indiana University Press, 289–97, 1974.

Roth, R., 'Politische Korruption in der Bundesrepublik – Notizen zum einem verdrängler', in Fleck, C. and Kuzmics, H. (eds), *Korruption. Zur Sozologie nicht immer abweichenden Verhaltens*, Frankfurt am Main, Athenaeum, 143–59, 1985.

Rose-Ackerman, S., *Corruption: A Study in Political Economy*, New York, Academic Press, 1978.

Rubin, P., 'The economic theory of the criminal firm', in Rottenberg, D. (ed.), *The Economics of Crime and Punishment*, Washington (DC), American Enterprise Institute for Public Policy Research, 1973.

Salmon, K., *The Modern Spanish Economy*, London, Pinter, 1991.

Santino, U. and La Fiura, G., *L'impresa mafiosa*, Milan, Angeli, 1990.

Sasago, K., *Seiji Shikin*, Tokyo, Gendai Kyoiku Bunko, 1989.

Sartori, G., 'La politica comparata: premesse e problemi', *Rivista italiana di scienza politica*, 1, 7–66, 1971.

Scheuch, H. and Scheuch, U., *Clinquen, Klingel und Karrieren*, Reinbek, 1992.

Schwarz, H. P., 'Die Ära Adenauer', in Bracher, K. D., Eschenburg, T., Fest, J. C. and Jäckel, E. (eds), *Geschichte der Bundesrepublik Deutschland, vol 3*, 261–72, Stuttgart, F. A. Brockhans, 1983.

Scott, J., *Comparative Political Corruption*, Englewood Cliffs, Prentice Hall, 1972.

Searle, G. R., *Corruption in British Politics 1895–1930*, Oxford, Clarendon Press, 1987.

Seibel, W., 'Necessary illusions: the transformation of governance structures in the New Germany', *Revue Tocqueville*, 13, 178–97, 1992.

Senato della Repubblica, XI legislatura, 'Richiesta di autorizzazione a procedere contro il senatore Severino Citaristi', Doc. 4, n. 113, 1992.

Shackleton, J. R., 'Corruption: an essay in economic analysis' *Political Quarterly*, 49, 25–37, 1978.

Smith, S. and Glaser, A., *Ces messieurs Afrique, le Paris-village du continent noir*, Paris, Calmann-Lévy, 1992.

Staudhammer, R., 'Bananen Republik Deutschland? Parteienfinanzierung im Zwielicht von Korruptionsaffären und Skandalgeschichten. Das Beispiel BRD', *Kriminalsoziologische Bibliographie*, 12, 44–73, 1985.

Subirats, J., 'Modernizing the Spanish Public Administration or

Reform in Disguise', Barcelona, Instituto de Ciencias Politicas y Sociales, Working Papers, (20) 1990.

Tezanos, J. F., 'El papel social y politico del PSOE en la España de los años ochenta. Una década de progreso y democracia', in Guerra, A. and Tezanos, J. F. (eds), *La década del cambio*, Madrid, Editorial Sistema, 1992.

Times Mirror Group Center for the People and the Press, *The Pulse of Europe: a survey of political and social values and attitudes*, Los Angeles, Times Mirror Center, 1991.

Tilman, R., 'Emergence of black-market bureaucracy: administration, development, and corruption in the new states', *Public Administration Review*, 28(5), 437–43, 1968.

Toharia, J. J., *Cambios recientes en la sociedad española*, Madrid, Instituto de Estudios Economicos, 1989.

Tollison, R. D., 'Rent-seeking: a survey', *Kyklos*, 35(4), 575–602, 1982.

Tribunale di Palermo, Sentence no. 411/90/RG, 17 January 1992.

Tullock, G., *The Economics of Special Privilege and Rent-seeking*, Kluwer Academic Publishers, 1989.

Tusell, J. and Sinova, J., *El secuestro de la democracia*, Barcelona, Plaza y Janés, 1990.

Vaksberg, A., *La mafia russe. Comment on dévalise le pays depuis 70 ans*, Paris, Albin Michel, 1992.

Van Wolferen, K., *L'énigme de la puissance japonaise*, Paris, Laffont, 1989.

Vannucci, A., 'Scambi e collusioni: analisi di un caso', *Il Progetto*, 74, 75–86, 1993a.

—, 'Fenomenologia della tangente: la razionalità degli scambi occulti', *Etica degli affari e delle professioni*, supplement in *L'impresa*, 1(3), 30–42, 1993b.

Wade, R., 'The system of administrative and political corruption: canal irrigation in South India', *The Journal of Development Studies*, 18(3), 287–328, 1982.

—, 'The market for public office: why the Indian state is not better at development', *World Development*, 13(4), 467–97, 1985.

Weber, M., *Economia e società*, Milan, Edizioni di Communità, 1981 (1st edn, 1922).

—, 'Politik als Beruf', in Weber, M., *Gesammelte Politische Schriften*. Tübingen, 493–548, 1958 (1st edn 1919).

Weingrod, A., 'Patron, patronage and political parties', *Comparative Studies in Society and History*, 10, 376–400, 1968.

Werner, S. B., 'New directions in the study of administrative corruption', *Public Administration Review*, 43, 146–54, 1983.

Wewer, G., 'Prolegomena zu einer Untersuchung der Korruption', in Benz, A., Seibel, W. (eds), *Zwischen Kooperation und Korruption. Abweichendes Verhalten in der Verwaltung*, Baden-Baden, Nomos, 295–324, 1992.

Wistrich, R., *Wer war wer im Dritten Reich?*, Frankfurt, 1987 (English edition, 1982).

Woodall, B., 'The Logic of Collusive Action. The Political Roots of the *Dango* System', *Comparative Politics*, 25(3), 197–312, 1993.

Yayama, T., 'The Recruit Scandal. Learning from the Causes of Corruption', *Journal of Japanese Studies*, 16(1), 93–114, 1990.

INDEX